GCSE
English in a Year
FOR AQA SPECIFICATIONS

Peter Turner

Hodder & Stoughton

A MEMBER OF THE HODDER HEADLINE GROUP

D1347258

KEIGHLEY CAMPUS LIBRARY
LEEDS CITY COLLEGE

KC05430

About the Author

Peter Turner is a lecturer at Brockenhurst College in the New Forest, teaching English to GCSE, A level and Access to Higher Education, and creative writing. He has also taught at secondary schools in North Devon, Nottingham and Leeds, a Further Education College in Bournemouth and Poole, and a college of Technical and Further Education in Sydney, Australia. He is the author of *Issues: A Course Book for Advanced Level English Language*, *Issues and Skills for A Level English* and *GCSE English in a Year*. He has also written for the magazine *New Internationalist*.

British Library Cataloguing in Publication Data

A catalogue record for this title is available from The British Library

ISBN 0 340 87166 0

First published 2003
Impression number 10 9 8 7 6 5 4 3 2 1
Year   2009 2008 2007 2006 2005 2004 2003

Typeset by Fakenham Photosetting Limited, Norfolk
Printed in Great Britain for Hodder & Stoughton Educational, a division of Hodder Headline, 338 Euston Road, London NW1 3BH by Martins The Printers Ltd.

CONTENTS

Author acknowledgements

I would like to acknowledge the enormous debt I owe to my wife, Lyn, in the preparation of this book, both practically, in allowing me to make use of her much-superior word-processing skills, and in the advice and support she has unfailingly and patiently offered me. I would also like to acknowledge the encouragement, support and advice of my step-daughter, Mel, throughout the gestation of the book, and I would like to thank the students who have cheerfully allowed me to use their personal writing in the book itself.

The author and publishers would like to thank the following for:

Copyright text:
Unit 1 pp. 3–4 © Celia Green and Charles McCreery, *Apparitions*, Institute of Psychophysical Research, 1989 (first published by Hamish Hamilton, 1975); distributed by Book Systems Plus, BSP House, Station Road, Linton, Cambridge CB1 6NW (tel. 01223 894870; e-mail: BSP2B@aol.com); pp. 5 & 7 *The Afterlife: An Investigation into the Mysteries of Life After Death* by Janny Randles and Peter Hough, Judy Piatkus (Publishers) Limited, 1993. **Unit 2** pp. 12–13 *Frank Skinner* © Frank Skinner, 2001. Avalon Management Group Ltd. **Unit 4** pp. 38–41 'Death' by Norman Mailer from *The Presidential Papers*, Penguin 1968. **Unit 5** pp. 45–47 *'Race' in Britain* ed. Charles Husband; pp. 48–51 *Who Do We Think We Are? Imagining the New Britian* by Yasmin Alibhai-Brown (Penguin Books 2001). Copyright © Yasmin Alibhai-Brown, 2002; pp. 54–55 *Inside the Third World* by Paul Harrison. **Unit 8 & 9** p. 99 © Roald Dahl, *Kiss Kiss*, Penguin Books Ltd; pp. 101–2, 106–7, 115–16 and 118–20 © Roald Dahl, *Someone Like You*, Penguin Books Ltd. **Unit 12** p. 154 © *Mail on Sunday*, 3 November 2002. **Unit 13** p. 179 *top* © *The Telegraph*, 1 November 2002, *bottom The Sun*, 1 November 2002 © News International Newspapers Limited, London; pp. 180–81 © *The Daily Mail*, 1 November 2002; pp. 182–83 © *Bella* magazine, H Bauer Publishing. **Unit 15** pp. 214–15 from *Penguin Book of 20th Century Speeches* by Brian MacArthur, Penguin. **Unit 16** pp. 220–22 © Bill Bryson. Extracted from *Neither Here Nor There* by Bill Bryson, published by Black Swan, a division of Transworld Publishers. All rights reserved; pp. 226–27 *The Road to Wigan Pier* by George Orwell (Copyright © George Orwell, 1936) Reproduced with permission of Bill Hamilton as the Literary Executor of the Estate of the Late Sonia Brownell Orwell and Martin Secker & Warburg Ltd. **Unit 17** p. 231 © Chinua Achebe, *Beware Soul Brother*, Heinemann Educational, 1972; pp. 233–34 Copyright © Grace Nichols 1984. Reproduced with permission of Curtis Brown Ltd, London on behalf of Grace Nichols.

Copyright photographs:
pp. 5 & 12 © CORBIS; p. 36 © Penny Tweedie/CORBIS; p. 40 © Popperfoto; p. 56 © Peter Turnley/CORBIS; p. 62 *left* © Popperfoto/Reuters, *right* © Library of Congress, USA; p. 63 © Popperfoto/Reuters; p. 64 © Henri Winterman; p. 79 © Archive Photos; p. 87 © Bettmann/CORBIS; p. 95 © Hulton-Deutsch Collection/CORBIS; pp. 97, 104 & 113, all © Anglia Television Ltd; pp. 124, 147 & 154 all © Ronald Grant Archive; p. 156 © BBC; p. 161 © Brooks & Bentley; p. 163 © US Eurolink Plc; p. 164 © Hewlett-Packard 2002; p. 165 © 2002 Casio Electronic Co. Ltd.; p. 169 © Rex Features Ltd; p. 182 © Paul Hardy/CORBIS; p. 183 Richard Clune/CORBIS; p. 214 © PA Photo; p. 221 © Nik Wheeler/CORBIS; p. 226 © Popperfoto; p. 231 © PA Photos/EPA; p. 233 © David Brooks/CORBIS.

Every effort has been made to trace copyright holders of material reproduced in this book. Any rights not acknowledged here will be acknowledged in subsequent printings if notice is given to the publisher.

A substantial number of students now sit GCSE examinations in English having taken only a one-year course in the subject. Such students can range from those who wish to improve their original grades achieved at the end of Year 11 in school, to adults keen to gain an increasingly important qualification and who have returned to learning later in their lives. Schools, colleges and adult centres are amongst the institutions that now cater for such students, offering them full-time, part-time or Open Learning courses during the day or in the evening. Despite the large number of diverse students (and methods of delivering courses) there are very few publications that offer specific help and guidance and that also demonstrate awareness of the constant time pressures under which such students work and study. You are now holding such a book.

This book is aimed at these students and their teachers and lecturers. Not only does it acknowledge these time pressures faced by one-year GCSE students, it has also been written to take account of the changes in Subject Criteria and Assessment Objectives for GCSE English beginning with the 2004 examination. The most popular of these GCSE specifications are those offered by AQA with its alternative A and B specifications together with the one that has been deliberately designed with mature candidates in view. It is sensible therefore that this book focuses on these AQA courses.

Examiners who have to assess the quality of work produced by one-year candidates are keenly aware of some of the weaknesses manifest in their scripts that, of course, preclude them from being awarded the grades that the students' hard work and aspirations may merit. In the 'Writing' category, such weaknesses can range from simple spelling errors to uncertainties about punctuation and syntax; from adopting an inappropriate voice in which to address the reader or listener to demonstrating a lack of awareness of the conventions of the specific genre in which they are asked to write. The other half of the assessment pairing, 'Reading', can also give rise to mark-lowering weaknesses. The AQA specifications demand that students read all texts (non-literary, literary and media) very closely indeed and that they pay careful attention to the way that writers have used language and to the conventions of the genre in which they are working. Candidates who read texts superficially or who present themselves for examination with only a limited acquaintance with their 'set' texts are, Humpty-Dumpty-like, heading for a fall. By working carefully through this book, students should become aware of such potential weaknesses in their work and will be encouraged and helped to eradicate them in a systematic way.

Throughout the book, there is a similarly helpful focus on speaking and listening activities, an area easy to neglect given the time-pressured circumstances of a one-year course. In addition, by using examples from students' own writing and providing suggestions for both coursework assignments and examination-based practice, this book will provide a thorough grounding in and preparation for the demands of all the three AQA GCSE English specifications.

John Shuttleworth

The requirements of the National Curriculum Orders for English for 2004 and beyond were not written with one-year courses in mind. To plan a course that covers all the requirements of the new specifications in a year will be an even more demanding task than it was for the 1998–2003 syllabuses.

Coursework responses to prose can no longer be based on the study of a couple of short stories, and empathic responses to the Shakespeare and prose texts will only be allowed for imaginative writing coursework. The study of a substantial body of poetry is now required as well, and the addition of a drama-focused activity for Speaking and Listening coursework is likely to further reduce the time available for covering all the other requirements.

The objective of this book is to offer approaches to tackling the specifications of AQA A and B and B (Mature) in ways that are stimulating for students, and which should make it possible for teachers to fit the whole course successfully into two and a half terms.

Each of the 17 units in the book is linked specifically to coursework and/or examination requirements of the AQA specifications. The units are arranged in such a way as to enable teachers who wish to use it as a course book to follow it through in unit order.

The early units are focused on the essential skills of Speaking and Listening, Writing and Reading. Approaches to the three coursework pieces that are common to each AQA specification are presented in Units 6 to 11. The final six units deal with aspects of the specifications that are covered by coursework in the one and terminal examinations in the other, and those which are examination requirements in both specifications.

Suggestions for Speaking and Listening activities are the major focus of three of the units, and are included in other units also, where they are usually linked to the subject matter of one of the unit sections. They can be identified easily through the Appendix on page 240. The final section of each unit is concerned with sentence structure, punctuation or spelling rules and exercises, which, while sometimes related to the unit in which they appear, can be used whenever there is time. These are also listed in the Appendix.

Coursework suggestions and examination practice exercises feature in nearly all the units. The book therefore covers all aspects of preparation for each of the AQA English specifications.

STRANGE ... BUT TRUE?

This first unit involves a lot of talking. There are two reasons for this. Firstly, finding out a bit about the other members of the class is obviously valuable in itself, and this is the main objective of the first activity. Secondly, talking (or 'Speaking and Listening', as it is called as an assessment activity) is a major aspect of the English GCSE course. It counts for 20 per cent of the assessment.

After the introductory conversation session, most of this unit is concerned with group discussion of a topic: the paranormal. This may be used as a first Speaking and Listening assessment. An introductory writing exercise is also suggested, as a follow-up to the discussion.

Conversation and report back

As an initial basic exercise in public speaking, and as a way of finding out about one another, the class should break up into pairs. For the next three minutes, talk to your partner about his or her life – family background, career history and/or aspirations, spare-time activities, likes and dislikes, feelings about school/college and so on.

Each of you will then be asked to report back to the rest of the class for between one and two minutes on what you have found out about the person you have been talking to. You might choose to arrange the conversation session as an interview, with the interviewer taking notes, or you might take a minute or so at the end of the conversation to jot down from memory the main things you intend to say about your partner. At the end of the activity, everyone should know at least something about everyone else.

Group discussion: the 'paranormal'

The three categories of Speaking and Listening activity for coursework assessment are: Individual Extended Contribution, Group Interaction, and Drama-Focused Activity. Group interaction will inevitably be taking place as a normal part of English classroom activity, and most of the interaction will not be assessed. A discussion of the paranormal would, however, provide the opportunity for you to get to know one another better and to lead to the first formal Speaking and Listening: Group Interaction assessment. The discussion could cover any of the three skill areas: 'explain, describe, narrate'; 'explore, analyse, imagine'; 'discuss, argue, persuade'.

The paranormal is defined in the *Oxford English Dictionary* as: 'phenomena or powers ... whose operation is outside the scope of the known laws of nature.' Obviously this is an enormous topic, covering all kinds of phenomena for which there is no accepted or satisfactory explanation. Examples would include:

➡ communicating with 'the other side' through mediums or ouija boards
➡ ghosts and haunted houses
➡ people who claim to have had previous lives
   or Near Death Experiences
➡ poltergeists
➡ Out of Body Experiences and levitation
➡ werewolves
➡ black and white magic.

You can tackle the topic of the paranormal through a free-ranging discussion with no particular structure, or you can deal separately with different phenomena.

As a possible stimulus to discussion, the unit continues with an exploration, through extracts from books and articles, of three of the commonest manifestations of 'paranormal' activity, after a general overview of the whole topic taken from a magazine article by Susan Blackmore.

THE LURE OF THE PARANORMAL

Why do so many people believe in the paranormal? The answer to this question, and the recent research exploring it, tell us little about the paranormal itself but much about the way our minds work.

There have been many surveys in the paranormal. The proportion of people claiming belief varies with the sample and the question asked but is usually well over half. More interesting is the main reason given: that people have had psychic experiences themselves.

There are three obvious explanations for this. First, they might really have experienced the paranormal. If this is true, we need to re-write much of science, and

soon. Secondly, they might be making it up. For anyone who has had these experiences, this does not seem a plausible explanation. Thirdly, they might be misinterpreting perfectly normal events – suffering from what we might call a 'paranormal illusion'.

Susan Blackmore, *New Scientist*, 22 September 1990

➡   Which of the three explanations of the paranormal offered above do you tend to support?

➡   Can you think of any other possible explanation?

Ghosts

Belief in ghosts goes back to the dawn of human history, and is common to virtually all cultures around the world. Most published accounts of ghostly visitations describe figures unknown to the person who encounters them; many of these 'ghosts' appear to 'haunt' a particular place. A substantial minority of reported 'ghosts' appear in the shape of known or loved ones.

Here are typical accounts of both, taken from a book called *Apparitions* by Celia Green and Charles McCreery.

APPARITIONS

As a nine-and-a-half year old, one of my more pleasant household 'chores' was to take the baby up to bed at six p.m., and sing him to sleep . . . The baby having duly fallen asleep, I levered myself gingerly off the bed, so as not to waken him, and quietly opened the bedroom door, still watching the baby to make sure he didn't 'disturb'. As I turned my head, I was gazing directly at the window on top of the stairs, along the landing from me. Sitting on the window-sill was a very old man. I was startled into immobility . . . He was very old, rheumy-eyed, grey haired. He wore old, dirty looking dark trousers, a cream Welsh flannel shirt without a collar, unbuttoned at the neck, an extremely dirty looking old 'weskit' which was food and grease stained. He had a muffler tied round his neck . . . On his head was an old bowler hat, black, and past its best by many a long day. The old man was leaning on a walking stick, his two old hands folded one on the other on top of the stick. His mouth was open slightly, and slack, as some old men look, and I'm sure that had he been a living man, I would have expected to hear his breathing quite clearly. As it was, I could only hear street noises from outside. The man's head was slightly inclined towards the window but he was not gazing out through the window. With hindsight, I realise now that he was *listening*, from his window seat. I suppose this apparition lasted about ten seconds . . . The apparition vanished as suddenly as a light goes out.

• • • • •

One night, about an hour after going to bed, I was awakened by the bedroom door being opened. Thinking it was my teenage daughter, who probably couldn't sleep, I raised myself up. Instead of my daughter, it was the full form of a very dear friend who had died a few weeks earlier. She was wearing a most beautiful green silk dressing-gown, which had a 'glow' about it. Her hand held the gown in place, and I noticed how white and thin the hand seemed to be. My eyes travelled up to her face, and I noticed that she looked so much younger than she was when she died.

I was so surprised – and as I began to say, 'I thought it was Valerie coming in' (Valerie being my daughter), my friend faded away.

She didn't speak to me, but her lovely brown eyes looked directly at me, with such love and understanding.

Celia Greene and Charles McCreery, *Apparitions*

➡ How do you respond to these accounts?
➡ Does anyone in the class think that they, or anyone they know, has seen a ghost?
➡ How do you explain stories of ghostly apparitions? If they are real, what are they?

Mediums and spiritualism

Spiritualism (communicating with the dead through mediums) is probably just about as old as religion. In a sense, it is a religion.

In a book called *The Afterlife: An Investigation into the Mysteries of Life After Death*, Jenny Randles and Peter Hough explain how spiritualism is supposed to work.

Haley Joel Osment in *The Sixth Sense*.

WHAT MEDIUMS DO

Mediums see themselves as radio receivers tuned into a particular frequency which carries information from the afterlife. They generally split into two types – 'mental' and 'physical' mediums.

Mental mediums utilise extra sensory perception (ESP) which enables spirit communications to take place. They receive mental impressions from deceased persons which they then try to interpret for the living. These impressions can be received 'clairaudiently' – spirit voices are paranormally 'heard', or 'clairvoyantly' – sensed or seen. Sometimes these communications take the form of automatic writing or drawing. Mental mediums are much more prevalent than their 'physical' colleagues.

Contact with the dead can take place during normal waking, or in a state of altered consciousness. This latter state can be achieved by staring at an object such as a glass of water or a crystal ball. Sometimes the services of a hypnotist are used. Mediums in the depth of trance often appear to have been temporarily possessed by a spirit. The entity vocalises using the medium's larynx; voice, facial expression and gestures emulate those of the deceased in possession of the medium's body.

Jenny Randles and Peter Hough, *The Afterlife: An Investigation into the Mysteries of Life After Death*

Mediums have been extensively researched, and often found to be fraudulent. However, this is by no means always the case. The implications of this are discussed by Richard Cavendish, in *The World of Ghosts and the Supernatural*.

For all the fraud and fakery, and the cheating and exploitation of the bereaved and the gullible by charlatans, psychical research seems to have demonstrated that some mediums possessed genuine paranormal abilities – and that some mediums who would cheat when they could get away with it would produce genuine phenomena when they could not. This did not necessarily mean that genuine mediums were in communication with the dead. The results could be put down to telepathy from the sitters, without the need to believe in the afterlife.

Richard Cavendish, *The World of Ghosts and the Supernatural*

➜ Has any member of the class visited a medium, or known someone who has? Was it a worthwhile experience?

➜ How do you explain the apparent ability of some mediums to give precise information about their clients' personal lives?

➜ How do mediums explain where they get their information from? Do you believe them? What are the implications, if what they say is true?

Near Death Experiences

There seems to be a surprising amount of agreement about 'out of body experiences' among people who have come very close to death, or who have actually been pronounced clinically dead and have 'come back to life'.

In a book called *Reflections on Life After Life*, Dr Raymond Moody constructed a model of 'Near Death Experiences' from people he interviewed who claimed to have had them. This is his model.

COMMON ELEMENTS OF NDE

You hear yourself pronounced dead by a doctor.
→ **You have an unpleasant buzzing or ringing sound in your head.**
→ **You feel yourself moving through a long tunnel.**
→ **Emotionally upset, you see your body from a distance, and watch the doctor and nurses attempt to revive you.**

→ You begin to notice that you still have a body, but of a different nature from the physical one.

→ Others come to meet you – relatives and friends who have already died.

→ A loving entity, a 'being of light', appears before you.

→ This being, without speaking, communicates to you the idea that you must now evaluate your life.

→ You see an instantaneous but highly detailed playback of your life.

→ You approach a barrier which seems to represent the dividing line between your previous life and the next one.

→ You feel you must go back to your previous life, even though you are intensely enjoying this 'after-life' experience and would like to continue it.

→ You find yourself back in your physical body.

→ You try to tell people afterwards about your experience, but find it hard to put into words.

→ The experience has changed your life, especially your attitude towards death.

Dr Raymond Moody, Reflections on Life After Life

A great many people claim to have had uplifting experiences of 'death', and to have experienced at least some elements of this model, but some report negative experiences. The following is a typical story.

International clairvoyant Peter Lee attracted a list of celebrity clients over the years, but it is his own personal experiences that stick most vividly in his mind.

'I was in Germany, and up the side of a mountain with some people. Suddenly I fell and was conscious of hundreds of little stones rolling beneath my body. I became aware of a clump of grass, or outcropping of some kind, and realised if I didn't grab it I was finished. Reaching out, I caught it firmly. I was relieved. Then it gave way ...

'As I fell, all the events of my life flashed before me like a roll of film unwinding. Then I was aware of a tunnel of light stretching before me. Instinctively, I knew this was a tunnel of life, not death. As I drifted along there were people I recognised who had passed away. Suddenly I was snapped back out of the tunnel, and I remember thinking; 'This doesn't feel much like Heaven ... there's pains in my head ... my legs hurt ... I realised I was still alive and on the mountainside.'

Jenny Randles and Peter Hough, The Afterlife: An Investigation into the Mysteries of Life
After Death

Many of the people who claim that their 'Near Death Experiences' have included a 'playback' of their lives have talked of viewing their actions and thoughts throughout their lives in terms of how they treated the people they came into contact with.

These are typical examples:

It seemed like this flashback was like a judgement was being made . . . it showed me not only what I had done but even how what I had done affected other people. And it wasn't like watching a movie projector because I could feel these things.

Quoted in Raymond Moody, *Reflections on Life After Life*

Then there was a review of my whole life. I can remember looking at it and assessing it and really judging myself. I felt no one else judged me. I judged myself.

Quoted in Claire Sutherland, *Transformed By the Light: Life After Near Death Experiences*

The consistency of people's accounts of Near Death Experiences around the world and throughout history has been viewed from two totally different perspectives, religious and scientific, as Dr Susan Blackmore explains in her book *Dying to Live*:

1 The Afterlife Hypothesis
NDEs are just what they appear to be – the soul's journey out of the body, through a tunnel to another world that awaits us after death.

2 The Dying Brain Hypothesis
Everyone has a similar brain, hormones and nervous system and that is why they have similar experiences when these systems fail.

Susan Blackmore, *Dying to Live*

➡ Is there anyone in the class who knows someone who has 'died' and come back to life? What was their experience?

➡ Do you regard NDEs as evidence for an afterlife, or do you believe in a scientific explanation?

Other paranormal phenomena

You could now go on to discuss some of the other manifestations of the paranormal listed on page 2, such as experiences of séances, Out of Body Experiences, poltergeists, and so on.

Writing

As an initial writing exercise you could attempt one of the following topics:

➜   Write about a personal experience or an account of someone else's experience of the paranormal, and comment on the significance of the experience.

➜   Give your views on the reality or otherwise of one or more of the paranormal phenomena discussed, and their significance.

Coursework

The first of the above exercises could be treated as an initial draft of a coursework piece for AQA B and B (Mature) Personal Writing: Non-Fiction – inform, explain, describe.

The important thing to remember in group discussion is that it is part of your Speaking *and* Listening assessment. Your examiner or teacher will therefore be watching and listening for your contributions to both parts of this aspect of English. Remember, too, that it's a *group* discussion and that you should neither seek to dominate proceedings by talking too much nor should you remain silent throughout, although you may well be listening attentively. Attentive listening means that you will be able to respond thoughtfully to what others have been saying and make your own contributions clear and helpful.

Working on Spelling

GCSE Assessment Objective (iii) for Writing requires you to demonstrate your ability to 'use a range of sentence structures effectively with accurate punctuation and spelling'. Unit 3 of this book concentrates on ensuring that you understand the basics of sentence structure, and in Unit 7 you can begin to work on varying your sentence structures.

You can begin working on your spelling now, and each subsequent unit ends with the examination of different aspects of either spelling or punctuation, with practice exercises.

Spelling is something you can work on frequently for brief periods of time, on your own. English spelling is not the most logical and consistent system of spelling in the world, but there *are* rules that you can learn and apply, and these are explained in later units. However, by far the best way to improve your spelling is to keep a systematic record of words you have spelt wrongly in your written work, and to check over the correct spelling regularly.

If you spell a word wrongly, the chances are that you have been spelling it wrongly for most of your life. You most probably have the wrong spelling imprinted in your consciousness. Only a conscious and determined effort to re-imprint the correct spelling will put it right.

Try the following suggestion. Buy a pocket-size book with blank pages and each time you make a spelling mistake, write the correct spelling of the word in the book. If your spelling is shaky, you'll soon have a substantial collection of corrected spellings. Get into the habit of looking at the words in your book when you have a few spare moments and maybe get someone to test you on the words you've written in the book from time to time. Eventually, the corrected spelling should become imprinted on your visual memory.

The fifteen words that follow are commonly misspelt. They are all spelt wrongly here. Write out the correct versions.

embarassed
definateley
arguement
sincerley
excitment
therfore
untill
begining

lonliness
completley
nuisence
buisness
occasionly
seperate
marrige

CHILDHOOD EXPERIENCES

Talking and writing about childhood takes up most of this unit. Three brief accounts of episodes from their childhood by different people are offered as stimulus for discussion, and your contribution to this discussion could be assessed for the Group Interaction category of Speaking and Listening coursework. The topic of childhood could also provide the opportunity for assessment in the Extended Individual Contribution category. Opportunities for group and individual writing about personal childhood experiences will also be presented.

The first extract for reading and discussion is an autobiographical account of an incident in the life of a young boy. Laurie Lee describes his first day at school in the village of Slad in Gloucestershire in 1920.

CIDER WITH ROSIE

The morning came, without any warning, when my sisters surrounded me, wrapped me in scarves, tied up my boot-laces, thrust a cap on my head, and stuffed a baked potato in my pocket.

'What's this?' I said.

'You're starting school today.'

'I ain't. I'm stopping 'ome.'

'Now, come on, Loll. You're a big boy now.'

'I ain't.'

'Boo-hoo.'

They picked me up bodily, kicking and bawling, and carried me up to the road.

'Boys who don't go to school get put into boxes, and turn into rabbits, and get chopped up Sundays.'

I felt this was overdoing it rather, but I said no more after that. I arrived at the school just three feet tall and fatly wrapped in my scarves. The playground roared like a rodeo, and the potato burned through my thigh. Old boots, ragged stockings, torn trousers and skirts, went skating and skidding around me. The rabble closed in; I was encircled; grit flew in my face like shrapnel. Tall girls with frizzled hair, and huge boys with sharp elbows, began to prod me with hideous interest. They plucked at my scarves, spun me round like a top, screwed my nose, and stole my potato.

I was rescued at last by a gracious lady – the sixteen-year-old junior-teacher – who boxed a few ears and dried my face and led me off to The Infants. I spent that first day picking holes in paper, then went home in a smouldering temper.

'What's the matter, Loll? Didn't he like it at school, then?'

'They never gave me the present!'

'Present? What present?'

'They said they'd give me a present.'

'Well, now, I'm sure they didn't.'

'They did! They said: "You're Laurie Lee, ain't you? Well, just you sit for the present." I sat there all day but I never got it. I ain't going back there again!'

But after a week I felt like a veteran and grew as ruthless as anyone else. Somebody had stolen my baked potato, so I swiped somebody else's apple.

Laurie Lee, *Cider with Rosie*

→ How did the child feel about the prospect of going to school? How did he feel on his first day at school? Pick out two or three phrases/sentences that capture the experience particularly well, and try to explain why you chose them.

→ Can you remember any particularly funny or frightening things that happened to you at your first school?

→ Do you remember your early days at junior, middle or secondary school? How much of a change was it, going to a new school? How soon did you adapt?

The next extract is also an account of an incident in the life of a five-year-old boy. The English comedian Frank Skinner tells of some private moments in his garden at home, in the West Midland town of Oldbury, near Birmingham, in 1962.

FRANK SKINNER

When I was five years old, I developed the urge to shout as loud as I possibly could; to really roar and scream and holler until I couldn't roar and scream and holler anymore. I can still remember the feeling of wanting to do it but knowing that my parents, understandably, would go crazy if I did. This was where having an outside toilet became a distinct advantage. Our kitchen, which operated as a living room, was at the back of the house, with a door leading into the back yard and garden. Just across the yard was the outside toilet. It had no light, so going at night involved a good deal of guesswork. In the early hours it was a long scary journey to have a mere wee.

. . . One night, I went to the kitchen door as if I was off to the toilet. It was dark outside. The air smelt sweet. One wall of the outside toilet was hugged by an enormous honeysuckle bush. I never really noticed the scent during the day, but at night it was intoxicating. To a five-year-old, it made the back yard a magical place. I walked through that back yard and into the garden. The only light source was from the kitchen window. I could still hear the sound of the telly and the voices of my family. As I walked further and further into the garden, both grew dimmer. It was dark at the end of the garden. I stood still and listened to the night. Distant mumble from our kitchen, almost inaudible traffic sounds. I waited, and even these sounds seem to fade like the stage was being cleared for me. It spooks me out a bit that I can still remember it so clearly. I stood very still. I mean, weirdly still. And then I started. Not with a big breath and an equivalent roar, but with an increasing murmur, slowly reassuring myself that it was OK to interfere with the silence. The sould developed from an 'Urrrrrrrrrnnnn . . .' to an 'Aaaaarrrrrrrgh . . .' This was the sound I was searching for. Once I'd found it, I let it get louder and louder. I stopped for breath. And then went again with the 'Aaaaarrrrrrgh . . .', thrilled at how loud it was. I spread my arms and leaned my head backwards into the darkness. I repeated my call about five or six times, then I stopped, very still, again, and listened to remind myself what the night sounded like without me. Then I went back into the house. They'd heard nothing over the sound of the television.

The next night I repeated the ritual. It became something I looked forward to and told no one about. Then, after about three weeks, the man who lived next door turned up at our house and explained to my parents that, the previous evening, he had let his dog out 'to do his business' and had heard shouting. In the gloom, he could make out a small figure, with arms outstretched, standing at the top of our garden. My dad asked me about it. I said I just felt like shouting that night. He told me not to do it again. And I didn't. So every night, the neighbour's dog was encouraged to go out into the garden, to stand still in the dark and slowly empty himself while I sat indoors and watched the telly.

Frank Skinner, *Frank Skinner*

➡   How does Frank Skinner bring the scene and the atmosphere of the back yard and the garden to life in this episode? Pick out two or three phrases/sentences that capture the child's impressions and feelings particularly well, and try to explain why you chose them.

➡   Can you remember any secrets that you tried to keep from your parents when you were very young?

➜ Can you remember an incident from your early childhood when you felt particularly embarrassed or humiliated?

The last piece describes an incident from early adolescence. In it, Kathleen Moore, who was a 16-year-old college student re-sitting GCSE English when she wrote it, tells of a traumatic episode at home, in Swanage, Dorset, in 1994, when she was 13.

ESCAPE

I was at Swanage Youth Club with my friend Tracey. She was staying at my house for the night, but we had to get home early because we had the school sponsored walk the next day. Tracey and I began to walk home. It was after nine, but it was late June so the sky wasn't yet too dark. Then I realised that I had left my key inside. I turned to face Tracey. She looked at my face, then asked, 'Have you got any cards?' When I was locked out we used to break in by using about five cards to push the lock down. We both fumbled through our wallets, taking out all the plastic cards. Mostly they were 'phone cards. Eventually we wedged the cards just in the right position, then 'bang', the door flew open.

'I'm starving. Can we make something to eat now?' Tracey begged.

'Let's get ready for bed in case Mum comes back. Then we'll make some rock buns,' I said.

We jumped into our pyjamas and then ventured to the kitchen. Tracey knocked up the mixture while I made the tea and put on the oven.

Footsteps were banging up the stairs, and then the door burst open. In walked Geoff with my Mum traipsing behind. They were both obviously drunk for a change. Geoff walked straight into the kitchen where Tracey was and said, 'Hello, fatty. Eating again?'

I felt my face burning. I was so ashamed of him, and embarrassed for Tracey. I confronted Mum. 'How can you let him talk to my friend like that? I'm not surprised no one comes round any more.'

'Oh, shut up,' Mum sighed.

Geoff heard that and thought that I was starting an argument. He was drunk and lost his temper. He was mumbling, and he threw the cakes all over the kitchen. I could see how enraged he was becoming so I followed Tracey into my bedroom. We weren't in there for more than two minutes when the door was shoved open. I was pushed onto my bed. My throat was being crushed by his clenched fist. I felt so claustrophobic, but I couldn't show any emotion, or speak at all. I think this is what enraged him even more, and made him do what he did next.

I felt him lift me, and then he spoke for the first time throughout the attack. 'I'm going to f——ing kill you, you little bitch!'

He lifted me towards my bedroom window. Although I was trying to withstand his strength he swung me towards the window, but I was kicking and punching too hard for him to keep me in the air, and in his drunken stupor I was dropped at Tracey's feet. She was sobbing uncontrollably. 'I thought he was going to kill you, so I stood in the way of the window.'

I was still in shock as I threw my clothes into a rucksack and pulled Tracey out of the front door. Tracey tripped down the stairs and she was really crying now, so I started to panic. Geoff had only gone to the bathroom, I think, because I had scratched his face, but I knew if he came out and caught us he would be even more angry, then go berserk. I dragged Tracey to her feet and we ran to a 'phone box. She 'phoned up her stepfather to come and get us, but he thought Tracey was acting like a drama queen and wouldn't come and get us. We went to a friend's house and sat up, telling her mum the story, until late. We were so tired that we missed the sponsored walk.

I couldn't go home, so I moved into my aunty's house. At thirteen, this was my first time of many of moving out of home.

Kathleen Moore, *Escape*

➡ How did you react to this account? Pick out some details or descriptions that you found particularly expressive or poignant, and try to explain why you chose them.

➡ Do you remember anything especially frightening or upsetting that happened to you when you were about 13?

Individual oral presentation

Individual students might choose to prepare for a Speaking and Listening assignment on a personal memory of childhood, to take place in a future lesson.

You should try to recall an incident from your childhood that stands out because it was funny, frightening, exciting, painful, or unusual in some other way, and jot down some notes about it. You will be called on to give an individual oral presentation lasting at least five minutes, which can be assessed in the 'explain, describe, narrate' category of Speaking and Listening coursework.

Group writing

This exercise requires someone in the class to give an outline account of a personal childhood experience. It could be funny, like the Laurie Lee piece, strange, like Frank Skinner's, or traumatic, like Kathleen Moore's.

The first section of the student's account will be written from the student's dictation on the whiteboard. The class will then discuss possible improvements to the account, to make it more dramatic, or descriptive, or expressive in whatever way any individual class member suggests, and changes made to the text on the board, until a consensus is reached on each suggested improvement. The completed section will then be copied by the class, before going on to the next section.

This procedure will be repeated, until the final draft is complete.

Personal writing

As an individual writing exercise, you could write an account of an experience from your childhood that stood out in some way. You should aim to write between one and two sides, and try to capture the experience as precisely and imaginatively as you can.

Coursework (Writing)

The exercise outlined above could be treated as an initial draft for a coursework piece for AQA A Original Writing – explore, imagine, entertain or AQA B and B (Mature) Personal Writing: Non-Fiction – inform, explain, describe.

Punctuation: the apostrophe

If used at all, apostrophes are often used inaccurately. There are some fairly simple rules for their use, and you should learn them.

The possessive apostrophe

The main use of the apostrophe is to indicate *possession*, to show that somebody or something *owns* something else. If you are referring to 'the cat belonging to Priscilla', you would normally say 'Priscilla's cat'. 'The pyjamas of my husband' would normally be referred to as 'my husband's pyjamas'. These are examples of the possessive use of the apostrophe. An apostrophe is placed before the 's' in 'Priscilla's' to show that you are talking about something belonging to Priscilla, and likewise with 'husband's'.

A small difficulty arises when an article(s) is possessed by more than one person or thing, as in 'the students' phone numbers'. There is a simple rule covering this. If the possessor is *singular*, the apostrophe goes *before* the 's':

e.g.   the cat's litter tray
         my cousin's house

If the possessor is *plural*, the apostrophe goes *after* the 's':

e.g.   the cats' litter trays
         my cousins' houses

In some cases the use of the apostrophe is essential for the meaning to be clear. Here is one example. In the following sentence, how many students are being referred to?

         The students essays were brilliant.

You can't tell whether one student has written the essays or several, unless you put an apostrophe before or after the 's' in 'students'.

If you're not in the habit of using apostrophes, there is a danger of *over-using* them at first, to write things like 'the student's essay's were brilliant'. You often see this outside shops, on signs like: 'We sell potatoe's.' You must think *why* you are using an apostrophe.

There is one further minor difficulty in the use of the possessive apostrophe. A few words in English form the plural not by simply adding an 's' but by changing the ending. Examples include: 'woman', 'man', 'child', 'person'. As the plural of 'woman' is 'women' rather than 'womans', there is no need for a possessive apostrophe after the 's' to show that it is more than one woman doing the possessing. So the possessive form of these irregular plurals goes like this:
         women's clothes
         men's problems

children's toys
people's expectations

Apostrophes are also needed in phrases like the following:
two weeks' holiday
tomorrow's football match
twelve hours' time

However, the following never have apostrophes:
yours   his
ours   hers
theirs   its (unless it is short for 'it is')

The apostrophe for contraction

The other use of the apostrophe is in words that have been contracted:

e.g.   it's (for 'it is')   I'd (for 'I would')
        shan't (for 'shall not')   wouldn't (for 'would not')
        they're (for 'they are')   who's (for 'who is')

The rule for placing the apostrophe is that it goes where the letters are missing.

Exercise

Put the missing apostrophes in the following sentences.
1 My dog has hurt its paw and its limping badly.
2 Wendys coat isnt in the hall where she left it.
3 Builders labourers are needed on site tomorrow.
4 Elephants are killed for their tusks.
5 The strikers goals saved United in Wednesdays match.
6 The cars horns were making a dreadful din.
7 I bought several childrens games for the Christmas party.

To achieve a good grade in GCSE English you need to have a clear understanding of how written English works. As well as being able to spell with a fair degree of accuracy, you need to be confident in your use of punctuation and you need to be able to write grammatically accurate sentences. You therefore need to know the ground rules of sentence structure and punctuation.

Detailed knowledge of the structure of the English language is not necessary for success in GCSE. However, in order to appreciate what you are doing wrong when you make mistakes in grammar and punctuation, it is necessary to understand the classification of words into different types. These types of words are called **parts of speech**. There are seven of them: nouns, pronouns, verbs, adjectives, adverbs, prepositions and conjunctions. This is where we shall begin.

Parts of speech

Nouns

These are commonly referred to as 'naming words'. They are words that *name* things, or people, or places, or abstract qualities. They can be subdivided into four main types: common nouns, proper nouns, collective nouns and abstract nouns.

Common nouns are words for things that you can identify with your senses (things that you can see, touch, smell, etc.). Examples include: desk, music, girls, shower, television, pig, wheels, gravy, tongue.

Proper nouns name *particular* people, places, months, etc. They always begin with a capital letter, for instance: Prince Charles, Hannah, River Thames, Buckingham Palace, September.

Collective nouns are the names given to *groups* of people, animals or things, such as: flock (of sheep), board (of directors), fleet (of taxis).

Abstract nouns are words for things that you cannot see, touch, etc., such as emotions, qualities, states of being. Examples include: beauty, hatred, death, deception, anger.

The vast majority of nouns are common nouns. A simple test to check whether or not a word is a common noun is to put 'the' in front of it (the desk, the music, etc.).

➜   Name ten more nouns in each category.

Pronouns

These are words that stand in place of nouns. The commonest pronouns are I, you, he, she, it, we, they, me, him, her, them, this, that, these and those.

Pronouns are most commonly used to avoid repeating a noun in a sequence of statements. Thus, instead of writing 'The boy (noun) was feeling ill. The boy (noun) decided to go home,' you could write 'The boy (noun) was feeling ill. He (pronoun) decided to go home.'

➜   Identify the nouns and pronouns in the following sentences:
The man called to the dogs.
They ran to him and he gave them some biscuits.
Anita sent Andrew a birthday card. He threw it in the bin.

Verbs

These are words that indicate actions. They are often referred to as 'doing' words. The basic form of a verb is the **infinitive** (for example, *to* see, *to* eat, *to* write). The infinitive is the form in which verbs appear in the dictionary.

From this basic form of the verb, *tenses* can be created. The tense of the verb tells you *when* something happens: in the past, present or future. Here are some examples of verbs with tenses (also know as **finite** verbs): he *ate*, he *was eating* (past); he *eats*, he *is eating* (present); he *will eat*, he *will be eating* (future.) Thus:

> I *ran* round the park (past tense of the verb 'to run'.)
> She *is* my girl-friend (present tense of the word 'to be'.)
> My aunt *will come* to stay this weekend (future tense of the verb 'to come'.)

➜   Name ten verbs in the infinitive. Give a past, present and future form of each.

Adjectives

These are often known as 'describing words'. To be more precise, they are words that *describe a noun*. You can check whether or not a word is an adjective by putting 'the' or 'a' in front of it and a noun after it. Thus:

a *beautiful* woman	the *youngest* son	a *frozen* chicken
a *terrifying* experience	a *red* rose	the *stupid* idiot

The words in italics in the following sentence are adjectives: The *lonely, frightened* child was crying; an *old* man, wearing a *dirty, brown, crumpled* jacket, was comforting him.

➡ Name the part of speech of each of the other words in the sentence above. (NB: the word 'the' is known as the **definite article,** and the word 'a' or 'an' is known as the **indefinite article.**)

➡ Name 20 more adjectives.

Adverbs

These are words that describe (or modify) any part of speech *other than* a noun. Most adverbs end in '-ly' and describe verbs (they are *ad*ded to a *verb*). They generally tell us *how* an action is done; they also tell us *when* or *where* an action is done.

Here are some examples:

She walked *gracefully* (describing the verb 'walked'; telling us *how* she walked).

He spoke *well* (describing the verb 'spoke'; telling us *how* he spoke).

We met *yesterday* (adding to the verb 'met'; telling us *when* we met).

I went *there* (adding to the verb 'went'; telling us *where* I went).

Examples of adverbs modifying parts of speech *other than verbs* are as follows:

It is a *completely* stupid idea (modifying the adjective 'stupid'; telling us *how* stupid the idea was).

He rose *very* suddenly (modifying the adverb 'suddenly'; telling us *how* suddenly he rose).

➡ Name ten more adverbs.

Prepositions

A preposition is a word that comes *before* a *pronoun* or a *noun phrase* in a sentence, and generally *after* a *verb*. These are examples:

He talked *to* me.

My friend came *round* the corner.

Most prepositions show the *position* of one person, or thing, in relation to another, and this is an easy way to identify them. Here are some examples:

The cow jumped *over* the moon.

I went *into* the supermarket.

Michael fell *off* his bike.

The same word can sometimes be a preposition and sometimes an adverb, depending on whether or not it is followed by a pronoun or noun phrase. In the last example above, the word 'off' is identifiable as a preposition because it is followed by the noun phrase 'his bike'. Look at this sentence, however:

He got back on his bike and rode off.

Here, the word 'off' is not followed by a pronoun or noun phrase, and it cannot, therefore, be a preposition. It is, in fact, an adverb.

Examples of prepositions that show the *position* of one person or thing in relation to another are:

above	below	by	off	round
across	beneath	in	on	towards
among	between	into	onto	through
around	beyond	near	over	under

Other common prepositions are:

| after | before | except | like | to |
| at | during | for | of | with |

➡ Identify the prepositions in the following sentences:

I went to the pub with my friends.
The old man got off the bus and walked into the park.
The wicket-keeper whipped off the bails and appealed against the batsman.
What are you doing under the table?

Conjunctions

These are often referred to as 'joining words'. They show a *junction*, or link, between words, phrases or statements. The commonest conjunction is 'and'; the next commonest is 'but'. Other conjunctions include:

although	if	since	then	until
as	nor	so	though	whether
because	or	than	unless	yet

Here are some examples of the use of conjunctions:

The match was abandoned, *because* the pitch was waterlogged. (Joining two statements.)
naughty *but* nice (joining two words).
violent gusts of wind *and* squalls of icy rain (joining two phrases).

➡ Identify the prepositions and conjunctions in the following sentences:

Although he was terrified, the young soldier went over the top and raced across no man's land into the enemy trenches.

You will go to church whether you like it or not.

Basic sentence structure

Of all the errors that you can make in written English, the most serious is the writing of improperly constructed sentences. Two types of sentence structure error are particularly common:

1   Running sentences together (with just a comma, or no punctuation mark at all, between them). Here is an example: 'My brother has broken his leg, it will be in plaster for the next two months.'
2   Writing incomplete statements, for example: 'Hundreds of people rushing round in a state of blind panic.'

The first type is the commonest of all; the second is particularly common in descriptive writing.

In order to be sure of avoiding this kind of error, it is necessary to understand what a sentence actually *is*. How do you define a sentence?

Most people could come up with a definition like this: 'A sentence is group of words that makes sense on its own'. This is true, but it doesn't get us very far. 'The Chinese restaurant' is a group of words that makes sense ... but it isn't a sentence. It is, in fact a **phrase**. Before we go any further with the attempt to define a sentence, perhaps we should define a phrase. A phrase is a group of words that makes sense, but it does not make complete sense. In other words, it does not make a *completed statement*. Here are some other examples of phrases: 'across the sea'; 'going to see my friends'; 'the silver earrings'.

A better definition of a sentence might therefore be: 'A sentence is a group of words that makes a complete statement'. There is a problem with this definition also, however. How can you be sure that you've made 'a complete statement'?

We need a more precise definition of a sentence than either of these. The following definition ought to be adequately precise, as long as you understand basic parts of speech:

A sentence is a group of words containing at least one complete statement, with a subject (a noun, noun phrase or pronoun) and a finite verb (a verb with a past, present or future tense).

A sentence can be any length, from two words to a virtually indefinite number of words. Many people make the mistake of thinking that a sentence has to be longer than just two or three words. It doesn't. As long as a group of words has a **subject** and a verb with a tense, it must be a sentence.

Most sentences, in addition to a subject and a finite verb, also contain further information about the subject of the action, or the action itself, but they don't have to.

Look at the following:

1 My brother was snoring.
2 My brother was snoring noisily in the armchair.
3 My bother was snoring noisily in the armchair, he was disturbing my concentration. I punched him to wake him up.
4 The ghost of my brother appeared at the top of the stairs.

Number 1 is a simple statement, containing a subject, 'My brother', and a finite (past tense) verb 'was snoring'.

Number 2 is slightly fuller: an explanation is added about how and where the action took place.

What about number 3? How many separate statements does it contain?

There are actually three sections to number 3, the first telling us *what* my brother was doing, the second telling us *the effect* of what he was doing, and the third telling us what '*I*' did as a consequence. It therefore contains *three separate statements*. Many people make the mistake of thinking that if a series of statements is made about the *same person or thing* they should merely be separated by commas, and that only when the *subject changes* should a new sentence be started. This is quite wrong. A single sentence *can* contain several statements, but only if a *link* is established between the statements.

There are two ways of establishing a link between complete statements. The more common way is by using a conjunction, or a linking phrase, like this:

> My brother was snoring noisily in the armchair, *and* he was disturbing my concentration. Or:

> My brother was snoring noisily in the armchair, so *that* he was disturbing my concentration.

The alternative is to use a **semi-colon** (a punctuation mark whose principal purpose is to **show** that two statements are closely linked), like this:

> My brother was snoring noisily in the armchair; he was disturbing my concentration.

If you do not indicate the link between the two statements in one of these two ways, then they have to be written as two separate sentences.

Number 4 contains a longer subject ('The ghost of my brother'). This is an example of a **noun phrase** forming the subject of a sentence.

Sentence structure exercises

1 Decide which of the following are incorrectly written. Make additions or alterations to those that are not proper sentences, so that they become grammatically correct. Explain why you have made the changes.

    The long and winding road.
    I left.
    Fluffy white clouds floating across a blue sky.
    The walls are very thin.
    She was feeling ill, she asked if she could go home.
    My mum wants me to get a job, because she thinks it's a waste of time for a girl to go to university when she'll get married and have kids by the time she's twenty-five.

2 The punctuation has been left out of the following passage, which is taken from Ian McEwan's novel *Atonement*. Your task is to write it out, adding all the full stops, commas and capital letters that you think it needs.

The passage describes an English soldier's attempts to keep a French woman and her young child out of the line of fire of a German bomber plane during the evacuation of Dunkirk in 1940.

The mother seemed incapable of running she was stretching out her hand and shouting the child was wriggling towards her across his shoulder now came the screech of the falling bomb they said that if you heard the noise stop before the explosion your time was up as Turner dropped to the grass he pulled the woman with him and shoved her head down he was lying across the child and the ground shook to the unbelievable roar the shock wave prised them from the earth they covered their faces against the stinging spray of dirt they heard the Stuka climb from its dive even as they heard the banshee wail of the next attack the bomb had hit the road less than eighty yards away he had the boy under his arm and he was trying to pull the woman to her feet

Descriptive writing

As was pointed out earlier, descriptive writing is particularly prone to errors of sentence structure. Partly as a test of your understanding of the basics of sentence structure, here is a descriptive writing exercise to attempt in class.

➜ Write a description of either a beach scene or a street scene in either summer or winter. Your description should be about ten to fifteen lines long, and be as detailed and expressive as you can make it. When you have finished, you could swap your description with a friend's, and check one another's sentence structure. If you are not sure whether a particular sentence is accurate, you could check with your teacher.

➜ As a companion exercise, which you might do at home after the first description has been checked, you could take the same scene in the opposite season, and try to capture a sense of how it has changed.

EXAMINER'S TIPS

It's important to leave some time (at least ten minutes in an exam) when you've finished your writing to check that you haven't made any mistakes. Your examiner will want to see that you've used accurate paragraphing, sentence construction, punctuation and spelling in your work. After all, it is a test of your English. To gain a grade C at least, you need to structure your paragraphs clearly, to ensure your punctuation clarifies your meaning and to make certain that your spelling is accurate. It is not therefore a waste of time for you to check through your work very carefully. Marks can be lost for inaccurate English (and for poor presentation!).

Spelling: homophones

A **homophone** is a word that is pronounced in the same way as another word but which is different in spelling and meaning. Homophones are almost designed to cause spelling problems!

Here are some of the commonest sources of confusion. As a test, write down each of them in a sentence to indicate its meaning:

to/too/two	affect/effect
there/their/they're	accept/except
whether/weather	piece/peace
practice/practise	not/knot
principle/principal	your/you're
no/know	hole/whole
may be/maybe	passed/past

When you read fiction or poetry or, in fact, any kind of creative writing, you will encounter a range of literary devices. Writers have been using these devices for thousands of years to make their writing more colourful and vivid, and to appeal to the reader's imagination. Such devices are often referred to as 'figures of speech'. There are two main kinds: figures of meaning (or images), and figures of sound.

In your examination papers you will be expected to comment on the effectiveness of the language used in both poetry and prose extracts. To do this convincingly, you will need to recognise the writer's use of imagery and figures of sound, and explain how they add to the impact of the poem or passage. In your coursework too, you will almost certainly need to discuss the language used in a work of prose fiction. You will, furthermore, have to produce a piece of imaginative writing of your own for coursework, and this could well be all the more effective if you can create your own figures of speech.

For all these reasons it is necessary to identify the most commonly used and important figures of speech, and know how to comment on and employ them.

Before going on to the study of figures of speech, which follows, it might be worth spending a few minutes looking at the passage entitled 'Death' on pages 39–41. After reading it, students might mark half a dozen phrases or sentences that had a particularly strong imaginative appeal. Each class member could choose one to read out to the rest of the class.

You can go back to this passage, and study it in greater detail, when you are familiar with the various literary devices dealt with in this chapter.

Images (figures of meaning)

Simile

If you want to create a more precise or vivid impression of something, you can do so by saying it is *like* something else. This is called a simile. A simile always contains the word 'like' or the word 'as'.

e.g.   **She wondered what Charlie would think of her pick-up; unquestionably she had landed him, rather as an angler struggling with a heavy catch finds that he has hooked nothing better than an old boot.**

(Graham Greene, 'Cheap in August')

The child was like ice in her womb.

(D.H. Lawrence, 'Odour of Chrysanthemums')

**Her rich attire creeps rustling to her knees:
Half-hidden, like a mermaid in sea-weed.**

(John Keats, 'The Eve of Saint Agnes')

➡   Identify the simile in each example. Try to work out the relevance of the image.

Metaphor

Like a simile, a metaphor is a comparison of one thing with another, intended to make an idea easier to imagine or visualise. Unlike a simile, the comparison is direct and does not use 'like' or 'as'.

e.g.   **My wife handed me the box of pills. 'Are these the ones?' I asked with a mask of ice on my face.**

(Italo Svevo, 'Generous Wine')

No one wanted him; he was outcast from life's feast.

(James Joyce, 'A Painful Case')

**But at my back I always hear
Time's winged chariot hurrying near:
And yonder all before us lie
Deserts of vast eternity.**

(Andrew Marvell, 'To His Coy Mistress')

➡   Identify the metaphors in each example. Try to work out their relevance.

Personification

Personification is a form of imagery in which objects that cannot literally experience any sensations are described as though they have human characteristics.

e.g. The stealthy moon crept slantwise to the shelter of the mountains.

(Katherine Anne Porter, 'Maria Concepcion')

The boat blew a long mournful whistle into the mist.

(James Joyce, 'Eveline')

If anything might wake him now
The kind old sun will know.

(Wilfred Owen, 'Futility')

➜   Try to explain why each of the above examples is used to illustrate personification rather than metaphor.

➜   Here are three further examples of imagery:

He was as quiet as a mouse.
She was a shadow of her former self.
He drinks like a fish.

➜   What kind of image is each? Do they appeal to your imagination as much as the examples used to illustrate the varieties of imagery? If not, why not? What term would you use for imagery of this kind?

Oxymoron

Oxymoron is the joining together of apparently contradictory ideas in the same statment.

e.g.   I am the enemy you killed, my friend.

(Wilfred Owen, 'Strange Meeting')

He said, 'This is the real world, Buddy.
Toughen up your ass or it'll break.'
I said, 'I'm not your buddy, Buddy,
And the real world is a fake.'

(Mike Scott, 'Let It Happen')

➡   Try to explain in what ways these examples illustrate oxymoron.

Figures of sound

Another way of making writing more colourful and vivid is through the use of various devices of sound patterning. These devices can heighten the emotional appeal or the atmosphere of a piece of writing. They should be used sparingly, but especially in poetry or descriptive prose, or at key moments in a narrative when a particular emotional impact is needed, they can add considerably to the power and effectiveness of writing.

Onomatopoeia

This is the use of a word, or several words in a sequence, in which the sound of the word or words closely resembles the meaning – like 'boom', 'crash', 'bang', 'splash', 'whisper'.

e.g.   **The two young women … were both in white, and their dresses were rippling and fluttering as if they had just been blown back in after a short flight around the house. I must have stood for a few moments listening to the whip and snap of the curtains and the groan of the picture on the wall. Then there was a boom as Tom Buchanan shut the rear windows and the caught wind died out about the room.**

(F. Scott Fitzgerald, *The Great Gatsby*)

The lavatories were given over to their own internal rumblings; the cistern gulped now and then.

(Nadine Gordimer, 'No Place Like')

> ... rifle-shots
> **Would split and crack and sing along the night**
> **And shells came calmly through the drizzling air**
> **To burst with hollow bang below the hill.**

(Siegfried Sasson, 'The Redeemer')

➡ Write a list of all the onomatopoeic words in the examples above.

➡ Write down as many onomatopoeic words resembling sounds as you can think of in five minutes. Compare lists.

Alliteration

Alliteration is the deliberate use of a number of words, placed close together in a sentence or sentences, all beginning with the same consonant sound, or in which the same consonant sound dominates.

A particular effect must be identifiable in the consonant repetition; if no particular sound colouring or emotional impression is created by the repeated consonants, then it is merely coincidence, rather than alliteration.

Some consonants tend to have a naturally gentle, soothing sound, such as 'f', 'n' or 'l', while others tend to create a much harsher, more intense or even violent sound impression, especially the consonants 'b' and 'd' and the hard 'c' (as in the word 'clasp') and 'k'. Repeated 'w' sounds can also sometimes sound soothing and sometimes sinister; the repetition of the 'r' consonant generally creates an impression of intensity.

e.g. **The frozen moisture of its breathing has settled on its fur in a fine powder of frost.**

(Jack London, 'To Build a Fire')

He could see her legs protruding from the open bedroom door. Beside her were the bodies of the black-backed gulls, and an umbrella, broken.

(Daphne du Maurier, 'The Birds')

> **I will arise and go now, for always night and day**
> **I hear lake water lapping with low sounds by the shore.**

> (W.B. Yeats, 'The Lake Isle of Innisfree')

Sibilance

This is a special term for alliteration using 's' sounds (the 's' consonant and the soft 'c' consonant). The sounds themselves are called sibilants, and the literary technique is called sibilance.

Sibilants can create different sound impressions dependant on the context in which they are used: they can sometimes be soft-sounding, sometimes create a kind of hissing sound, and sometimes sound quite sinister.

e.g. **And then she began to dance, a slow sensuous movement, the smoke of a hundred cigars clinging to her, like the thinnest of veils.**

> (Ralph Ellison, *The Invisible Man*)

> **He sipped with his straight mouth,**
> **Softly drank through his straight gums, into his slack long body,**
> **Silently.**

> (D.H. Lawrence, 'Snake')

➡ Look again at the examples used to illustrate alliteration and sibilance.
   – Write down all the words that contain repeated identical consonant sounds.
   – Try to comment on the mood or atmosphere created in each sentence and extract of poetry, and consider how this is enhanced by the use of alliteration or sibilance.

Assonance

This is the deliberate use of a number of words, placed close together in a sentence or sentences, all containing the same vowel sound.

If the same vowel sound recurs in a sequence of words, then this sound is likely to be dominant. It has to be the same *sound*, however, and not just the same letter. For instance, 'ancient caves' is an example of assonance, but 'ancient caverns' is not, because the 'a' sound is different in the latter phrase.

Some vowel sounds tend to create a light sound impression, especially the short 'i' vowel sound (as in the word 'lift'), while the long 'i' vowel sound (as in the word 'light') often creates an impression of intensity. The longer 'o' vowel sounds (as in the words 'crow' and 'ghoul') tend to create a heavier, more sombre sound impression. The short 'a' vowel sound (as in the word 'cat') often creates a rather harsh sound impression.

e.g. **On the lake, the loon lifted its piercing cry into the evening gloom.**

(Stephen King, *Gerald's Game*)

Heaps of entangled weeds that slowly float
As the tide rolls by the impeded boat.

(George Crabb, 'Peter Grimes')

Watching, we hear the mad gusts tugging on the wire,
Like twitching agonies of men among its brambles.
Northward, incessantly, the flickering gunnery rumbles.

(Wilfred Owen, 'Exposure')

➜ Look again at the examples used to illustrate assonance.
   – Write down all the words that contain the same vowel sounds.
   – Comment on how the use of assonance adds to the feeling and atmosphere of the illustrative extracts.

Detailed analysis of literary devices

Extracts from the works of two of the major American writers of the twentieth century are offered here to give you a chance to test your understanding of the literary devices we have been exploring, and your awareness of their value in certain kinds of writing.

To illustrate how to write an analysis of a passage, commenting on the use of literary devices, we shall explore a brief extract from John Steinbeck's short novel (or novella), *The Pearl*.

Here is a summary of the novel up to the point at which the extract appears:

Kino, a pearl diver in a small town in South America, has found a magnificent pearl. He is hurrying through the jungle to the city to sell his pearl and to pay for a doctor to cure his sick baby. He is pursued by three men who intend to kill him and steal the pearl. At night, Kino rests with his baby in a cave. Below him are his pursuers, who are  waiting for daylight so that they can pick him out and shoot him. Two of them are sleeping, while the third is awake and watching for any signs of movement in the rocks above. Kino decides that he must creep silently down the mountain face and stab the men before the moon comes up. The moon rises, however, as he is preparing to leap down on his pursuers and stab them with his long knife. At the same moment, his baby cries, and one of the men below cocks his rifle and raises it towards the cave from which the wailing noise is coming. Kino reacts instantly.

Kino was in mid-leap when the gun crashed and the barrel-flash made a picture on his eyes. The great knife swung and crunched hollowly. It bit through neck and deep into chest, and Kino was a terrible machine now. He grasped the rifle as he wrenched free his knife.

His strength and his movement and his speed were a machine. He whirled and struck the head of the seated man like a melon. The third man scrabbled away like a crab, slipped into the pool, and then he began to climb frantically, to climb up the cliff where the water pencilled down. His hands and his feet threshed in the tangle of the wild grapevine, and he whimpered and gibbered as he tried to get up.

But Kino had become as cold and deadly as steel. Deliberately he threw the lever of the rifle, and then he raised the gun and aimed deliberately and fired. He saw his enemy tumble backwards into the pool, and Kino strode to the water. In the moonlight he could see the frantic frightened eyes, and Kino aimed and fired between the eyes.

John Steinbeck, *The Pearl*

Here is a detailed analysis of the use of literary devices in the extract:

In the first sentence, the sound of the gun is captured by onomatopoeia, in the word 'crashed'. The onomatopoeic effect is heightened by assonance in 'barrel-flash', using the same harsh, short 'a' consonant as in the word 'crashed'. A similar effect is produced in the second sentence, with the onomatopoeic effect of the word 'crunched' reinforced by the assonance of 'swung and crunched'.

Assonance is used again in the third sentence to emphasise the violence of the killing, in the repeated short 'e' sounds in 'neck' and 'chest'. The power and inhuman brutality of Kino's actions are captured by the metaphor of a 'terrible machine'. Alliteration using 'r' sounds helps to reinforce the feeling of violent intensity in the final sentence of the first paragraph, in the words 'grasped', 'rifle' and 'wrenched'.

The syntax of the paragraph is varied, which adds to the fluency and intensity of the writing. The flowing first sentence is followed by a short single statement. The third and fourth sentences repeat the same pattern of a longish sentence followed by a dramatic short sentence.

Now you can attempt your own stylistic analysis of the *second* paragraph. You should try to identify and comment on the effects produced by as many as you can of the following features:

➜ simile
➜ metaphor
➜ onomatopoeia
➜ assonance
➜ alliteration
➜ sibilance
➜ rhetorical repetition
➜ syntax.

You might also pick out two or three particularly powerful words that are not used in any of the literary devices you have analysed, and explain why you have chosen them.

You are advised to use the analysis of the first paragraph, above, as a guide.

Before you begin, there are two terms in the list of stylistic features above that need explanation. The device of **rhetorical repetition**, which features in the second and third paragraphs of the quoted passage, involves repeating a word or phrase in a sentence or sequence of sentences, the effect of which is generally to create an extra feeling of intensity, excitement or tension at a dramatic moment in a text. The device is used in the paragraph that precedes the passage you are studying from *The Pearl*. A cry is heard from the cave, and one of the men waiting below says, 'What is it?' The man who is watching the cave replies, 'It sounded like a cry, almost like a human – like a baby.' The repetition of the word 'like' is not necessary to get the point across – he could just have said, 'It sounded like the cry of a baby'. The moment is made more dramatic, however, by the rhetorical repetition.

The other new term is **syntax**. This is another term for sentence structure. The syntax of the first paragraph of the quoted episode from *The Pearl* is discussed in the sample analysis, where comment is made on the use of short sentences. This aspect of syntax is also discussed and illustrated at greater length in Unit 7, on page 86. Short sentences generally add punch and extra impact, and often, as in the extracts discussed in this unit and the next, increased dramatic effect. It is a good idea to look out for short sentences in prose extracts, and to try to comment on the impact they create.

When the exercise is completed, you might compare your analysis of the second paragraph with those of your classmates, in class discussion of words, phrases and stylistic features selected by individuals.

As a further reinforcement of the analytical skills you have developed, you might attempt a stylistic analysis of the *third* paragraph, along similar lines to the first two.

For further analysis of stylistic devices, read the following essay by Norman Mailer, describing an actual event. It is a description of a World Welterweight Championship boxing match that took place in the 1960s between Benny Paret, who was the world champion, and his challenger, Emile Griffith. For reasons which will become obvious, it was one of the most notorious fights ever.

DEATH

The rage in Emile Griffith was extreme. I was at the fight that night. I had never seen a fight like it. It was scheduled for fifteen rounds, but they fought without stopping

from the bell which began the round to the bell which ended it, and then they fought after the bell, sometimes for as much as fifteen seconds before the referee could force them apart.

Paret was a Cuban, a proud club fighter who had become welterweight champion because of his unusual ability to take a punch. His style of fighting was to take three punches to the head in order to give back two. At the end of ten rounds, he would still be bouncing, his opponent would have a headache. But in the last two years, over the fifteen-round fights, he had started to take some bad maulings.

This fight had its turns. Griffith won most of the early rounds, but Paret knocked Griffith down in the sixth. Griffith had trouble getting up, but made it, came alive and was dominating Paret again before the round was over. Then Paret began to wilt. In the middle of the eighth round, after a clubbing punch had turned his back to Griffith, Paret walked three disgusted steps away, showing his hindquarters. For a champion he took much too long to turn back around. It was the first hint of weakness Paret had ever shown, and it must have inspired a particular shame, because he fought the rest of the fight as if he were seeking to demonstrate that he could take more punishment than any man alive. In the twelfth, Griffith caught him. Paret got trapped in a corner. Trying to duck away, his left arm and his head became tangled on the wrong side of the top rope. Griffith was in like a cat ready to rip the life out of a huge boxed rat. He hit him eighteen right hands in a row, an act which took perhaps three or four seconds, Griffith making a pent-up whimpering sound all the while he attacked, the right hand whipping like a piston rod which had broken through the crankcase, or like a baseball bat demolishing a pumpkin. I was sitting in the second row of that corner – they were not ten feet away from me, and like everybody else, I was hypnotised. I had never seen one man hit another so hard and so many times. Over the referee's face came a look of woe as if some spasm had passed its way through him, and then he leaped on Griffith to pull him away. It was the act of a brave man. Griffith was uncontrollable. His trainer leaped into the ring, his manager, his cut man, there were four people holding Griffith, but he was off on an orgy, he had left the Garden[1], he was back on a hoodlum's street. If he had been able to break loose from his handlers and the referee, he would have jumped Paret to the floor and whaled on him there.

And Paret? Paret died on his feet. As he took those eighteen punches something happened to everyone who was in psychic range of the event. Some part of his death reached out to us. One felt it hover in the air. He was still standing in the ropes, trapped as he had been before, he gave some little half-smile of regret, as if he were saying, 'I didn't know I was going to die just yet,' and then, his head

leaning back but still erect, his death came to breathe about him. He began to pass away.

As he passed, so his limbs descended beneath him, and he sank slowly to the floor. He went down more slowly than any fighter had ever gone down, he went down like a large ship which turns on end and slides second by second into its grave. As he went down, the sound of Griffith's punches echoed in the mind like a heavy axe in the distance chopping into a wet log.

Paret lay on the ground, quivering gently, a small froth on his mouth. The house doctor jumped into the ring. He knelt. He pried Paret's eyelid open. He looked at the eyeball staring out. He let the lid snap shut. He reached into his satchel, took out a needle, jabbed Paret with a stimulant. Paret's back rose in a high arch. He writhed in real agony. They were calling him back from death. One wanted to cry out, 'Leave the man alone. Let him die.' But they saved Paret long enough to take him to a hospital where he lingered for days. He was in a coma. He never came out of it. If he lived, he would have been a vegetable. His brain was smashed. But they held him in life for a week, they fed him chemicals, and made exploratory operations into his skull, and fed details of his condition to The Goat. And The Goat kicked clods of mud all over the place, and spoke harshly of prohibiting boxing. There was shock in the land. Children had seen the fight on television. There were editorials, gloomy forecasts that the Game was dead. The managers and the prize fighters got together. Gently, in thick, depressed hypocrisies, they tried to defend their sport. They did not find it easy to explain that they shared an unstated view of life which was religious.

Norman Mailer, *Death*

[1] **Madison Square Garden, in New York, where the fight was held.**

After discussion of the passage, possibly along the lines suggested on page 38, you might write an analysis of the passage, picking out two or three similes, and an example of metaphor and personification, and say whether and in what way you found them effective.

You could also comment on some examples of the writer's uses of:

➜   alliteration
➜   sibilance
➜   onomatopoeia
➜   assonance
➜   rhetorical repetition
➜   dramatic short sentences.

 **EXAMINER'S TIPS**

The important thing to remember when writing about literary devices such as the ones mentioned in this unit is that your examiner expects you to comment on the effect that these devices have in the text. It's not enough just to point out that the writer uses, for example, a simile here or alliteration there; nor is it enough just to quote an example of imagery or of oxymoron and leave it at that. The highest marks are awarded to those candidates who can comment on the effects created by the use of these devices. Remember to make your comments as specific as possible as examiners loathe reading empty observations such as 'It makes the poem flow better'.

Punctuation: the comma

The ability to punctuate accurately is an absolutely central aspect of effective writing. For this reason it is a central aspect of GCSE assessment. The most problematic and complicated of all the punctuation marks is the comma, and to be confident of using commas accurately requires careful study.

Perhaps the best way to study commas is to learn the rules governing their use, and to try to make sure that you apply them in your own writing.

The uses of the comma

1 To separate words or phrases in a list:
   e.g. She had eggs, bacon, sausage, tomatoes and fried bread for breakfast.
   His face was thin, pale and drawn.
   We went across several fields, over a stream, past a dairy and along a dirt track to get to the farmhouse.

   N.B. There is no need for a comma before 'and' in a list, unless the list is unusually long or complicated.

2 To mark off a person addressed (by their name, a title or some other description) in direct speech:
   e.g. 'You can go, Wendy, when you've apologised.'
   'I think so, sir.'
   'Get out of my sight, you disgusting creature.'

3 To mark off a **parenthesis** or an aside that interrupts a statement. A parenthesis has the function of providing an explanation of the subject of a statement, or information about it:
   e.g. Thomas Hardy, a great novelist, lived in Dorset.
   Guy Fawkes, who tried to blow up the Houses of Parliament, was hanged.
   I took my dog, a labrador, to the vet.
   He is, I would imagine, as deaf as a post.

4 To mark off a word or phrase that shows a direct connection between two statements. The main ones are: 'however', 'moreover', 'therefore', 'nevertheless', 'for instance', 'for example', 'in fact', 'on the other hand'. (N.B. When they appear in the *middle* of a statement, words like 'however' have a comma before *and* after them.)

e.g. I wanted to go clubbing. However, my boyfriend wanted to go home.

I wanted to go clubbing. My boyfriend, however, wanted to go home.

She was afraid of the dark. She asked me, therefore, if I would walk home with her.

5 In sentences beginning with a phrase introduced by a present participle (a verb ending in '-ing'), a comma is needed to mark off this phrase from the main statement to which it is linked:

e.g. Arriving early, she found she had time to make herself a coffee.

Having eaten a huge breakfast, he had no appetite for lunch.

6 To separate the two halves of a sentence, when the first half begins with one of the following conjunctions: 'when', 'as', 'if', 'though', 'although', 'unless', 'because':

e.g. Although he was very poor, he always gave money to beggars.

When you've had enough, let me know.

If you think you're so clever, why don't you put your money where your mouth is?

7 In a sentence which consists of two statements joined by a conjunction, a comma is put before the conjunction if it is needed to make the meaning clear:

e.g. The play was very long, and I fell asleep in the second act.

She was deeply upset by his rudeness, but she tried not to show it.

He always gave money to beggars, although he was very poor.

8 To separate spoken words from the verb of saying ('he said', 'she shouted', etc.) in a sentence of direct speech:

e.g. 'I can't come to the concert,' she said, 'because I can't get a baby-sitter.'

'For God's sake put your head down,' he yelled, 'or you'll get it blown off!'

9 To mark off interjections, like 'yes', 'no', 'please', 'thank you', 'well', 'to tell you the truth':

   e.g. 'Well, yes, er, I'd like one, please.'

   'I think he's, sort of, given up, if you know what I mean.'

10 To separate phrases such as 'don't you?', 'aren't they?', 'isn't it?' which are tagged on at the end of a statement or question:

   e.g. 'You like me, don't you?'

   'They'd like to come to the party, wouldn't they?'

Exercises in the uses of the comma

Fill in the commas in the following sentences. Before each sentence write down the number of the rule that applies to it. (N.B. Two of the sentences do not need a comma at all.)

1 Los Angeles is I believe the most polluted city in America.

2 She felt very ill yet she went to work.

3 If you don't like peanut butter don't eat it.

4 Although he's very clever he often makes silly mistakes.

5 I like playing squash but my girlfriend prefers to play tennis.

6 You can talk to your uncle can't you?

7 Taking a short cut he quickly found that he was lost.

8 There are many people however who never read newspapers.

9 He got into his car drove towards the town centre turned off just before the church and headed in the direction of the river.

10 The old palace which has been standing for over four hundred years is badly in need of renovation.

11 Unless you work a lot harder you will fail your exams.

12 'Listen to me boy when I'm talking to you!'

13 The cats and dogs were all making a tremendous noise.

14 Almost everyone young and old enjoyed the film.

15 'When you leave the building' she said 'please lock all the doors.'

16 I like reading watching television listening to records and going to the pub in the evenings.

17 There are millions of people who cannot read or write.

18 I went to the theatre and my friends joined me later.

19 He would never for instance go to the cinema on his own.

20 'Let me know Peter if you can join us this evening.'

The main focus of this unit is Speaking and Listening coursework. The material is intended to provide stimulus for two separate Group Interaction sessions. The race relations section is designed to cover the skill areas 'discuss, argue, persuade', and the world poverty section could cover the same skill area, or that of 'explore, analyse, imagine'.

The ideas and information contained in the sets of extracts on both themes can be used as source material for AQA B and B (Mature) coursework (Personal Writing – inform, explain, describe), and for examination practice for each AQA specification.

Race

Extracts from two books about race relations in Britain will be the focus of this section of the unit. Each set of extracts is followed by questions that might form the basis for discussion. Alternatively, a free-ranging discussion of some of the issues raised in the extracts might be preferred.

In a book called 'Race' in Britain, published in 1982, edited by Charles Husband, a young British man of West Indian origin talks about his life in Britain from earliest childhood. This is his autobiographical account.

'RACE' IN BRITAIN

Ever since I can remember, and this is going way back, early 1960s, from being very small I was always aware of being dark – black – and for a six-year-old it wasn't very pleasant being called 'darkie' and 'monkey'. Because if you're dark then you're stupid – a fool – and I wasn't stupid, I wasn't a fool, but I was quiet and different. I remember wanting to be white when I grew up because being black was something bad and awful, and in all my dreams I was white and I'd go round in space from planet to planet in my spaceship doing good deeds and rescuing people. Then we moved to Leeds and Leeds was a big frightening place ...

I remember the first day I went to school in Leeds. I don't know why – perhaps it was because I spoke differently or looked different, but this white kid came up and started to pick on me. All the resentment, all the fear and frustration of coming to Leeds just came out and I found myself attacking him. I'd never done anything before

like that in my life and I haven't since, but I had to be dragged away. Since then nobody ever picked on me, which was surprising because there were kids who were stronger than me who got picked on and cowed. I still wanted to be white and most of my friends were white, I suppose, and then we moved to junior school which was just across the playground. There I had to be much more aware of black kids because we all seemed to be lumped together in the same class, and I suppose because we were all black we just got on – it wasn't a question of making friendships but I still went around with my white friends. I felt I didn't belong to either group – white or black, I was in a sort of limbo of my own . . .

The weird thing was that, although I had this attitude in me that I wasn't going to be a 'blackie' no matter what, the people I used to go round with used to come out with 'nigger' jokes. It was okay because I was supposed not to mind. 'It's all right, he doesn't take offence.' I was part of their group so I had to accept it. I did mind, but I didn't say, because it was something apart from me. I wasn't what they were talking about – I was almost like them. It was a really strange attitude when I look back on it now – I don't understand it – but at the same time I wasn't going to conform to what other people wanted me to be. I wasn't going to be a 'happy nigger' or an athlete, or a footballer. I wanted to be something that everyone else was – everyone white that is. As far as I could see there were no black guys doing A Levels and writing essays, they were all playing football – and I wanted to be somebody . . .

Racism doesn't exactly help you feel secure as a person; I've been followed by the police and I don't look your sort of heavy dread guy. I've had the police follow me in a car all the way up Roundhay Road at ten o'clock at night, just cruising by the side of me not saying a word. It was really eerie and I just carried on walking, because I knew that if I stopped or jumped over a wall or something they'd have got me and there'd have been no witnesses. And I've had people in the middle of town trying to run me over and other people don't believe it. Patti and I have suffered abuse from people – it happens all the time, and when we tell people they're so amazed. Drivers have made U-turns to come back at me, shouting 'you wog, you bastard, you nigger', and people just walk on – I just walk on, I mean I'm so hardened to it now. I've been attacked in Safeways in Headingley and nobody did a thing – and that was when I was out with one of the children from the home where I work. You can't go into a shop without being the focus of attention because people expect you to steal something. If you go into a restaurant for a meal then you are shunted off into a corner where you won't offend the other all-white clientele.

Being a mixed couple we tend to move in racially mixed circles when we can, except where we have to move in all-white ones because of work or colour reasons.

This means that for a lot of the time we are with a lot of white people and we stand out. We have to fight continuously against people's stereotyped ideas about us as a racially mixed couple. When you are out, you are always aware of people because they are always aware of you. They are always staring and making comments and you learn to sum people up in one go, because you have to for your own survival, otherwise you could be walking straight into trouble. You learn to read body language – you immediately know if someone is being friendly or not, then you have to decide how to deal with it . . . For the majority of white people who see us in the streets, we just fulfil their idea of the sexual stereotype – white girls who go with black men must be of 'loose morals', just looking for sexual excitement.

I'm a lot more secure now in my black identity than I have ever been, but it took a long time getting there, through a lot of stages. It was easier to get along without any hassle by conforming to a stereotype because you were being what people expected of you, whereas it was harder and more threatening if you were something that was close to them. If you wear a woolly hat and spend your time building a sound system, then you also conform to the stereotype, but if you aspire to be something else, a substitute white, an imitation white as they see it, wanting to study and do well, then you are threatening because you have the ability to take people's jobs away and be in a position of telling other people – especially white people – what to do. But in doing that you don't feel comfortable on either side of the fence because you're not black and you're not white . . .

Most of the things I've been talking about are psychological – how people see themselves and how they see other people. Black people in Britain in my opinion are still slaves, but the chains are not on their bodies but on their minds, and black kids especially need someone to help them break out of these chains, because otherwise they've got no future, they've got nothing. They've got to learn, but more important, white people have got to learn to accept them for themselves, then perhaps we can learn to accept each other.

'Race' in Britain, ed. Charles Husband

→ Why do you think the young man in 'Race' in Britain was always white in his childhood dreams?

→ Why do you think he felt he was 'in a sort of limbo' when he moved to junior school?

→ How do you explain his attitude to 'nigger' jokes when he was at school?

→ Do you think the kind of racism that he describes in the paragraph beginning 'Racism doesn't exactly make you feel secure as a person' is still going on nowadays? Do you know of anyone who has had similar experiences to the ones described?

➡ Do you think the kind of sexual stereotyping that he describes in the paragraph beginning 'Being a mixed couple', and the paragraph following it, is still prevalent?

➡ In the paragraph beginning 'I'm a lot more secure in my black identity', he claims that most white people prefer blacks to conform to the stereotype, rather than 'wanting to study and do well'. Why do you think this is? Do you think the attitude is becoming less common? Do you understand the attitude of whites, as he describes it?

➡ What do you think he means by saying 'black people in Britain . . . are still slaves'?

➡ Do you think his hope, expressed in the final sentence, is gradually being fulfilled?

In a book published in 2000, entitled *Who Do We Think We Are? Imagining the New Britain*, the writer and journalist Yasmin Alibhai-Brown considers some of the issues concerning race relations in Britain at the beginning of the twenty-first century. She interviewed hundreds of British people from different ethnic backgrounds in the course of research for the book, and some of their views are presented below.

One of the issues tackled in the book is that of the possibility or desirability of the *cultural integration* of people of non-British ethnic origin into mainstream British society. Another is *racial violence* and its causes and effects.

Integration

Here are the feelings on the issue of integration of four of the people interviewed for the book. Firstly, the view of a middle-aged Asian British woman:

Never let their ideas poison your minds, East is best. Our girls and boys know modesty, they don't need dirty things like sex before marriage. Their civilization is finished. Just mind our own business and don't have much more to do with them.

➡ Do you understand why some people feel the urge to retain their ethnic traditions and avoid 'contamination' by the western lifestyle? How realistic are they being? Are they wrong to try to do this?

Secondly, the view of the son of a multimillionaire from India:

This is England and I am happy to get a top-class English education. I don't want all this crap about Diwali and that like in those state schools. All the men in my family have had this kind of education. We are Hindus at home. But here, we do as the English do. This opens so many doors for me. That is all it is about.

➡   Do you understand why this young man has adopted the opposite attitude from that of the woman quoted above? Is *he* being realistic?

Thirdly, the view of a young white man called Ian, whom the author met 'carrying his sweet blonde baby (on whose arm he had drawn a swastika with a biro.)'

Look, why don't you lot just understand that this is our country? We built it and made it. You were nothing, slaves and our servants for centuries. We don't want you here. And if our politicians don't get rid of you, then a day will come when you will regret it. If I don't do it, this son will do it. You have no future with us. Your children are in danger – you saw what the Serbs did to those Muslim bastards. I have nothing against you. I just don't understand why you are here. Go and write this and tell your stupid people.

➡   Why do you think people like Ian harbour such violent feelings about Black and Asian Britons? How common do you think this attitude still is?

Finally, a young Muslim woman called Halima, who was studying science at London University.

I am twenty-two. I have talents, feelings, poetry in my heart which I wish to give to this nation, my nation. Will they let me? Can they let me or would it be like asking them to let the cleaner into their beds? What they will see is a young woman who has skin which is darker than it should be; a Muslim who can never be one of them. Well I am. But not on their terms nor on those imposed by my father. Whoever we are, Muslims in Britain have been profoundly changed in the years we have been living here. None of us would go to Saddam's country or to Iran or Algeria. I want to share my life and my dreams with this, my country. I want us to discuss, to fight and then make up. I want them to take me into their arms, with my difference, with all the light and shade I will bring with me. In exchange I am willing to do the same.

➜   What kind of society is this young woman hoping Britain will become? How realistic is her dream? How far do you share it?

Racial violence

Another issue taken up by Yasmin Alibhai-Brown is that of racially motivated violence against individuals and groups.

Community violence

The significance of periodic explosions of community violence, such as the race riots that erupted in the north of England in 2001, is discussed in this extract from the book.

It is perhaps no accident that across Britain young people are increasingly involved in inter-ethnic, inter-religious and inter-racial violence. A seminar I held at the Institute for Public Policy Research in 1998 to discuss this issue confirmed that, in the views of the Home Office Research Unit, community activists, the police and academics, these tensions and community flashpoints are a symptom of some deep sense of dislocation which we must take seriously.

Unmesh Desai, one-time fiery community activist, was one of the main speakers, and this is how he interpreted the problem:

> **How are we to explain today the situation of 'gangs' of one communal origin attacking another communal origin? The way I see it is that the tensions are inevitable in dispossessed communities living side by side in conditions of urban deprivation. Partly it arises out of a desire to be in a gang, to feel powerful and to adjust to the brutal realities of the streets; partly it is because there is nothing else to do; partly it is a response to racism that goes overboard. But much more importantly it speaks of the failure of leadership, both at community and state levels to address these issues in a principled and courageous way.**

Yasmin Alibhai-Brown, *Who Do We Think We Are? Imagining the New Britain*

➜   How do you explain the rioting and fighting that periodically flares up between racially-aligned gangs?

➜   Do you think more can be done at national and local level to prevent it?

Asylum seekers

Violence against asylum seekers is a recent development considered in the book. The author argues that such violence is inflamed by coverage in the press:

This kind of coverage is not only shameful for such a self-regarding profession, but is considered by groups monitoring racist violence to have incited violence against asylum seekers. Suresh Grover of the Southall Monitoring Group told me:

We have started to get so many lies about refugees in the local and national papers, it is creating a backlash. We get many calls from asylum seekers, families, lone mothers with small children who cannot go out at all or take the children to school. They get worse in the days after such stories appear.

Yasmin Alibhai-Brown, *Who Do We Think We Are? Imagining the New Britain*

➡️   Do you think that the press is actually encouraging attacks on asylum seekers by biased reporting?

➡️   Do you think government policy towards asylum seekers should change?

Writing coursework suggestions

Using the information and opinions on racial issues contained in this first section of the unit, and other material which you obtain from your own research, you could choose one of the following topics for AQA A Personal Writing: Non-Fiction (inform, explain, describe) coursework. You might find it useful to look at the section on magazine article writing in Unit 14, pages 192 to 196, if you decide to pursue the first of these suggestions.

➡️   Write a magazine article on the theme of race relations in Britain.

➡️   Write a piece expressing your personal feelings and explaining your point of view on the state of race relations in Britain today.

Examination practice

The topic of race relations in Britain could provide useful timed writing practice for the examinations in each AQA specification. This would be best left until near the end of the course. It would be advisable to study the sections on Persuasive Writing and writing a speech, in Unit 15, pages 212 to 215, before attempting the first of these practice questions.

You should spend no more than 50 minutes on your answer.

➡   Write a speech for a debate, arguing for or against this motion: 'Relations between the different races in Britain are an example to the rest of the world.' (AQA A, B and B (Mature): Writing to argue, persuade and advise).

➡   Write an essay in which you analyse and comment on the issue of race relations in Britain today. (AQA B and B (Mature): Writing to analyse, review, comment).

World Poverty

In the second half of this unit, the stimulus material is again chiefly focused on Speaking and Listening assessment. This could take the form of an exploration and analysis of the global situation of the 'haves' and 'have nots', and if this is the focus of the session, then it can be assessed for the skill areas 'discuss, analyse, imagine'. If the focus is more on discussing the issues raised, then it can be assessed for the skill areas 'discuss, argue, persuade'. In reality, of course, there is likely to be considerable overlap, and either set of skill areas can apply.

Living conditions in the developing world

To give a sense of the scale of the problem of world poverty over the past thirty-five years or so, the following passages should give you something to think about.

While you are reading these words, four people will have died of starvation, most of them children.

From the front cover of Paul Ehrlich's book, *The Population Bomb*, 1968

World Bank figures show that 'on average the one billion people in the countries with per capita incomes below $200 consume only about 1 per cent as much energy per capita as the citizens of the United States'. The Bank's Mr McNamara also hopes that 'once the people of the United States understand that they, with 6 per cent of the

world's population, consume about 35 per cent of the world's total resources, and yet in terms of economic assistance as a percentage of Gross National Product rank 14th among the 16 developed nations, they will not turn away in cynicism and indifference'.

Susan George, *How the Other Half Dies*, 1976

Wage rates in underdeveloped countries are often one twentieth or one thirtieth of those in the richer countries, for the same type of work. Today the World Bank says that there are about 800 million people, or almost 40 per cent of the population of the so-called developing countries, who live in 'absolute poverty': 'a condition of life so characterised by malnutrition, illiteracy and disease as to be beneath any reasonable definition of human decency'. In some countries one child in four dies before the age of five. Millions of people live in houses or huts made of corrugated tin, cardboard boxes and other 'impermanent' materials. They have no running water and no toilets. Electricity is a luxury. Health services are rarely within walking distance, and have to be paid for. Primary education may be available and free, but often children are needed to work. There is generally no social security or unemployment pay, and many people, some 300 million according to the International Labour Organisation, are without any kind of employment.

Teresa Hayter, *The Creation of World Poverty*, 1981

Britain's 0.2 per cent annual population growth rate adds 116,000 people per year to its population. By contrast Bangladesh, with a 2.4 per cent growth rate, adds 2.7 million. But every person in Britain uses more than 80 times as much fossil fuel as a Bangladeshi, so Britain's population growth effectively contributes 3.5 times as much carbon dioxide to the global atmosphere as Bangladesh's.

Sanjay Kumar, *New Scientist*, 6 November 1993

The total external debt of developing countries rose from $90bn in 1970 to almost $2000bn in 1998: 2.8bn of the world's 6bn people live on less than $2 a day; 1.2bn on less than $1 a day.

Between 30–35,000 children under five die every day of preventable diseases. The gap between the richest 20 per cent and the poorest 20 per cent of the world's population has doubled over the last 40 years, with the assets of the world's top three billionaires exceeding the GNP of all the 48 least developed countries (population: 600 million) . . .

In recent decades nearly one-fifth of the world's population has regressed – arguably one of the greatest economic failures of the twentieth century. World Bank economist Branco Milanovic recently pondered 'how long such inequalities (of income) may persist in the face of ever closer contacts . . . ultimately the rich may have to live in gated enclaves while the poor roam the world outside these few enclaves.'

Mike Bygrave, *The Observer*, 14 July 2002

A poor family in Brazil

To get some sense of what it must be like to be born to a poor family in a developing country, here is a description of a family that the British journalist and writer, Paul Harrison, met in Brazil. The extract is taken from his book, *Inside the Third World*.

Francisco's mother Fatima is small for her age. She is visibly weak, distant, yet easily irritated by the children. Years of pregnancy and menstruation, along with an iron-poor diet of maize, have made her chronically anaemic. Her husband Jaime is a landless labourer, with a low, erratic income barely enough to keep them all alive and clothed. No-one eats enough, and when there's not enough to go round, Fatima goes without, even when she's pregnant. And that is frequently, as the couple use no form of contraception. They have had ten children, six of whom survived to adulthood.

Fatima went through several periods of under-nourishment while Francisco was in her womb. There were times when Jaime could not get regular work and everyone went hungry. Fatima also had several attacks of stress and anxiety when Jaime beat her. Francisco probably suffered his first bout of growth retardation, both mental and physical, before he even saw the light of day.

He was born underweight, and his brain was already smaller than normal size. For the first few months he was breast-fed and suffered few infections, as he was partly protected by the anti-bodies in his mother's milk. Then he was weaned onto thin gruels and soups, taken off the breast and put onto tinned evaporated milk, thinned down with polluted water from the well. His diet, in itself, was inadequate. Then he started to get more and more infections, fever, bronchitis, measles and regular bouts of gastro-enteritis. With well-fed children these pass within a few days, but in his case, they went on for weeks and sometimes a month or more. In these periods he could tolerate no milk and few solids, and so was given weak broths, tea or sugar water. By now he was 25 per cent underweight. Because of poor nutrition, he was even more susceptible to infection, and each time he was ill, he lost his appetite and ate even less. Then he got bronchitis which developed into pneumonia. But Fatima borrowed money off a relative, went to town and got antibiotics for him. So he survived. But malnutrition made him withdrawn and apathetic. His mother got no reward for playing with him, so he received little of the stimulation his brain needed to develop properly. As he grew older, infections grew less frequent, but by the time he went to school, aged eight, he was already a year behind normal physical development and two years behind mentally. The school, in any case, was a poor one, with only three classes, no equipment, and a poorly qualified teacher.

As Francisco was continually worried about whether and what he was going to eat that day, he was distracted, unable to concentrate, and seemed to show little interest in schoolwork. The teacher confirmed that he was a slow learner, and could not seem to get the hang of maths or reading and writing. As the family was poor, they did not want to keep him on at school. He was doing so badly anyway that there seemed no point. He did a year, then was away for three years helping an uncle who had a farm, then did another year, then left for good, barely able to read or write more than a few letters. He soon forgot what little he had learned. So, like his father, he began tramping round the local ranches asking for work. Without any educational qualifications or skills, that was all he could ever hope for. And because so many were in the same boat, pay was low. When he was twenty-two he married a local girl, Graciela, aged only fifteen. She too had been under-nourished and was illiterate. She soon became pregnant and had to feed another organism inside her before she herself had fully developed. Graciela had heard about family planning from a friend, but Francisco would not let her use it and anyway she was not sure she wanted to. So by the age of only twenty-five, Graciela already had five children and had lost two. The children had every prospect of growing up much as Francisco and Graciela did, overpopulating, underfed, in poor health and illiterate.

Paul Harrison, *Inside the Third World*

Group discussion

The following questions may be used as a basis for a Speaking and Listening: Group Interaction assessment on the issue of world poverty.

➡️   What conditions of life constitute 'absolute poverty'?

➡️   What is stopping people in developing countries from breaking out of 'absolute poverty'?

➡️   What do you imagine happens to families in developing countries when the breadwinner has no regular paid employement?

➡️   Why do you think the birth rate tends to be higher in Third World countries than in developed countries?

➡️   Why are the literacy levels so much lower in most Third World countries than in developed countries?

➡️   Why do you think that wage rates are so much lower in Third World countries than in developed countries?

➡️   Do you think that major world fund-raising efforts like the Live Aid, Sport Aid and Comic Relief campaigns have any significant effect on relieving hunger in the Third World?

➡️   Do you think that the development projects of charities like Oxfam and Christian Aid are helpful?

➜ Do you think governments in the developed world should offer more aid to help development in the Third World?

➜ Should the rich nations cancel Third World debt?

➜ Should the developed countries do more to cut back on the use of fossil fuels and natural resources? What might happen over the next few decades if they do not?

➜ What might happen in the next few decades if the gap in the levels of affluence and poverty between the developed and developing countries does not significantly narrow?

Writing coursework suggestion

You might choose to use the information contained in this section of the unit, and material that you obtain from your own research, to write a coursework piece for AQA A Personal Writing: Non-Fiction (inform, explain, describe). Here is a suggested topic:

➜ Describe your feelings and explain your point of view on the conditions experienced by the poor in developing countries.

Examination practice

The topic of world poverty could provide useful timed writing practice for the 'argue, persuade, advise' section of the examinations in each AQA specification. This would be best left until near the end of the course. It would be advisable to study the sections on persuasive writing and writing a speech, in Unit 15, pages 205 to 208, before attempting this question.

You should spend no more than 50 minutes on your answer.

➜ Write a speech for a debate, arguing a case for or against this motion: '"Charity begins at home". We should solve the problems in our own country before we start worrying about the problems of others.'

Punctuation: semi-colons, colons, exclamation marks and question marks

The semi-colon

The main use of the semi-colon was illustrated in Unit 3, on page 26. It shows that there is a link between two completed statements that could otherwise be written as separate sentences, or linked with a joining word or phrase.

For example, the two statements that follow are clearly dependent on one another to make a point:

Life is short. We are fools if we don't make the most of it.

This can be written as two separate sentences, as above. However, to establish the link, the statements can be brought together in a single sentence, by using a joining word, thus:

Life is short, and we are fools if we don't make the most of it.

A more punchy way to make the link, however, would be by using a semi-colon:

Life is short; we are fools if we don't make the most of it.

Semi-colons should not be over-used, and you must be careful not to use them instead of *commas*. Used carefully and occasionally, they can add style and sophistication to your writing.

The colon

The most important use of the colon is to introduce a list, when a pause is required before the list.

An example would be:

You will need to bring several items with you into the exam: a pen, a pencil, an eraser, the pre-release booklet, and your brains.

However, in a construction in which the list is fitted into the sentence without a pause, a colon is not needed:

> You will need to bring a pen, a pencil, an eraser, the pre-release booklet and your brains into the exam.

A colon is always needed after the phrase 'the following', as in:

> You will need to bring the following into the exam: a pen, a pencil, etc.

The colon is also needed when you are introducing an extended quotation. For example:

> Hamlet picks up the skull of the old court jester and says: 'Alas, poor Yorick! I knew him, Horatio.'

If (a) brief quotation(s) are simply fitted into a sentence, however, without a pause, you would not need a colon. For example:

> Hamlet addresses the skull as 'poor Yorick', and tells Horatio that he 'knew him'.

A further common use of the colon is in a sentence in which a second statement backs up or explains an opening statement. For example:

> There can be no doubt about one thing: we're never going to one of Jane's parties again!

In this kind of construction, the colon is an alternative to writing 'that is' or 'namely'.

A capital letter is not needed after a colon.

The exclamation mark

An exclamation mark is needed when strong feeling or shock or surprise is being expressed.

Here are some examples:
> My God! My ex-wife's at the door!
> I hate Mondays!
> Don't do it! You'll kill him!

In formal writing, exclamation marks should be used sparingly, although in informal writing, such as in a letter to a friend, they tend to be used as an expression of intimacy, so that any kind of emotion can be pointed up by an exclamation mark.

The question mark

The question mark is used to show that a direct question is being asked, for example:

> 'Did you hear the thunder?' she asked.

If a question is not asked directly, but is merely *reported*, there is no need for a question mark. This is called an indirect question. Here is an example:

> She asked him if he had heard the thunder.

The main objective of this unit and the next one is to prepare you for the AQA A Original Writing/AQA B and B (Mature) Personal Writing: Fiction coursework tasks. These cover the National Criteria GCSE requirement: Writing to imagine, explore, entertain. You will study and practise the art of writing a short story, leading up to producing a piece of imaginative fiction of your own.

As a human activity, storytelling is as old as speech. All human beings tell stories. Every time we talk about something that happened to us in the past, we are telling a story. From the simplest verbal anecdote to the most sophisticated written fiction, there are common ingredients in all storytelling.

So what are the basic essentials of a story? They can be summarised thus:

➜ characterisation
➜ setting
➜ plot
➜ lively use of language
➜ point of view (first person/third person)
➜ period (past/present).

Let us look at each.

Characterisation

Every story has to focus on some*body*, and his/her interactions with others. This is the essence of the story. The characters you create must be interesting to your readers.

It must be possible for your readers to imagine them in their mind's eye, hear them in their mind's ear, and identify with them in one way or another. It is therefore vital that you can imagine them clearly yourself and make them seem real.

Study the pictures over-page. Choose one of the pictures, then answer the questions, perhaps in groups of three or four.

➜ How would you describe the person's appearance?
➜ What impressions of his/her character can you get from his/her face?

➡ What do you think s/he might have been doing just before the picture was taken?

➡ What do you think s/he might have been planning to do in the next few weeks after the picture was taken?

Now study the picture on the facing page.

➡ How would you describe the mood and feelings of the people in the picture?

➡ Where are they?

➡ What has just happened?

➡ What is about to happen?

➡ What are they saying to one another?

As the last exercise may have shown, characterisation, setting and plot are inextricably linked, and one of the best ways of bringing an imaginary situation to life is through dialogue between characters.

However, let us stay with characterisation for the moment.

The characters you create in your stories may be drawn partly from your experience of real people, or wholly from your imagination. Either way, it is necessary for your *reader* to be able to imagine them. It is thus essential to include a brief physical description of each character in your story. There are all sorts of ways of introducing them. Here are two examples.

As she dialled the number, I noticed that her finger-nails were painted emerald green, a colour unfortunately chosen, for it called attention to her hands, which were much stained by cigarette-smoking and as dirty as a little girl's. She was dark enough to be Fritz's sister. Her face was long and thin, powdered dead white. She had very large brown eyes which should have been darker, to match her hair and the pencil she used for her eyebrows.

Christopher Isherwood, *Goodbye to Berlin*

... his face slowly re-emerged into light. It was an old man's face, very bony and hairy. The moist blue eyes blinked at the fire and the moist mouth fell open at times, munching once or twice mechanically when it closed.

James Joyce, 'Ivy Day in the Committee Room'

→ What impressions of the two characters as people did you get from the description of their physical appearance?

→ Which of the two descriptions appealed most to your imagination? Why?

→ Now you might try introducing (a) character(s) of your own creation, by writing a physical description of one of the following:
  – a woman walking her dog
  – a man stepping out of a lift
  – a little girl lost in a crowd
  – two teenagers at a club
  – a drug dealer waiting for an appointment with a client.

→ If the characters and situation have appealed to your imagination, you might expand on them, and make the exercise the starting point for a complete short story.

Setting

Just as the readers of your story need to be able to picture your characters, they also need to be able to visualise the setting in which you place them. This is an important way of creating atmosphere in your story.

Look at the picture on page 64.

➡ Where do you think this scene might be? Why?
➡ How would you describe the setting?
➡ What impressions do you get of the two men?
➡ If this was a scene from a story, and they were planning something, what do you think it might be? Why?

Here is an illustration of how a vivid visual impression of a setting can be created in a few words:

I was shocked by the gloomy, dingy house, and by his room at the top of it. There was a smell of sour milk, and the window looked onto a wall, so that he was obliged to keep the light on the whole time – a muddy, low-watt bulb. He had plenty of furniture – huge, dark oak furniture, cluttered into the small space. On the table was a brown suitcase and a woman's blonde, curly wig.

Susan Hill, 'Ossie'

➡ The room belongs to the title character of the story from which this extract was taken. What sort of person would you imagine the owner of the room might be, from the description? Why?

Plot

A story stands or falls on its plot. The reader must be interested in your storyline, and must want to keep on reading to find out what happens at the end.

A well-constructed plot usually builds up to a climax near or at the end of the story. In the next unit you will find tips about starting and ending stories, and other aspects of plotting.

To get you started on working out a plot for an original story, you could join with two or three other students in a group exercise. Working with the theme of 'silence' or of 'obsession', try to work out the main stages of a story plot in summary form.

Here are some possible approaches to each title. These are only offered as illustrations. Your storyline must be original.

Silence

➡   The central character could be someone who is placed in an eternally noisy setting, dreaming of silence, and finally achieving it, with unexpected consequences.

➡   The story could focus on a Roman Catholic priest who hears a confession by one of his parishioners. The priest is tempted, or pressurised, to break his vow of confidentiality, with dramatic consequences.

➡   The central character could be someone in possession of secret information which other characters are determined to get him/her to reveal. S/he could be forced to break his/her silence, with the consequences forming the climax of the story.

Obsession

➡   The story could centre on someone who is obsessed with Internet chat rooms, leading to unexpected complications.

➡   The central character could be someone who is obsessed with discovering his/her birth parents, with a surprising or distressing outcome.

➡   The obsession could take the form of an addiction to gambling, leading to a potentially ruinous or life-threatening climax.

Lively use of language

Adopting a writing style that suits the story you are writing is essential if the story is to be effective. The story must come alive through the way you describe character and incident; you must strive to make it possible for the person who is reading your story to *see* people and events in his or her mind's eye. Having said that, writing style is a personal matter. It is not something that can be taught. Any attempt to alter your natural style to comply with a model of supposedly 'good' writing is bound to take much of the enjoyment and naturalness out of the act of writing. The ideas that follow are not designed to make you abandon your personal writing style, but merely to encourage you to look at it in a slightly more critical light, and see if there are any ways in which you can make what you have written more lively and effective.

Let us begin with adjectives. They are the principal 'describing words', as probably most people will have been aware since early childhood. The adjective is also the most commonly over-used part of speech. Here is a suggestion: when you are reading through a piece of writing that you have completed in draft form, look out for unnecessary adjectives and adverbs, and see if there are any that you can remove. (If you are not sure of the distinction between these two types of 'describing words', look at Unit 3, page 21.)

Look at this piece of writing.

The strange young man was watching her with an eerily malevolent expression in his sinister eyes.
  'What the hell are you staring at?' she yelled, angrily.

➔   Read and/or write it out with all the adjectives and adverbs removed.
➔   Comment on the difference. Which of the describing words actually weaken the impact?

Well-chosen adjectives can, on the other hand, greatly enhance the effectiveness of your writing. It all depends on the words you choose. It is a good idea always to check through what you have written and to try to replace boring or obvious adjectives with more precise and interesting ones. In particular, you might try to think of more original alternatives for adjectives that are used so frequently with particular nouns that they have lost all force and effect. Here are some examples:

> a bitter argument
> a tragic accident
> an ugly situation
> a brutal assault.

It is worth bearing in mind that adjectives and phrases that capture a precise sense impression are almost always more vivid and effective than abstract words. As a general principle, you could say that a word picture of a situation is always more effective than a statement about it. Look at these two versions of the same scene:

1   **She entered the room, and was shocked at what she saw. It was a disgusting mess. It looked as if a bomb had hit it. There were old newspapers and clothes and dirty plates everywhere, and the revolting smell made her feel sick.**

2 **She entered the room, and was shocked at what she saw. Her immediate reaction was that the house had been burgled. Crumpled shirts and underpants and yellowing newspapers littered the floor, and dishes and plates, smeared with coagulated remnants of bacon and egg, or decomposing meat, lay under the sofa and on the sideboard. The room was filled with the sickly, fetid stench of decay.**

➡ Which of these two versions is more effective? Why?

Here is another passage.

He could hear shouting coming from the lighted house, which made him more scared than ever. He plucked up courage and rang the bell. A fat man with rippling muscles under a dirty T-shirt opened the door and let him into the hall, which was full of junk, and smelt disgusting.

➡ Write an improved version.

A useful habit to develop would be to think about the relative strengths and weaknesses of *all* the important words you use, and not just the adjectives. Verbs and nouns also need to convey appearance, emotion, movement, sound and so on, as exactly as you can make them. Think about the words you use: try to make sure they're not clichéed, dull or vague, but precise and expressive.

The English language is uniquely rich in the range of its vocabulary, with words indicating the subtlest and most precise degrees and shades of meaning. You could try to draw on this richness. If someone in a story you are writing is frightened, don't just plump for the obvious word. They might just be frightened, but a word indicating a stronger degree of fear may be called for: they could be terrified, horrified, paralysed with fear.

A **thesaurus** is an extremely useful tool in this respect. It will provide you with all possible alternative options for any word. You could have one handy whenever you are engaged in imaginative writing.

Another useful habit would be to read out loud the completed draft of a piece of writing, and ask yourself if the sentences run smoothly and easily. You can then make any changes that seem necessary and finally read the whole piece out loud again to check how well it flows after your revisions.

Here are two passages taken from short stories.

Men are hunting deer up in the hills, and the noise of the shots volleys across the field with greater clarity because of the soundlessness created by the snow.

Again, on their way back, they pass the snarling dogs and they literally run down a hill and across a stubbled field to take a short cut home.

Edna O'Brien, 'Ways'

We looked around apprehensively. The professor was gone. A harassed guard threw open the front door from the outside to yell that the professor had escaped. He brandished his pistol in the direction of the gates, which hung open, limp and twisted.

In the distance, a speeding government wagon topped a ridge and dropped from sight into the valley beyond. The air was filled with choking smoke, for every vehicle on the grounds was ablaze. Pursuit was impossible.

'What in God's name got into him?' bellowed the general.

Mr Cuthnell, who had rushed out onto the front porch, now slouched back into the front room, reading a pencilled note as he came. He thrust the note into my hands.

Kurt Vonnegut Jr., 'Report on the Barnhouse Effect'

➡ Which word in the Edna O'Brian passage stands out for you as being the most expressive and effective in conveying atmosphere? Try to explain why.

➡ On a copy of the Kurt Vonnegut Jr. extract, underline all the verbs and adjectives. Discuss their effectiveness.

➡ Write a passage, no more than half a page long, capturing as vividly as you can the dramatic possibilities of one of the following situations:
an escape
the scene of a fire
a car smash and its immediate aftermath
a confrontation between a thief and a policeman.

Point of view

When you are writing, or for that matter telling a story, you are a narrator. If you are narrating an anecdote about yourself, then you are telling the story in the first person (using the pronoun 'I'). It is possible to fulfil the AQA requirement for coursework which is designed to 'explore, imagine or entertain' by writing an account of an incident that actually happened to you, and a suggestion for such a coursework piece is offered on page 16. However, we are concerned with writing narrative fiction in this unit.

If you are writing a fictional narrative in the first person, you will need to think yourself into the mind of a character who is *different* from you, and invent a story for your character to tell. The character's *voice* will need to be distinctive, and probably different from your own, so you need to be able to really imagine the character and hear him/her speaking in your head, if the story is going to be convincing.

The alternative, and probably easier option, is to write a third person narrative, focusing on named characters who you refer to as 'he' or 'she'. It is usual to limit yourself to the viewpoint of one of the characters, and enter the mind of this viewpoint character only, as you tell the story, but you still refer to this character as 'he' or 'she'.

The stories that follow illustrate the use of both first and third person narrators.

Past or present

Most stories are written in the past tense, and it is generally less complicated to use this tense. What you absolutely must *not* do is switch from present tense to past and back again. Decide on the timescale of your story and stick to it.

Sample stories

Here are two stories to read and discuss in terms of narrative technique. They were both written by college students. The first is a third person narrative and the second is written in the first person.

SILENCE

In the grimy room, lit by flickering candlelight, the woman frantically searched through the cupboards looking for her lifeline. Neither food nor drink interested her; only drugs could stimulate her interest now. Her scarred and painfully thin arms searched in vain through cupboards rendered bare by her desire for the heroin which had already destroyed her senses and her instinct to protect the baby she was carrying inside her.

The woman had the physical appearance of an unkempt teenager; she wore leggings and an oversized, stained tee-shirt stretched across her swollen belly, but the look in her dead eyes peeping beneath a greasy fringe of hair contradicted the initial impression of youth. Her eyes, like most junkies', mirrored too many, best for-gotten experiences which haunted her when she tried to sleep at night, and each time the nightmares returned she swore silently she would inject no more. It was always a hollow promise.

After making an attempt to tidy her matted hair with an almost toothless comb she grabbed a grey, threadbare coat, and leaving the syringe-littered room, she ven-tured onto the street. Her body began to shake, warning her she needed a fix. She knew what she had to do.

The first two men she approached turned away in disgust when she offered her-self to them: their revulsion was obvious, but she was too desperate to dwell on it, and even if she did it would not have bothered her.

She walked further down the street, past winos and other drug users in the door-ways, and turned the corner. And there he was! The person she needed the most. The pusher looked stylish in his new coat, and as he drew on his out-sized cigar, a gold watch and bracelet glistened on his wrist. As soon as he noticed her, an irritated look flashed across his face and he turned to one of his minders and whispered something in his ear. All the time his eyes never left the woman's direction, but now the irrita-tion turned to disgust.

'I need some gear,' the woman whined in a too-loud whisper. 'Please help me, I beg you. I promise I'll pay you soon.'

The pusher sneered his loathing at her. 'No money, no gear,' he spat as he turned away. Fear rose in her throat. Her fix was disappearing. Fast. She grabbed his arm in desperation, 'We were good together once. Come back to my place, we can be good together again'.

The dealer inclined his head slightly at one of his henchmen. He was aware the woman was creating too much attention, and attention was the last thing he wanted – especially from the police.

'Get rid of her,' he hissed. 'Now'.

The minder half pushed and half dragged her to an alleyway. The woman grabbed his arms as he threw her to the ground, causing him to fall on top of her. The man stared at her splayed legs and felt no pity for the pathetic creature, only rising, primitive violence. He discarded his coat and unzipped his trousers. The rape was over within a few seconds. The man heard a noise and, fearing the police, he panicked and ran away, leaving his coat behind.

The woman was not too traumatised by the rape. She had experienced such violations before with a much greater degree of violence. She summoned her strength and sat up – the discarded coat was now her prime interest. Rifling through the pockets she found something much more valuable to her than money – heroin and a syringe. She injected herself and within moments felt relief; but a few seconds later the relief was replaced by pain in her womb.

The couple who found her were taking a short cut through the litter-strewn alleyway. The woman accompanying the middle-aged man wanted to leave her where she was (after all, few people give sympathy to a junkie). But the kindly man was touched by her youth and condition and insisted they phone for an ambulance.

At the hospital the unconscious woman was attended by a doctor, a qualified midwife and a trainee midwife. The trainee had only attended a handful of births, all producing healthy, noisily wailing infants. She, of course, knew she would, one day, experience the birth of a dead baby. She had attended training lectures and knew what to expect; the grieving parents being brought even closer together, the Polaroid snapshot of the infant who looked perfect, if small. She had even prepared the words to say to the parents. Sadness would be there, but she would concentrate on offering support to the parents. Yes! A sad event, she thought, but one which could be made so much better by behaving as the professional she was.

The junkie's labour progressed; unnaturally long, and fraught with problems. The pregnant woman was oblivious to it all, lost in her fuddled fantasy world. The best technology was used of course, indeed the best that could be offered in a modern hospital. The situation even looked cautiously optimistic for a while, but after a few hours all those in the room knew there was going to be no joyous ending. No one, however, neither the doctor nor the experienced midwife, and definitely not the young trainee midwife, were prepared for the sight of the baby.

No cry came from its mouth, indeed it had no mouth, just a gaping hole where its nose should have been. The hideously swollen head and undersized body, deformed by drug abuse, was still. The grotesquely half-formed limbs did not move. The mother and child, silent partners in death, accompanied the shocked silence of the medical team. The trainee midwife, her shallow speech forgotten, opened her mouth to scream, but horror had struck her dumb.

Lyn Turner, 'Silence'

Discussion of 'Silence'

The opening paragraph establishes a lot about character, situation and setting.
➜ What do we learn about the woman?
➜ How does the writer provide us with this information?

The second paragraph gives us a detailed impression of her appearance.
➜ What do the details of her appearance suggest about her life?

The next two paragraphs establish the degree of her degradation.
➜ How is this revealed?
➜ Why is her approach to the two men not developed more fully?

The next section of the story deals in more detail with her approach to the drug dealer and her rape by his 'minder'.
➜ What is the effect of the physical description of the dealer?
➜ What is your impression of the character of the dealer? How does the writer's use of language create this impression?
➜ How is the sense of her desperation created?
➜ What is the point of the rape episode, in terms of characterisation and plot?
➜ What is the point of the paragraph about the couple finding her in the alley?

The paragraph beginning 'At the hospital' switches the focus of the story from the junkie to a trainee midwife.
➜ Does this slow the story down too much?
➜ What is the point of it?

The last two paragraphs bring the focus of the story to the title word.
➜ In the description of the baby, the writer is using a kind of poetic licence: the baby could not really be born so deformed as a result of

its mother's drug abuse! Does this matter? Does it create an effective climax?

➜   What is the point of re-introducing the midwife in the final sentence?

➜   The central character is never given a name. What effect is created by keeping her nameless?

THE SIGNS

Was it my fault? I think it was. I knew teenagers were difficult. I was told plenty of times. But I was out of my depth. I didn't even know what was going on, really. Oh, family? Yes, they have been kind and understanding. You know, the usual stuff: 'Oh, I'm sorry dear', and 'Fancy you not knowing!' I didn't know. There were no signs. Chris, my husband, says it would have happened even if we hadn't chucked him out of his home. I can't see that though. He must have been so alone and depressed.

I'll never forget the day we made him leave. He had been dismissed from college, lost his part-time job and had had a visit from the father of one of his ex-girlfriends, angrily telling him he was going to be a father too. I couldn't take any more. I was on medication from the doctor, and we were scraping the bottom of the barrel in order to keep him. We had given him advance warning and a little money. In fact it was all we had left. The bills we had to pay because of damage or theft he'd committed had taken a heavy toll.

That night, we didn't have to wait up for him. The house was quiet and lonely.

For the first time, I didn't have to take my sleeping tablets before going to bed. I slept soundly. When morning came, I woke to find the house had been turned upside down, and anything that was of value was gone. There was no forced entry and I knew who had done it! Some people said I should have shopped him. Chris nearly did. But that night, my son returned, and we saw the state that he was in and our hearts nearly broke.

Of course he denied the whole thing. We knew that by now the things he'd taken were in some pawn shop. But he had no money. He asked for more money, but Chris refused. I asked him to come back home. What else could I do? He was my son, for God's sake. I loved him! I know now that it was foolish and only made things worse, but at the time . . .

The final crunch came when I caught him breaking open our gas meter. I did nothing, just broke down and cried. It was Chris that blew his top. At one point, they nearly came to blows. I put myself in between them, to protect my son.

That was the last time I saw him. Funny really. I had longed for him to leave, but when he did I missed him so much. True, I gained a little health, but I had lost a son, who I loved even with his faults.

Two weeks later the police came to see us. We were expecting him to be in more trouble. We usually had a visit at least once a month. The curtains were twitching non-stop in our street. The neighbours loved it! The first question the police asked was, 'Did you know your son was taking drugs?' Like I said – no signs.

At the funeral, everyone was saying, 'What a shame!' and 'He was such a nice boy'. But I couldn't help feeling hatred towards the son I had loved so much that I would have died for him. He had left my husband and me in extreme poverty and debt, and all for an addiction. Could I have helped him? I know my husband feels bad about sending him away. If only we had known, we might have understood. It's the signs, you see, you have to know the signs . . .

Louise Guppy, 'The Signs'

Discussion of 'The Signs'

→ What do you notice about the syntax of the first paragraph? How does it help to bring the character to life?

→ How would you describe the *style* of narration? What impression do you form of the narrator from the way she tells the story? Pick out some examples of clichés. Does the use of clichés add to or detract from the effectiveness of the story?

→ The third paragraph consists of just two short sentences. Is it acceptable to write such a short paragraph? Why do you think the author chose to separate these two sentences off in this way?

→ How does the writer create a sense of the narrator's emotions in this story? Are they powerfully conveyed?

→ How is the story structured? How much do we know about the situation at the end of the opening paragraph? At what point do we find out the reason for her son's behaviour?

→ What hints are given of the strain put on the marriage by the son's behaviour? Do you think it should have been made more explicit?

→ Do you think the ending is effective?

→ Do you think the mother's ignorance of her son's drug addiction is realistic?

Coursework suggestions

As a follow-up to the story ideas worked on in this unit, here are some suggestions for a first draft of a coursework task to produce an original short story.

→   Write a story entitled 'Silence'.

→   Write a comic or serious story about an obsession.

→   'Too Late!' Write a first person narrative focusing on a discovery that comes too late.

At the end of the next unit, on pages 91–92, you will find a further twelve suggestions for short story writing. You might start planning a response to one of these suggestions instead.

Vocabulary extension: adjectives of degree

The English language contains an enormous range of adjectives, making it possible to express the subtlest and most precise shades of meaning in descriptive writing.

Here is an exercise in the recognition of variety and degrees of strength of adjectives. This can be done as a class exercise, drawing up a series of lists on the board, and perhaps recording them in a vocabulary book. Think of as many adjectives as you can, indicating degrees of the following:

     fat, thin, big, small, hungry, frightened

Re-arrange the list in an ascending order of degree, from least fat, etc. to most fat, etc.

Individual orals

Preparation for individual Speaking and Listening coursework might begin in this unit. Here is a suggestion.

Over the next few weeks you should choose a work of fiction, autobiography or travel writing to talk about. The talk should last about five minutes, or a little more. The idea of the talk is to 'sell' the book to the rest of the class, so that they want to read it as well. A good way to do this would be to pick out brief extracts from the book to read aloud, to show what is good about the book and the way it is written. What you must *not* do is to simply summarise the story, without explaining *why* you think it is good. What you are trying to convey is *what you like about the book* and *why other people might want to read it.*

Revision of sentence structure

Here are two exercises to test your understanding of basic sentence structure, and as a revision of Unit 3.

➜   Write out the sentences below. Tick the correctly constructed ones, and add words to those that are incorrect, to make them into proper sentences.

Dogs barking and howling in their pens.
He went home.
Laughing and joking and having a wonderful time.
She is eating far too much.
The car coughed and spluttered up the hill.
Men and women wandering round in the dark, searching for somewhere to rest.

➜   Correct the following passages, either by changing the punctuation or adding conjunctions:

1   The little girl was looking for her mother, they had become separated in the crowd, she began to cry, a tall man with horn-rimmed spectacles spoke to her, he asked her what the matter was, 'I've lost my mummy,' the little girl sobbed, the kind-hearted man took her to the nearby police station.

2   The police were looking for a brown Jaguar, suddenly they saw it, they immediately accelerated and chased the car, it also accelerated, both cars were travelling at twice the speed limit, the Jaguar roared through a red traffic light, it smashed into the side of a yellow Datsun, with a sickening crash, the police car arrived seconds later, to drag the victims from the smash, the Datsun driver was badly hurt, bleeding from wounds to the head and wrist, the Jaguar driver was concussed, they had caught him.

NARRATIVE WRITING TECHNIQUE: SOME HINTS

In this unit we shall go on to explore other methods used by writers to make their narratives lively and interesting. It is hoped that by looking at examples of how these aspects of the narrator's art have been used by published writers and students, you may feel encouraged to try to employ them in your own writing.

Before we go any further, though, it should be made clear that we are not talking about *rules* for short story writing. There *are* no rules. The hints that follow are merely offered as suggestions

A lively opening

Somehow or other you need to capture your reader's interest from the very opening lines of your story. If you start a story in the obvious way, by *telling* the reader about a situation and characters, in a sort of summary, there is a danger that s/he will be bored by the end of the first paragraph. You *will* have to clarify the situation and explain who the characters are, of course, but there is no need to do so straight away.

Beginning your story with an actual incident, *showing* your characters in action, is likely to capture the reader's interest from the start. Dialogue between the characters can be included at the beginning. You can then use flashback to explain about the characters and situation. This is a favourite technique of short story writers.

Generally speaking, the reader is more likely to want to know about your characters once s/he has seen them in action.

Here are three openings to short stories for exploration in terms of narrative technique.

Two gentlemen who were in the lavatory at the time tried to lift him up: but he was quite helpless. He lay curled up at the foot of the stairs down which he had fallen. They succeeded in turning him over. His hat had rolled a few yards away and his

clothes were smeared with the filth and ooze of the floor on which he had lain, face downwards. His eyes were closed and he breathed with a grunting noise. A thin stream of blood trickled from the corner of his mouth.

James Joyce, 'Grace'

→ What is Joyce trying to establish with this opening?

→ What impressions do you get of the character and situation described here? Pick out the descriptive details/phrases that create the most vivid impression for you.

→ What questions are you asking yourself by the time you've finished reading this opening passage?

→ Do you think this is a good beginning to a story? Why?

Thomas withdrew to the side of the window and with his head between the wall and the curtain he looked down the driveway where the car had stopped. His mother and the little slut were getting out of it. His mother emerged slowly, stolid and awkward, and then the little slut's long slightly bowed legs slid out, the dress pulled above the knees. With a shriek of laughter she ran to meet the dog, who bounded, overjoyed, shaking with pleasure to welcome her. Rage gathered throughout Thomas's large frame with a silent ominous intensity, like a mob assembling.

Flannery O'Connor, 'The Comforts of Home'

→ Do you think this is a good opening to a story? Why/why not?

→ From whose point of view is the situation being viewed? How do you know?

→ What is the effect of the way the young woman is introduced to the reader?

→ What questions are you asking yourself at the end of this opening paragraph?

→ How do you think the story might develop?

'I think I must move out of where I'm living,' he said. 'I have this problem with my landlady.'

He picked a long, bright hair off the back of her dress, so deftly that the act seemed simply considerate. He had been skilful at balancing glass, plate and cutlery too. He had a look of dignified misery, like a dejected hawk. She was interested.

'What sort of problem?'

A. S. Byatt, 'The July Ghost'

➡   Is this opening effective in arousing your interest? Why?
➡   Look at the descriptions of the man's (a) appearance and (b) behaviour.
➡   What impressions do you get of him from each?
➡   Pick out phrases that convey these impressions.

A strong ending

When a person reads a story, what keeps them reading, more than anything else, is the desire to know what is going to happen at the end. It is extremely important, therefore, that the ending of the story represents a natural development from what has happened before, and that it is powerful. It can be dramatic or funny, surprising or shocking, ironic or weird, but it *must* have punch. Nothing irritates a reader of a story so much as a weak ending. The major incident in a story, towards which everything else leads, is generally referred to as the climax. The great majority of short stories have a single climax, close to, if not right at, the end. One of the commonest failings of short stories written by students is that *too much* happens in the story. Too many incidents, too much drama, tends to weaken the climax. There is no need to write action-packed stories; very often a simple idea, interestingly developed, leading to an unexpected, poignant, etc., climax or revelation, makes the best story.

What is absolutely essential is to keep the reader *guessing* about what is going to happen in the end. You can, of course, lead the reader to *expect* a certain outcome, then provide an unexpected twist. A skilfully handled twist can create a very memorable ending. What you must *not* do is to provide the reader with clues which are so strong that s/he actually does guess the ending half way through. This is likely to result in an **anticlimax**.

The ultimate expression of the device of the unexpected twist at the end of the story is to leave the twist or revelation until the very last sentence. A good illustration of the technique at its most gruesomely dramatic is 'The Boarded Window', a short story by the late nineteenth-century American writer Ambrose Bierce. A short summary of the story is needed for the twist to be appreciated.

The wife of an American frontiersman of the early nineteenth century has just died of a fever. The couple had lived contentedly in a lonely cabin in the woods, and the man is described preparing his wife's body for burial. His task finally completed, he lays the body out on the kitchen table and falls asleep, exhausted, as a long wailing sound is heard in the woods surrounding the cabin. He awakes, hours later, in pitch darkness, as the table, on which he is slumped, shakes, and he hears the sound of bare feet on the floor. A heavy body seems to be hurled against the table, which seems to be empty. The man grabs his rifle and fires randomly into the darkness. This is how the story ends:

By the flash which lit up the room with a vivid illumination, he saw an enormous panther dragging the dead woman towards the window, its teeth fixed in her throat! Then there was darkness blacker than before, and silence; and when he returned to consciousness the sun was high and the wood was vocal with songs of birds.

The body lay near the window where the beast had left it when frightened away by the flash and report of the rifle. The clothing was deranged, the long hair in disorder, the limbs lay anyhow. From the throat, dreadfully lacerated, had issued a pool of blood not yet entirely coagulated. The ribbon with which he had bound the wrists was broken; the hands were tightly clenched. Between the teeth was a fragment of the animal's ear.

Ambrose Bierce, 'The Boarded Window'

➡   How do you explain the last sentence?

The use of dialogue

If you summarise a conversation between characters, you can cover a lot of ground quickly. If, on the other hand, you invent a conversation for them, in direct speech, although it will take longer, you can make your characters and situation come to life. The extra time and effort that it takes to invent dialogue rather than merely reporting it can be fully rewarded in the variety, conviction and sense of immediacy that it adds to the narrative.

The most commonly quoted principle in creative writing is 'showing not telling'. What this means is actually *creating* incidents and situations through *action*, rather than merely telling the reader about them or summarising what happened. Dialogue is an important aspect of 'showing not telling', as long as it is effectively and convincingly handled.

You should, if you can, try to imagine *how* each of your characters would speak. You can tell a great deal about a person from the way they speak. This necessitates being able to imagine the characters themselves before you start writing about them.

Here is an example of the way in which action and dialogue can work together to create dramatic immediacy. It is taken from a story called 'An Outpost of Progress' by Joseph Conrad.

The story is set in the Belgian Congo in the nineteenth century. The two characters in the episode that follows are left in charge of a remote ivory trading station for six months, until the steamer that brought them there returns to relieve them. Kayerts is placed in overall authority, and Carlier, an ex-soldier, is his assistant.

The six months pass, during which the other permanent member of the trading company's staff, an African called Makola, gets the ten Africans who are working on fixed-term contracts drunk on palm wine, and trades them for ivory. The two whites are shocked by this 'slave-dealing', but as time passes their consciousness of the money that the ivory will bring them gradually overcomes their moral scruples. The men's health deteriorates, their veneer of civilised behaviour becomes increasingly stripped away and their provisions sink so low that they are forced to live on plain rice and coffee without sugar. Still the steamer fails to arrive. They get closer and closer to breaking point. The moment at which they crack is captured in this episode:

AN OUTPOST OF PROGRESS

They waited. Rank grass began to sprout over the courtyard. The bell never rang now. Days passed, silent, exasperating and slow.

When the two men spoke, they snarled; and their silences were bitter, as if tinged by the bitterness of their thoughts.

One day, after a lunch of boiled rice, Carlier put down his cup untasted, and said, 'Hang it all! Let's have a decent cup of coffee for once. Bring out that sugar, Kayerts!'

'For the sick,' muttered Kayerts, without looking up.

'For the sick,' mocked Carlier. 'Bosh! . . . Well! I am sick.'

'You are no more sick than I am and I go without,' said Kayerts in a peaceful tone.

'Come, out with that sugar, you stingy old slave-dealer!'

Kayerts looked up quickly. Carlier was smiling with marked insolence. And suddenly it seemed to Kayerts that he had never seen that man before. Who was he? He knew nothing about him. What was he capable of? There was a surprising flash of violent emotion within him, as if in the presence of something undreamt-of, dangerous and final. But he managed to pronounce with composure –

'That joke is in very bad taste. Don't repeat it.'

'Joke!' said Carlier, hitching himself forward on his seat. 'I am hungry, I am sick, I don't joke! I hate hypocrites. You are a hypocrite. You are a slave-dealer. I am a slave-dealer. There's nothing but slave-dealers in this cursed country. I mean to have sugar in my coffee today, anyhow!'

'I forbid you to speak to me in that way,' said Kayerts with a fair show of resolution.

'You! What?' shouted Carlier, jumping up.

Kayerts stood up also. 'I am your chief,' he began, trying to master the shakiness of his voice.

'What?' yelled the other. 'Who's chief? There's no chief here. There's nothing here: there's nothing but you and I. Fetch the sugar you pot-bellied ass.'

'Hold your tongue. Go out of this room,' screamed Kayerts. 'I dismiss you, you scoundrel!'

Carlier swung a stool. All at once he looked dangerously in earnest. 'You flabby, good-for-nothing civilian, take that!' he howled.

Kayerts dropped under the table, and the stool struck the grass inner wall of the room. Then, as Carlier was trying to upset the table, Kayerts in desperation made a blind rush, head low, like a cornered pig would do, and over-turning his friend, bolted along the veranda and into his room. He locked the door, snatched his revolver, and stood panting. **In less than a minute, Carlier was kicking at the door furiously, howling. 'If you don't bring out that sugar, I will shoot you at sight, like a dog. Now then, one, two, three. You won't? I will show you who's the master.'**

Joseph Conrad, 'An Outpost of Progress'

➜   What impressions do you get of Carlier from what he says and the way he speaks?

➜   What impressions do you get of Kayerts?

➜   Look at the narrative passage between the two sections of dialogue ('Kayerts looked up quickly' etc.). What is the purpose and effect of this passage?

➜   Look at the way the dialogue is presented:
   - Is the speaker always named?
   - How many variations are there in the representations of *how* words are spoken, such as verbs of saying ('he said, he shouted', etc.). List them.
   - For what reasons does the writer begin a new paragraph?
   - How are actions by characters *within* sections of dialogue set out on the page?

As the above exercise will probably have shown, it is not always necessary to use a verb of saying at all. Quite often, several lines of dialogue can follow one another on the page without any indication of who is speaking. You should be careful, however, not to let this kind of unattributed dialogue go on so long that the reader loses track of which line is being spoken by whom. It is irritating and distracting for the reader to have to count back to the beginning of the dialogue to find out who is speaking.

A note of caution should also be sounded on the question of finding alternatives to 'he/she said'. The passage by Joseph Conrad that we have just looked at rings the changes on the verb of saying several times, as you will no doubt have noticed. But there is always a good reason for using verbs like 'howled' and 'shouted' instead of 'said'. The alternative verb of saying captures the exact tone or emotion of a character's utterance.

Perhaps the best advice would be to try to think of alternatives to 'he/she said' only if there is a good reason for doing so, or else to dispense with the verb of saying altogether.

With regard to the matter of setting out dialogue on the page, there are conventions of which you should be aware, as follows.

A new paragraph for a new speaker

The basic principle of layout is that you start a new paragraph every time the speaker changes. Any *action* by the character who has just spoken or is about to speak is written on the same line. Check back to the Conrad passage if you are still not quite sure how this works.

Single or double inverted commas

The only clear-cut convention about this is that you should distinguish between the words that your characters are actually saying, and other quotations. Thus, if you use single inverted commas for speech, you should use double inverted commas for everything else that needs them. For example:

'I know!' he said. 'Let's go to the 'Crown and Anchor'. It says in the 'Advertiser' that it's got "the best range of real ales in town". How's that sound?'

A couple of further points about the use of dialogue are worth making. You should only write dialogue if it adds something to the story. Rambling dialogue about nothing in particular detracts from the effectiveness of a story. It would be a good idea to read your dialogue out loud to yourself or someone else after you have written it. You need to get the rhythm of speech right, and the ear catches awkwardness of rhythm and stilted dialogue more easily than the eye.

Finally, you must try to punctuate your dialogue accurately. Dialogue is notoriously difficult to punctuate without making mistakes. If you are not certain of the rules for punctuating dialogue, it would be worth studying the last section of this unit, headed 'Punctuation: inverted commas', and attempting a practice exercise. It would be foolish to throw away marks for the faulty punctuation of an otherwise effective passage of conversation.

When you *do* use dialogue in a story, you might find it useful to check the rules to make sure that your punctuation is as accurate as you can get it.

You could now try writing some practice dialogues. Here are a few suggestions.

→   Write a dialogue that takes place at midnight between a mother and her teenage daughter, who had promised to be home by eleven.

→   Write a dialogue in which a boy confronts his girlfriend with his suspicions that she has secretly been seeing one of his friends.

→   Add another ten to twenty or so lines to this extract:

'Since I've waited so long you could at least let me in,' she said.

   'It's awfully late . . .'

Miriam regarded her blankly. 'What difference does that make? Let me in. It's cold out here and I have on a silk dress.' Then, with a gentle gesture, she urged Mrs Miller aside and passed into the apartment. She dropped her coat and beret on a chair. She was indeed wearing a silk dress. White silk in February. The skirt was beautifully pleated and the sleeves long; it made a faint rustle as she strolled about the room. 'I like your place,' she said. 'I like the rug. Blue's my favourite colour.' She touched a paper rose in a vase on the coffee table. 'Imitation,' she commented warmly. 'How sad. Aren't imitations sad?' She seated herself on the sofa, daintily spreading her skirt.

   'What do you want?' asked Mrs Miller.

   'Sit down,' said Miriam. 'It makes me nervous to see people stand.'

   Mrs Miller sank to a hassock. 'What do you want?' she repeated.

   'You know, I don't think you're glad I came.'

Truman Capote, 'Miriam'

→   You might now like to write a complete story, using the characters, situation and dialogue you have just created.

Varying your sentence structure

Sentence structure (or **syntax**, as it is also known) is an important element of writing style. To avoid monotony, it is a good idea to vary the lengths of your sentences. This applies particularly to moments of drama or heightened emotion in narratives. Short sentences stand out. A short sentence surrounded by longer sentences becomes a focus of the reader's attention. It is likely to be more dramatic than a longer sentence; to have more punch. It is therefore worth thinking of interspersing short and longer sentences, especially at moments of climax, special intensity or poignancy in your narrative writing. Let us look at a dramatic moment in a short story and see how the syntax helps to create dramatic impact. The story is by Daphne du Maurier and is called 'The Little Photographer'.

The female character in this extract has married into the French aristocracy and become a marquise. She has been conducting an extra-marital affair with the little photographer of the title while on holiday at a seaside resort. He has fallen in love with her, and after they have had intercourse in their usual love nest, in bracken, near a cliff's edge, he declares his love. She spurns him contemptuously, and in anger and despair the little photographer threatens to tell her husband, Edouard, everything. This is what happens next:

He reached for his coat, he reached for his hat, he slung his camera around his shoulder, and panic seized the Marquise, rose from her heart to her throat. He would do all that he threatened to do; he would wait there, in the hall of the hotel by the reception desk, he would wait for Edouard to come.

'Listen to me,' she began, 'we will think of something, we can perhaps come to some arrangement . . .'

But he ignored her. His face was set and pale. He stooped, by the opening at the cliff's edge, to pick up his stick and as he did so the terrible impulse was born in her and flooded her whole being and would not be denied. Leaning forward, her hands outstretched, she pushed his stooping body. He did not utter a single cry. He fell and was gone.

The Marquise sank back on her knees. She did not move. She waited. She felt the sweat trickle down her face, to her throat, to her body. Her hands were also wet. She waited there in the clearing, upon her knees, and presently, when she was cooler, she took her handkerchief and wiped away the sweat from her forehead, and her face, and her hands.

It seemed suddenly cold. She shivered. She stood up and her legs were firm; they did not give way, as she feared. She looked about her, over the bracken, and no one was in sight. As always, she was alone upon the headland. Five minutes passed and then she forced herself to the brink of the cliff and looked down. The tide was in. The sea was washing the base of the cliff below. It surged, and swept the rocks, and sank, and surged again. There was no sign of his body on the cliff face, nor could there be, because the cliff was sheer. No sign of his body in the water and had he fallen and floated it would have shown there, on the surface of the still blue sea. When he fell he must have sunk immediately.

Daphne du Maurier, 'The Little Photographer'

→   On a copy of the passage, underline all the sentences that you would consider short.

→   Can you work out any reasons why the writer might have chosen to make these particular sentences short?

Some final thoughts on narrative writing

1   A story is likely to have more impact if there is an original idea behind it, rather than reliance on an obvious situation with a hackneyed resolution.

2   Most effective stories end up revealing something interesting about human relationships; in other words, they leave the reader thinking about the situation and train of events that they have just been reading about.

3   Too many characters and incidents tend to destroy the impact of a story and weaken its climax. Stories tend to work best if they focus on one main character, and some conflict or dilemma with which s/he is concerned.

4   One absolute essential is to make sure that the story you write is clearly related to the title. If the reader gets to the end of the story and is left wondering what it has to do with the title, then, in an essential respect, the story has failed. You would be well advised to think carefully about this before you start.

5   You should never end a story with the alarm clock beside the bed ringing and the discovery that it was all a dream! This ending is always an anti-climax for the reader.

6   On a basic, practical level, it would be a good idea to develop the habit of reading your narrative to yourself slowly when you have finished it and checking for mistakes of spelling, sentence structure and punctuation, especially the punctuation of dialogue.

7   You might then read your story once more, out loud, preferably to someone else, and decide whether there is anything else that you need to change.

8   On the issue of *planning* a short narrative, no definite advice can be given. As a general rule, it is safest to map out your story-line before you begin writing. If you do not have a clear idea of how the story is going to develop, and what is going to happen in the climax, then you run the risk of writing a story that has little shape or coherence, and of the ending seeming contrived. Having said this, it should be borne in mind that, once begun, stories have a tendency to take on a life of their own. For many people the best advice, as far as planning is concerned, would be to start with a guiding idea, and to rely on their imagination and creativity to

guide them towards the climax. For others, a clear idea of the story-line would be helpful. It is impossible to generalise about this.

As a final example of short story writing, here is another story written by a college student. The task this time was to write a story entitled 'Paradise'. Before you read it, you might brainstorm ideas for different ways this title could be treated as a basis for a short story.

PARADISE

The sun cast long shadows on the glass still water, as John sipped the last remaining drops of milk from the coconut and lay back, looking out towards the warm glow of the horizon.

It was almost a year ago that he had first landed on the white sands of the island, and lay exhausted and heavy in the heat of the burning sun, unable even to lift his head and thank God that he was alive. He lay quite still, his heart beating with just enough strength to carry oxygenated blood to his tired brain, and he slept. It was almost twenty four hours later that he managed to open his eyes and see the island that was to be his home for the next ten months: a blur of colour and shapes so vivid and exciting that even through his exhausted vision they seemed out of place away from the artist's canvas.

He stood on legs of rubber and stared into the wondrous scene, marvelling at the cascade of colour bombarding his retina. Palm trees thrust their hairy trunks skyward and opened their leaves towards the sun; in the shadow of the palms, smaller, vibrantly coloured flowers caught the morning dew, and everywhere was silent.

Standing on the warm sand, greeted by this scene of tranquillity, John almost forgot the horror he had escaped: the screams, the blood, the noise, the terror, the panicked scramble for the lifeboats, the desperation for survival as man trampled man (women and children first) in a bid for freedom from the mangled metal and twisted steel of the two ships.

He had reached the island, half swimming, half drifting, half conscious. Others must have survived, been rescued and flown home to their families. John had drifted. He had no family anyway. The reason he was on the tragic ship was to escape the memory of the previous six months, during which John had lost his family, in a road accident in his car, his pals and his girlfriend. He wanted to escape the hurt and pain, to 'get away from it all'. He smiled as he realised the chronic irony of the situation.

'Well, you can't get further away from it all than this,' he said to himself and smiled again. He thought of what his next move should be. Breathing in the warm air and scanning the beauty of the island, he could do nothing. His brain swam, a kaleidoscope of images: panic, blood, sea, sand, death, paradise. He should look for food, build shelter, for he never knew what horned beasts inhabited this strange and wonderful land or if the temperature plummeted to arctic levels at night or rose to bake him while he slept, but he could do nothing but smile and bask in the sun's rays. He was alive.

The night came and went with little change of temperature and without attack from wild creatures. In the light of a fresh day the island looked even more beautiful, but John was hungry. Not even here in Eden can you simply bask and relax all day; there was food to be found. It wasn't long before he discovered a fresh water pool. He drank thirstily and washed his blood and sweat encrusted face, suddenly realising how tired and filthy he had become, and so spent a long hour bathing in the crystal waters and forgetting his hunger as the beauty of the scenery again engulfed him.

'This is the life,' John told himself as he crawled from the revitalising pool and sat back against a palm tree, cracking a nearby coconut and lapping its cool milk and tasting its welcome flesh. 'I could stay here forever.'

Almost a year had passed now as John again found himself leaning back against a palm sipping milk from a coconut and looking towards the warm glow of the horizon. He sat. The sun shone. Behind him he could hear the whisper of the wind gently blowing through the tops of the tall palm trees and below them through the dense, uninhabited jungle of inedible vegetation. 'I ... I could stay here forever,' he stammered through cracked lips, and coughed violently, sending his thin and distorted, malnourished body into spasm. He closed his eyes to the warm glow of the horizon. The sun beat down. All was silent.

Spencer Wakeling, 'Paradise'

Discussion points

The structure

→   Trace the changes of time sequence in this story.

→   Try to work out why the writer chose to vary the time sequence in this way.

The style

This is a story that depends for its effectiveness partly on its evocation of atmosphere and its vividness of description.

➜ Choose three or four sentences or phrases that create a particularly vivid atmosphere or sense impression.

➜ Try to explain why you have chosen them.

The use of irony

➜ Try to find examples of the use of irony in the story.

➜ Try to explain how this adds to the effectiveness of the story.

The last paragraph

➜ Re-read the last paragraph of the story and comment on:
  - the sentence structure
  - the repetition of phrases and ideas used earlier in the story
  - its effectiveness as an ending to the story.

Coursework story: final draft

If you have followed up any of the suggestions for short stories already offered in this unit, now is the time to write your final draft. Think about all the narrative writing hints that you have been looking at and decide on any alterations and improvements you might usefully make in the plot, structure, characterisation, expression, etc., of your story. Redraft it in final form.

Additional suggestions for narrative writing coursework

➜ 'Blind date'.
➜ 'The river'.
➜ Write a story featuring revenge.
➜ Write a story that centres on the occurrence of something mysterious or inexplicable.
➜ Write a story, making full use of dialogue, in which a quarrel figures prominently.
➜ Write a story about enchantment.

→ Write a story about something ludicrous or embarrassing that is told in the first person.
→ Write a story that focuses on an act of betrayal.
→ 'Paradise.'
→ 'Envy'.
→ 'The grass is always greener on the other side'.
→ Write a story featuring at least one of the characters and settings, and at least two of the sources of conflict and significant items listed over.

Characters	Setting
working mother	city suburb
rebellious teenager	coastal village
adopted child	waiting room
cinema usherette	beach

Sources of conflict	Significant items
divorce	letter
money	piece of jewellery
education	item of clothing
pregnancy	photograph
alcohol or drugs	hat
diet	animal
passion	old banger

 **EXAMINER'S TIPS**

Before beginning to write your narrative, it's always worth taking some time to plan it carefully by making some brief notes about its overall shape and structure, about who's going to be telling the story and on any important points of focus in it. A well-shaped and organised narrative is bound to improve your mark. Don't use the opening of your story for what examiners call 'throat-clearing', whilst making up your mind what it's really going to be about. Remember, too, that a variety of sentence lengths and structures will create a positive impression, if they are used purposefully.

Punctuation: inverted commas

The main use of inverted commas (or quotation marks as they are sometimes called) is in punctuating dialogue.

When you are writing dialogue, you put inverted commas round the words that someone is speaking, like this:

> 'I hope you won't forget to buy Amy's present.'

> 'Do you think I'm a complete idiot? Of course I won't!'

> 'You forgot last year, and I had to rush out on Christmas Eve and get it myself.'

As the above passage indicates, you begin each spoken sentence with a capital letter, and start a new line each time the speaker changes.

If you include a verb of saying with the spoken sentence (he *said*, she *whispered*, they *shouted*, etc.) you must put a *comma* between the spoken words and the verb of saying:

> 'I hope you won't forget to buy Amy's present,' he said.

The comma must come *before* the inverted commas. Make sure it is clearly before and not *under* the inverted commas.

If the spoken sentence is a question, then you use a question mark before the verb of saying, instead of a comma. You should never put a question mark first and then a comma:

> 'Do you think I'm a complete idiot?' she replied.

Notice that 'she' begins with a small letter even though it comes after a question mark. This is because 'she replied' is part of the complete sentence. The same applies with an exclamation mark.

If the verb of saying comes between two spoken sentences, it is followed by a full stop, and the second spoken sentence begins with a capital letter:

> 'Do you think I'm a complete idiot?' she replied. 'Of course I won't!'

However, if the verb of saying is placed *within* a spoken sentence, it is followed by a comma, and the second half of the spoken sentence begins with a small letter:

> 'You forgot last year,' he retorted, 'and I had to rush out on Christmas Eve and get it myself.'

To make sure that you are quite clear about punctuating dialogue, look at the following passage and answer the question:

> 'I hope it won't cost too much,' she said. 'If it's more than ten pounds I can't afford it.'

> 'You're so stingy,' he scoffed, 'that it's a wonder you bought anybody any presents!'

➡   Why is the first verb of saying followed by a capital 'I' and the second verb of saying followed by a small 't'?

Inverted commas are also used for the following:
 1 Quotations from books, plays, speeches, etc. For example: A famous play by Shakespeare begins: 'If music be the food of love, play on.'
 2 The titles of books, plays, films, radio and television programmes, newspapers, magazines, etc. and the names of pubs, restaurants, ships, etc., such as Shakespeare's 'Twelfth Night', 'The Sunday Mirror', 'EastEnders', 'HMS Invincible'. It should be noted that italics rather than inverted commas are the norm for the above, if they are word-processed rather than handwritten.

Inverted commas exercise

➡   Rewrite the following sentences putting in inverted commas, capital letters, commas and any other necessary punctuation:

Can I have some of your crisps the boy asked I'm ever so hungry.

We saw the film harry potter and the chamber of secrets one evening when we were crossing the atlantic in the queen elizabeth.

I would like to know why you insist on humiliating me in public. I don't she replied its just your paranoid imagination.

PROSE STUDY (1): ROALD DAHL'S 'LAMB TO THE SLAUGHTER', 'THE LANDLADY' AND 'NECK'

This unit and the next cover the Prose Study requirements of each AQA specification, which are identical. All students of GCSE English are now required to study a novel or a minimum of five or six short stories from the English literary heritage, and in AQA this requirement is covered by coursework.

Roald Dahl's *Tales of the Unexpected* have been chosen for this section of the course. There are several reasons for this. Dahl's stories are brilliantly crafted, and are universally recognised as classics in their startling linking of the grotesque and the comic. They are entertaining and approachable, and lend themselves perfectly to the study of short story technique. The stories are substantial, without being particularly long, which has to be a significant consideration on a one-year course.

The five stories suggested for study are separated into two groups: in this unit three stories that culminate in acts of unexpected violence are linked together, and the next unit links two stories in which the suspense and drama are focused on a wager.

A follow-up suggestion for a Speaking and Listening: Drama-Focused Activity is also offered in each unit.

Introduction to Roald Dahl

Roald Dahl is generally recognised as the most important children's writer of the twentieth century, and his classics like *Charlie and the Chocolate Factory*, *James and the Giant Peach* and *The BFG* have delighted generations of children and adults with the quirky brilliance of his imagination. He also wrote five collections of short stories for adults: *Someone Like You*, *Kiss Kiss*, *Twenty-Nine Kisses from Roald Dahl*, *Switch Bitch* and *Ah! Sweet Mystery of Life*. All of them were world-wide best sellers, and some of the best stories from these collections were dramatised in the TV series *Tales of the Unexpected*, and published under that title.

The son of Norwegian parents, Roald Dahl was born in Wales in 1916. He was educated at public school, a horrifying experience brought vividly to life in his autobiographical work *Boy*. He joined the RAF on the outbreak of World War II, and suffered serious injuries in a crash.

At the end of the war he moved to America and began writing short stories for adults. When he died in 1990, *The Times* called him 'one of the most widely read and influential writers of our generation'. *The New York Times Book Review* commented that Dahl had a 'masterful hand with nuance and an ability to keep the reader off balance through sheer astonishment', and a review in the *Saturday Review* aptly said, 'These bizarre stories are heightened by the matter-of-fact and realistic method with which the author approaches his surprise endings.' It is his dazzling cocktail of the grotesque, bizarre and comic that makes Roald Dahl perennially popular the world over.

Studying the stories

The approach taken to the study of Roald Dahl's stories in the Prose Study units is to take them section by section, possibly after reading the complete story at home first.

Study questions are offered for each of the five selected stories. At the end of each set of study questions is a section of text headed 'Detailed analysis'. This is also followed by a set of study questions, and significant words and phrases in the text, in terms of these questions, are highlighted.

The purpose of these 'Detailed analysis' sections is to give students the chance to explore key passages in greater detail than is possible to sustain through the study of five complete stories, given the time constraints of a one-year course. These sections could be drawn on for special focus in coursework answers, in terms of analysing the *ways* Roald Dahl creates the effects on which his stories rely.

These sections also include analytical notes on a couple of the highlighted passages, as examples of the kinds of analytical note-making that the questions are aimed at producing.

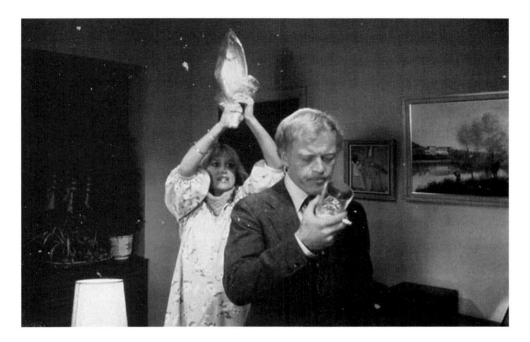

Lamb to the Slaughter

The room was warm ... to ... until the whisky had taken some of it away.

➜ What impressions do you get of Mary Maloney's relationship with her husband in this section?

➜ How does the image of 'a sunbather' capture her feelings towards him?

➜ What kind of person does she seem to be?

➜ What is the first hint that this won't be an ordinary day?

'Tired, darling?' ... to ... She stood up and placed her sewing on the table by the lamp.

➜ Do you find Mrs Maloney's husband's responses to her surprising or suspicious?

➜ How does the narrator emphasise the strangeness of his behaviour with the whisky?

'Sit down,' he said. 'Just for a minute sit down' ... to ... this time he didn't stop her.

➜ Why are we not told what he tells her? What do you think it was?

➜ How do you react to the husband in the paragraph beginning: 'So there it is'?

➜ How do you explain her immediate reaction to the story, in the paragraph beginning: 'Her first instinct ...'?

When she walked across the room ... to ... Then he crashed to the carpet.

➜ In what state of mind is Mrs Maloney when she takes the leg of lamb out of the freezer?

➜ What provokes her to attack her husband with the leg of lamb?

The violence of the crash ... to ... down the garden into the street.

➜ How does she react to the realisation that she has killed her husband? How do you explain this reaction, taking into account her feelings about him in the first section of the story?

➜ What provokes her to start planning an alibi?

It wasn't six o'clock ... to ... 'How are you, darling?'

➜ How did you react to her when she goes to the grocers and buys the vegetables and cheesecake?

➜ Why does she call out to her husband when she gets back?

She puts the parcel down ... to ... when she felt better, she would move.

➜ How does she manage to keep up the deception when the police arrive?

➜ Does her ability to lie so convincingly about her husband's death mean that she never really loved him?

So they left her then ... to the end.

➜ How does she persuade the policemen to eat the leg of lamb?

➜ What does the conversation between the policemen at the dinner table add to the effectiveness of the story?

➜ At what point in the story did you realise what her plan was?

➜ Did you think the story was believable, in terms of Mrs Maloney's motivation and the execution of her plan?

➜ Could her alibi work?

➜ Did you enjoy the story? What did you like/dislike about it?

DETAILED ANALYSIS

When she walked across the room she couldn't feel her feet touching the floor. She couldn't feel anything at all – except a slight nausea and a desire to vomit. Everything was automatic now – down the stairs to the cellar, the light switch, the deep freeze, the hand inside the cabinet talking hold of the first object it met. She lifted it out, and looked at it. It was wrapped in paper, so she took off the paper and looked at it again.

Repetition – creates sense of dazed state of mind, like a zombie.

A leg of lamb.

All right then, they would have lamb for supper. She carried it upstairs, holding the thin bone-end of it with both her hands, and as she went through the living-room, she saw him standing over by the window with his back to her, and she stopped.

'For God's sake,' he said, hearing her, but not turning round. 'Don't make supper for me. I'm going out.'

Long sentence without pauses – sense of acting automatically, without pause for thought.

At that point, Mary Maloney simply walked up behind him and without any pause she swung the big frozen leg of lamb high in the air and brought it down as hard as she could on the back of his head.

Matter-of-fact description of violence makes it more startling.

She might just as well have hit him with a steel club.

She stepped back a pace, waiting, and the funny thing was that he remained standing there for at least four or five seconds, gently swaying. Then he crashed to the carpet.

The violence of the crash, the noise, the small table overturning, helped bring her out of the shock. She came out slowly, feeling cold and surprised, and she stood for a while blinking at the body, still holding the ridiculous piece of meat tight with both hands.

All right, she told herself. So I've killed him.

Roald Dahl, 'Lamb to the Slaughter'

→ The first paragraph is notable for the use of repeated words and phrases. How does this repetition add to the dramatic effect, and the sense of Mrs Maloney's state of mind?

→ What is the effect of using a short, incomplete statement as a free-standing paragraph to follow the opening paragraph?

→ What is the significance of the phrase 'with his back to her' in the third paragraph?

→ What is the effect of the final phrase of the third paragraph: 'and she stopped'.

→ What is the impact of her husband's last words?

➜   What would you say about the style of narration of the paragraph in which Mrs Maloney kills her husband? Does it come as a shock? Is it dramatic? Is it effective?

➜   How does the use of language and syntax in the penultimate paragraph help to create the sense of her coming 'out of shock'?

➜   Is the final sentence, showing her initial reaction to the murder, surprising, shocking, predictable?

The story could be used in coursework questions on the following topics:

➜   comparison of stories focusing on an act of unexpected violence

➜   the exploration of male/female relationships

➜   the theme of deceit

➜   the creation of suspense

➜   the creation of atmosphere and drama.

The Landlady

Billy Weaver had travelled ... to ... They were amazing.

➜   Why is Billy looking for somewhere to stay?

➜   What is the effect of the repetition of the word 'new' and variants of the word 'brisk' in the paragraph beginning: 'Billy was seventeen years old'? What does it suggest about Billy?

There were no shops ... to ... reaching for the bell.

➜   What impression of the area Billy is walking through is created in the first paragraph of this section? How is it created?

➜   What attracts Billy to the 'bed and breakfast'?

➜   How does Billy's dithering over the choice of lodgings for the night add to the impact of this section of the story?

He pressed the bell ... to ... 'I knew you would. Do come in.'

➜   Is there anything about the woman that ought to make Billy feel suspicious?

She seemed terribly nice ... to ... This is a bit of all right.

➜   How does Dahl build up a feeling of unease about the landlady in the section, by what the narrator tells us, and by what she says and her way of saying it?

➡ How does Billy's impression of the landlady differ from yours? How does this divergence of reaction add to the tension?

Now, the fact that his landlady . . . to . . . waiting for him to come over.

➡ How is the sinister atmosphere built up in this section?

He crossed the room . . . to the end.

➡ What clues are there that he is in mortal danger?

➡ How do you explain his failure to realise what the landlady is planning to do?

➡ What is the impact of the discovery about the parrot and the dachsund?

➡ Do you think the ending is effective?

DETAILED ANALYSIS

As a matter of fact, now he came to think of it, he wasn't at all sure that the second name didn't have almost as much of a familiar ring about it as the first.

'Gregory Temple?' he said aloud, searching his memory. 'Christopher Mulholland? . . .'

'Such charming boys,' a voice behind him answered, and he turned and saw his landlady sailing into the room with a large silver tea-tray in her hands. She was holding it well out in front of her, and rather high up, as though the tray were a pair of reins on a frisky horse.

'They sound somehow familiar,' he said.

'They do? How interesting.'

'I'm almost positive I've heard those names before somewhere. Isn't that queer? Maybe it was in the newspapers. They weren't famous in any way, were they? I mean famous cricketers or footballers or something like that?'

'Famous,' she said, setting the tea-tray down on the low table in front of the sofa. 'Oh no, I don't think they were famous. But they were extraordinarily handsome, both of them, I can promise you that. They were tall and young and handsome, my dear, just exactly like you.'

Once more, Billy glanced down at the book. 'Look here,' he said, noticing the dates. 'This last entry is over two years old.'

'It is?'

'Yes, indeed. And Christopher Mulholland's is nearly a year before that – more than *three years* ago.'

Chilling, discovery – we realise he's in danger.

'Dear me,' she said, shaking her head and heaving a dainty little sigh. 'I would never have thought it. How time does fly away from us all, doesn't it, Mr Wilkins?'

'It's Weaver,' Billy said. 'W-e-a-v-e-r.'

'Oh, of course it is!' she cried, sitting down on the sofa. 'How silly of me. I do apologize. In one ear and out the other, that's me, Mr Weaver.'

'You know something?' Billy said. 'Something that's really quite extraordinary about all this?'

'No, dear, I don't.'

'Well, you see – both of these names, Mulholland and Temple, I not only seem to remember each one of them separately, so to speak, but somehow or other, in some peculiar way, they both appear to be sort of connected together as well. As though they were both famous for the same sort of thing, if you see what I mean – like . . . well . . . like Dempsey and Tunney, for example, or Churchill and Roosevelt.'

'How amusing,' she said. 'But come over here now, dear, and sit down beside me on the sofa and I'll give you a nice cup of tea and a ginger biscuit before you go to bed.'

'You really shouldn't bother,' Billy said. 'I didn't mean you to do anything like that.' He stood by the piano, watching her as she fussed about with the cups and saucers. He noticed that she had small, white, quickly moving hands, and red finger-nails.

'I'm almost positive it was in the newspapers I saw them,' Billy said. 'I'll think of it in a second. I'm sure I will.'

There is nothing more tantalizing than a thing like this which lingers just outside the borders of one's memory. He hated to give up.

'Now wait a minute,' he said. 'Wait just a minute. Mulholland . . . Christopher Mulholland . . . wasn't *that* the name of the Eton schoolboy who was on a walking-tour through the West Country, and then all of a sudden . . .'

'Milk?' she said. 'And sugar?'

'Yes, please. And then all of a sudden . . .'

'Eton schoolboy?' she said. 'Oh no, my dear, that can't possibly be right because *my* Mr Mulholland was certainly not an Eton schoolboy when he came to me. He was a Cambridge undergraduate. Come over here now and sit next to me and warm yourself in front of this lovely fire. Come on. Your tea's all ready for you.' She patted the empty place beside her on the sofa, and she sat there smiling at Billy and waiting for him to come over.

Roald Dahl, 'The Landlady'

Confirms for reader that Mr M. was Eton schoolboy. B. still doesn't realise – suspense!

➔ What is the effect of the landlady suddenly breaking into his thoughts in the fifth line?

➔ What impression of her is created by the description of her entrance with a tea tray? You might comment on the use of metaphor and simile in this paragraph.

➔ How does her saying, 'They were tall and handsome, my dear, just exactly like you' increase the sense of menace?

➔ What is the dramatic effect of Billy's discovery that the previous two guests stayed at the house two and three years ago?

➔ In the context of Billy seeming to be about to remember the connection between the two names in the guest book, what is the effect of the landlady saying, 'How amusing' and inviting him to sit and drink tea with her?

➔ What does Billy fail to realise about her reaction to his remembering that Mulholland was the name of an Eton schoolboy who disappeared?

➔ How does the final sentence add to the developing drama?

The story could be used in coursework questions on the following topics:
➔ comparisons of stories focusing on an act of unexpected violence
➔ the theme of deceit
➔ the creation of suspense
➔ the creation of atmosphere and drama.

Neck

When, about eight years ago ... to ... realised what was happening.
➔ What makes Sir Basil Turton such a good 'catch'?
➔ What is the narrator of the story suggesting about the women who show an interest in Sir Basil, by his imagery in paragraphs three to five? How would you describe the tone of these paragraphs?

You can imagine ... to ... triumph in her walk.
➔ What assumptions would you make about the relationship between Sir Basil and Lady Turton from what we are told in the first paragraph of this section?
➔ What is suggested about Lady Turton's character in the way the narrator describes her appearance and her demeanour?

A few minutes later ... to ... the early winter evening was beginning.

➜ How does the narrator come to be invited to the Turtons' manor house?

I went slowly ... to ... a faint smell of embrocation.

➜ How does the narrator feel about the house when he gets inside? What atmosphere is created by this?

➜ What is the effect of the introduction of Jelks, the butler, into the story? What impressions of him did you form, from the narrator's description of his appearance, and from the conversation about an alternative form of tipping?

➜ What is the effect of the narrator's description of the way Jelks talks about Major Haddock and Lady Turton?

Shortly after seven ... to ... no chance of an explosion.

➜ What further impression is created of Lady Turton by the way she talks to the narrator in this section?

➜ How does she appear to treat her husband?

➜ Do you accept the narrator's judgement that there was 'no chance of an explosion'?

➜ What are the ingredients of a potential 'explosion'?

After dinner I was ordered ... to ... and went to sleep.

➜ How would you imagine Sir Basil would be feeling about the way his wife speaks to him?

➜ What do you make of Jelks' behaviour?

The next morning ... to ... a shilling a day and they worked ten hours.

➜ Does Sir Basil seem to be at peace, as he walks around the estate with the narrator? What appears to make him happy?

➜ What effect is created by Dahl introducing 'a woman dressed in red', seen by the narrator in 'the far distance'?

➔ The focus shifts back and forth between the narrator and Sir Basil, and 'the woman in the red dress', in consecutive paragraphs. What is the effect of this? What development has occurred in the far distance?

In the clear sunlight ... to ... 'Yes,' he said. 'Of course'.

➔ What further developments occur as the two figures in the distance get closer?

➔ How is the attitude of the man and woman towards the sculpture revealed?

➔ What do you deduce about the relationship between the man and the woman?

➔ What dramatic development occurs at the end of the section?

I noticed now that something ... to ... small and clear through the sunlight.

➔ How does the narrator capture the freakishness of the situation by his use of language in the first paragraph?

➔ How does he make us aware of the danger that the woman is in, in the rest of the section?

Out of the corner ... to ... 'My beautiful Henry Moore'.

➔ How do you explain Sir Basil's reaction to what is happening, before they go to try and help?

➔ How has Sir Basil's tone in addressing his wife changed? What is the dramatic impact of this change?

➔ What is the likely effect on Sir Basil of the 'small smudge of red' on Major Haddock's moustache?

➔ Who do you sympathise with in the discussion of destroying the Henry Moore to free Lady Turton?

At this stage ... to ... and he sprang to life.

➔ How is Lady Turton's abuse of her husband likely to affect him, given the situation?

➔ What is the effect of the narrator's description of Jelks? What is ominous about his facial expression?

➔ What is the significance of Jelks' movements when he comes back with the axe and chopper?

For me, after that ... to the end.

➡   How does Dahl build up the dramatic tension in the first paragraph?

➡   What do you think Sir Basil has done?

➡   He blames Jelks for the 'accident'. Was it Jelks' fault?

DETAILED ANALYSIS

In the clear sunlight it was not difficult to follow the movements and gestures of the two figures on the lawn. They had turned now towards the piece of sculpture, and were pointing at it in a sort of mocking way, apparently laughing and making jokes about its shape. I recognized it as being one of the Henry Moores, done in wood, a thin smooth object of singular beauty that had two or three holes in it and a number of strange limbs protruding.

'When Beaumont planted the yew trees for the chess-men and the other things, he knew they wouldn't amount to much for at least a hundred years. We don't seem to possess that sort of patience in our planning these days, do we? What do you think?'

'No,' I said. 'We don't.'

The black object in the man's hand turned out to be a camera, and now he had stepped back and was taking pictures of the woman beside the Henry Moore. She was striking a number of different poses, all of them, so far as I could see, ludicrous and meant to be amusing. Once she put her arms around one of the protruding wooden limbs and hugged it, and another time she climbed up and sat side-saddle on the thing, holding imaginary reins in her hands. A great wall of yew hid these two people from the house, and indeed from all the rest of the garden except the little hill on which we sat. They had every right to believe that they were not overlooked, and even if they had happened to glance our way – which was into the sun – I doubt whether they would have noticed the two small motionless figures sitting on the bench beside the pond.

B's devotion to garden and sense of order it seems to represent – couple mocking it.

'You know, I love these yews,' Sir Basil said. 'The colour of them is so wonderful in a garden because it rests the eye. And in the summer it breaks up the areas of brilliance into little patches and makes them more comfortable to admire. Have you noticed the different shades of green on the planes and facets of each clipped tree?'

'It's lovely, isn't it?'

The man now seemed to be explaining something to the woman, and pointing at the Henry Moore, and I could tell by the way they threw back their heads that they were laughing again. The man continued to point, and then the woman walked around the back of the wood carving, bent down and poked her head thorugh one of its holes. The thing was about the size, shall I say, of a small horse, but thinner than that, and from where I sat I could see both sides of it – to the left, the woman's body, to the right, her head protruding through. It was very much like one of those jokes at the seaside where you put your head through a hole in a board and get photographed as a fat lady. The man was photographing her now.

'There's another thing about yews,' Sir Basil said. 'In the early summer when the young shoots come out ...' At that moment he paused and sat up straighter and leaned slightly forward, and I could sense his whole body suddenly stiffening.

'Yes,' I said, 'when the young shoots come out?'

The man had taken the photograph, but the woman still had her head through the hole, and now I saw him put both hands (as well as the camera) behind his back and advance towards her. Then he bent forward so his face was close to hers, touching it, and he held it there while he gave her, I suppose, a few kisses or something like that. In the stillness that followed, I fancied I heard a faint faraway tinkle of female laughter coming to us through the sunlight across the garden.

'Shall we go back to the house?' I asked.

'Back to the house?'

'Yes, shall we go back and have a drink before lunch?'

'A drink? Yes, we'll have a drink.' But he didn't move. He sat very still, gone far away from me now, staring intently at the two figures. I also was staring at them. I couldn't take my eyes away; I *had* to look. It was like seeing a dangerous little ballet in miniature from a great distance, and you knew the dancers and the music but not the end of the story, nor the choreography, nor what they were going to do next, and you were fascinated, and you *had* to look.

'Gaudier Brzeska,' I said. 'How great do you think he might've become if he hadn't died so young?'

'Gaudier Brzeska.'

'Who?'

'Yes,' he said. 'Of course.'

Roald Dahl, 'Neck'

Narrator's matter-of-fact description of kissing – makes us more aware of outrage B. must be feeling.

Almost hear sound of woman's laughter through soft 'f' alliteration and onomatopoeia – effect on B.!

→ What hint is given in the first paragraph that Sir Basil is likely to be angry and upset if he finds out who the woman is?

→ How does Sir Basil's remark about 'patience' add to the feeling of tension?

➡ The narrator discovers what the black object in the man's hand is. How does this add further to the tension?

➡ What do the couple fail to realise? Why is this significant?

➡ Sir Basil continues to talk about the garden, and how the colour of the yews 'rests the eye'. What is the significance of this in the context of what is happening on the far side of the garden?

➡ What do the woman and man do next? What does this show about their attitude to the priceless sculptures belonging to Sir Basil?

➡ What is the effect of Sir Basil stopping talking in mid-sentence?

➡ How does Dahl suggest, by the language he uses to describe the sights and sounds across the garden, the effect on Sir Basil of what is happening?

➡ What is the effect of the sentence: 'But he didn't move', and the description of him in the following sentence?

➡ How does the narrator feel at the end of the extract about what is happening? How does this increase the dramatic effect still further?

➡ What is the significance of Sir Basil's final words?

The story could be used in coursework questions on the following topics:

➡ comparison of stories focusing on an act of unexpected violence
➡ the exploration of male/female relationships
➡ the theme of deceit
➡ the creation of suspense
➡ the creation of atmosphere and drama.

Coursework suggestion

Here is a coursework suggestion that focuses on the three stories studied in this unit. You will find four more coursework suggestions for which at least two of the stories in this unit would be suitable, in Unit 9 on page 121.

➡ Write an essay comparing the different treatments of the theme of unexpected violence, in two or three of the stories in this unit.

Preparing a coursework answer on prose fiction

Before working on your coursework answer, you should give some thought to the marking criteria. The key general criterion for Reading coursework is that you refer with as much precision as possible to language, theme and structure in your work on texts.

What this means in terms of specific Prose Fiction marking criteria is that, as well as showing how characters and themes are revealed in the *events* of a story, you also discuss *how* the writer creates the *effects* on the reader, by the way the plot is structured and developed, and the way the language is used. The more you display your ability to analyse the effects of language, style and structure the higher your mark is likely to be.

Here is a suggestion as to how you might prepare your coursework answer, before you start writing it. The coursework suggestion for this unit will serve as a sample topic: 'Write an essay comparing the different treatments of the theme of unexpected violence, in two or three of the stories.'

You should begin by working out a plan for the essay, in terms of paragraph themes, for example:
- The nature of the violence.
- The build up to the violence.
- The act of violence.
- The point in the story at which the violence occurs, and the effect of this on the development of the story.
- My personal reaction to the perpetrators of the violence.
- The effectiveness of the ending of the story.

You might then draw up a grid, like the one on page 110. The sample grid has been partly filled in, as a guide.

	Lamb to the Slaughter	*The Landlady*	*Neck*
Nature of violence			
Build-up		Series of stronger and stronger hints that she's insane, and has killed 2 previous lodgers. Give 2 or 3 examples.	
Reasons			Realisation that wife is having an affair. Disgust at her rejection of all he stands for.
When it occurs and effect	Half way through story. Focus of story is not murder itself but her creation of an alibi and deception of police by cooking murder weapon.		
Personal reaction			
Ending			

A sample paragraph

As an illustration how to write a coursework piece on prose fiction, here is an example of how the third paragraph of the essay plan above might be written. The coursework title is: 'Write an essay comparing the different treatments of the theme of unexpected violence in two or three of the stories'. The paragraph topic is 'The act of violence'.

The murder itself is an impulsive, unplanned act in both 'Lamb to the Slaughter' and 'Neck'. Mrs Maloney takes the leg of lamb with which she kills her husband out of the fridge in a trance-like state. She picks it up without even seeming to realise what it is, emphasised by the use of repetition: 'She lifted it out, and looked at it. It was wrapped in paper, so she took off the paper and looked at it again'. She still seems to intend to cook it for dinner, until her husband says: 'Don't make supper for me. I'm going out'. She just seems to snap then: she 'swings' the frozen leg of lamb in the air and brings it 'down on his head as hard as she could'. In 'Neck', it is the butler who provides the murder weapon, offering Sir Basil a saw and a lethal axe to free his wife's neck from the sculpture. However, Jelks seems to secretly put the idea into Sir Basil's mind of murdering his wife, pushing the axe forwards and giving 'a little offer, a little coaxing offer that was accompanied by an infinitesimal lift of the eyebrows'. Repetition is used this time to emphasise the subtle pressure he is putting on Sir Basil. The decision is instantaneous: 'the instant he felt the handle in his grasp he seemed to realise what was required of him and sprang to life', and he brings it down on his wife's neck. In 'The Landlady' the murder is planned. We are left at the end of the story to assume that Billy is going to die from drinking the poisoned tea, and end up preserved on the third floor with the previous lodgers.

All the important assessment objectives for Writing are met in this paragraph.

Assessment Objective (i) requires: 'making appropriate references to texts and developing and sustaining interpretations of them'. In this paragraph the interpretation is developed by backing up each point with reference to the text, either through explanations of incidents, or by direct quotation. This is absolutely central to successful textual analysis.

Assessment Objective (iv) requires you to 'make cross-references'. This is obviously done by exploring similarities and differences between the stories, which is also essential when you are studying a short story collection.

The relevant requirement of Assessment Objective (v) is to 'understand and evaluate how writers use linguistic devices to achieve their effects'. This is dealt with in the sample analysis by mentioning the device of repetition, and explaining the different effects it creates in two of the stories. This also illustrates cross-referencing between stories.

Speaking and Listening: Drama-Focused Activity

'Lamb to the Slaughter' could be used as a stimulus for a group improvisation to fulfil the requirement of a drama-focused activity covering the skill area: 'explore, analyse, imagine'.

Five students could play the roles of Mrs Maloney and the four detectives who arrive at her house after she has called to report her husband's death. The students playing the detectives should write out a set of questions that each of them is going to ask about the death of Mr Maloney, and the student playing Mrs Maloney should improvise answers. This should, of course, be performed without a script, and will largely involve improvisation from all the students involved.

Punctuation: revision exercise

Write out the following text and punctuate it correctly:

I went to see shakespeares macbeth at taunton arts centre yesterday it was difficult to understand but it was pretty dramatic stuff macbeth who starts out as a hero turns into a villain after three witches have predicted that hell become king of scotland he kills the king whos called duncan to fulfil their prophecy and ends up becoming a tyrant whats the point my girlfriend said afterwards of watching a play written hundreds of years ago

because its good I said

shes thick

PROSE STUDY (2): ROALD DAHL'S 'MAN FROM THE SOUTH' AND 'TASTE'

This unit focuses on two further stories from *Tales of the Unexpected*. They are linked by the theme of a dangerous wager. There is another suggestion for a Drama-Focused Activity for Speaking and Listening, based on one of the stories.

Man from the South

It was getting on ... to ... tipping them up by their legs.

➜   What kind of atmosphere is created in this first section, and how is it created through the use of language?

Just then I noticed ... to ... 'No', I said. 'I am not.'

➜   What is your first impression of the old man?

Suddenly one of the American cadets ... to ... 'I promise you it never fails.'

➜   Is there anything odd about the behaviour of the old man in this section?

'One momint, pleess' to ... 'Den we forget it, yes?'

➜ What is the effect of the narrator saying, '... and at the same time I had the feeling that he was relishing a private little secret all his own'?

➜ How is the tension and drama built up as the boy and the old man discuss the size and nature of the bet?

➜ How did you react when the old man suggests that the boy bets 'de little finger of your left hand'?

➜ How does the boy's reaction to this suggestion add to the dramatic effect?

The boy sat quite still ... to ... Soon he was tapping with one of his feet as well.

➜ How does Roald Dahl release and then begin building up the tension again in this section?

'Now just let me check ...' to ... 'You come and watch.'

➜ Why do you think the boy brings up the subject of the bet again?

➜ What is the effect of the discussion of the precise arrangements for the bet?

➜ Why do you think the old man says, 'But I see you are not a betting man. Americans never are.'?

The little man led the way ... to '... in de pocket of de car.'

➜ Very little happens for the next two pages. Does this weaken the dramatic impact?

➜ How does the maid add to the dramatic impact?

➜ How do the narrator and the girl respond to the situation? How do you explain the boy's determination not to be dissuaded from going through with the bet?

Then the coloured maid ... to ... with the chopper in his hand.

➜ How would you describe the old man's behaviour as he prepares to begin the wager?

➜ At the end of this section, did you have any idea what was going to happen when the counting began?

We are all ready? ... to the end.

➜ How is dramatic tension created up to the moment when the woman bursts in?

→ How does Dahl create a sense of the violence of the woman's behaviour towards the old man by his use of language?

→ Do you think the ending of the story is effective?

DETAILED ANALYSIS

'We are all ready?' he said. 'Mister referee, you must say to begin.'

The English girl was standing there in her pale blue bathing costume right behind the boy's chair. She was just standing there, not saying anything. The boy was sitting quite still, holding the lighter in his right hand, looking at the chopper. The little man was looking at me.

'Are you ready?' I asked the boy.

'I'm ready.'

'And you?' to the little man.

'Quite ready,' he said and he lifted the chopper up in the air and held it there about two feet above the boy's finger, ready to chop. The boy watched it, but he didn't flinch and his mouth didn't move at all. He merely raised his eyebrows and frowned.

'All right,' I said. 'Go ahead.'

The boy said, 'Will you please count aloud the number of times I light it.'

'Yes,' I said. 'I'll do that.'

With his thumb he raised the top of the lighter, and again with the thumb he gave the wheel a sharp flick. The flint sparked and the wick caught fire and burned with a small yellow flame.

Repetition of 'thumb' emphasises difficulty.

'One!' I called.

He didn't blow the flame out; he closed the top of the lighter on it and he waited for perhaps five seconds before opening it again.

He flicked the wheel very strongly and once more there was a small flame burning on the wick.

shows he's nervous

'Two!'

No one else said anything. The boy kept his eyes on the lighter. The little man held the chopper up in the air and he too was watching the lighter.

tension

'Three!'

'Four!'

'Five!'

'Six!'

'Seven!' Obviously it was one of those lighters that worked. The flint gave a big spark and the wick was the right length. I watched the thumb snapping the top down on to the flame. Then a pause. Then the thumb raising the top once more. This was an all-thumb operation. The thumb did everything. I took a breath, ready to say eight. The thumb flicked the wheel. The flint sparked. The little flame appeared.

'Eight!' I said, and as I said it the door opened.

Roald Dahl, 'Man from the South'

→ How do each of the characters behave at the beginning of this passage, up to '"Yes', I said, 'I'll do that."' How does this add to the build-up of tension and drama?

→ How do you react to the description of the boy's first attempt to ignite the lighter?

→ What is different about the boy's second flick of the lighter's wheel? What does this suggest about his state of mind?

→ What do you notice about the syntax of the section between 'Two!' and 'Eight'? What do you notice about the use of language? How does the way this passage is written create dramatic impact?

→ What is the effect of the last sentence of the passage?

This story could be used in coursework questions on the following topics:
→ stories focusing on a wager
→ the creation of suspense
→ the creation of atmosphere and drama.

Taste

There were six of us ... to ... the first warm oozings of saliva to my mouth.
→ What impression of Richard Pratt is created in the second paragraph?

As we sat down ... to ... tell him about the village of Geierslay.
→ What impression do you form of Mike Schofield in this section? Why is it important to him to display his knowledge and discrimination in wine?

But Richard Pratt did not taste ... to ... 'Excuse me now, will you, while I fetch it.'
→ What do you think of Pratt's behaviour in this section? How does Louise respond to him? How are their reactions captured by Dahl's use of language?

→ What is Mike's reaction to his guest's behaviour? How is it captured by the use of language?

→ What is the significance of the passage of conversation, in terms of the ending of the story?

The thought of another ... to ... 'I'll bet you anything you like.'

→ How do the words and phrases chosen by Dahl to describe Pratt's physical appearance in this section affect your response to him?

→ How is the sense of danger built up in this section?

The three women and I ... to ... 'the hand of your daughter in marriage.'

→ Why do you think Mike Schofield is so willing to up the stakes?

→ The announcement of the wager is delayed for thirty lines after Mike has agreed to bet 'anything you like'. What is the effect of the delay?

→ How do you react to Pratt's announcement of the wager, when it finally comes?

Louise Schofield gave a jump ... to ... 'But I don't want to hear it.'

→ What appears to be happening in the first twenty lines of this section?

→ How does Mike react immediately after Pratt has offered 'both my houses'? How does this add to the atmosphere of the story?

→ How does Louise's refusal add to the drama?

'Louise! Please!' ... to ... 'It's a bet.'

→ Are you convinced by Mike's insistence that 'It's impossible' for Pratt to name the wine?

→ What does the conversation between Mike and his wife and daughter reveal about him?

→ What is the effect of the last line of this section?

Immediately, Mike picked up ... to ... Mike did not smile back.

→ How effective is Dahl in creating a sense of the grotesque by his use of language in the description of Pratt's face in the first paragraph, and of his smelling the bouquet of the wine in the second paragraph of this section?

→ What is the effect of the description of his tasting performance in the fourth paragraph?

→ What else did you find repulsive in this section?

First, then, which district ... to ... 'This is the little Château Branaire-Ducru.'

➜ The pace of this section is quite slow. Do you think this detracts from or adds to the impact?

➜ Were you expecting Pratt to come up with the right answer? Why?

Mike sat tight ... to ... 'Go on and turn it round.'

➜ How do you react to Louise's call to her father to turn the bottle round? What does this show about her?

➜ What is the dramatic effect of the description of Mike's face, after he says 'Just a minute'?

Then this happened ... to the end.

➜ Is the maid telling the truth? How can you tell?

➜ How does Dahl capture a sense of the maid's anger, by the use of language in the description of her appearance, in the paragraph beginning: 'But the maid didn't go away.'?

➜ What is the significance of her revelation?

➜ What do you think is likely to happen next?

DETAILED ANALYSIS

'First, then, which district in Bordeaux does this wine come from? That's not too difficult to guess. It is far too light in the body to be from either St Emilion or Graves. It is obviously a Médoc. There's no doubt about *that*.

'Now – from which commune in Médoc does it come? That also, by elimination, should not be too difficult to decide. Margaux? No. It cannot be Margaux. It has not the violent bouquet of a Margaux. Pauillac? It cannot be Pauillac, either. It is too tender, too gentle and wistful for Pauillac. The wine of Pauillac has a character that is almost imperious in its taste. And also, to me, a Pauillac contains just a little pith, a curious dusty, pithy flavour that the grape acquires from the soil of the district. No, no. This – this is a very gentle wine, demure and bashful in the first taste, emerging shyly but quite graciously in the second. A little arch, perhaps, in the second taste, and a little naughty also, teasing the tongue with a trace, just a trace of tannin. Then, in the after-taste, delightful – consoling and feminine, with a certain blithely generous quality that one associates only with the wines of the commune of St Julien. Unmistakably this is a St Julien.'

He leaned back in his chair, held his hands up level with his chest, and placed the fingertips carefully together. He was becoming ridiculously pompous, but I thought that some of it was deliberate, simply to mock his host. I found myself waiting rather tensely for him to go on. The girl Louise was lighting a cigarette. Pratt heard the match strike and he turned to her, flaring suddenly with real anger. 'Please!' he said. 'Please don't do that! It's a disgusting habit, to smoke at table!'

realisation of ·hat he'll be ·e if he wins ·ager – con- ·olling bully.

She looked up at him, still holding the burning match in one hand, the big slow eyes settling on his face, resting there a moment, moving away again, slow and contemptuous. She bent her head and blew out the match, but continued to hold the unlighted cigarette in her fingers.

'I'm sorry, my dear,' Pratt said, 'but I simply cannot have smoking at table.' She didn't look at him again.

'Now, let me see – where were we?' he said. 'Ah, yes. This wine is from Bordeaux, from the commune of St Julien, in the district of Médoc. So far, so good. But now we come to the more difficult part – the name of the vineyard itself. For in St Julien there are many vineyards, and as our host so rightly remarked earlier on, there is often not much difference bween the wine of one and the wine of another. But we shall see.'

He paused again, closing his eyes. 'I am trying to establish the "growth",' he said. 'If I can do that, it will be half the battle. Now, let me see. This wine is obviously not from a first-growth vineyeard – nor even a second. It is not a great wine. The quality, the – the – what do you call it? – the radiance, the power, is lacking. But a third growth – that it could be. And yet I doubt it. We know it is a good year – our host has said so – and this is probably flattering it a little bit. I must be careful. I must be very careful here.'

He picked up his glass and took another small sip.

'Yes,' he said, sucking his lips, 'I was right. It is a fourth growth. Now I am sure of it. A fourth growth from a very good year – from a great year, in fact. And that's what made it taste for a moment like a third – or even a second-growth wine. Good! That's better! Now we are closing in! What are the fourth-growth vineyards in the commune of St Julien?'

akes him em like a ptile – dehu- anises him.

Again he paused, took up his glass, and held the rim against that sagging, pendulous lower lip of his. Then I saw the tongue shoot out, pink and narrow, the tip of it dipping into the wine, withdrawing swiftly again – a repulsive sight. When he lowered the glass, his eyes remained closed, the face concentrated, only the lips moving, sliding over each other like two pieces of wet, spongy rubber.

Simile and sibilants create impression of a grotesque puppet.

'There it is again!' he cried. 'Tannin in the middle taste, and the quick astringent squeeze upon the tongue. Yes, yes, of course! Now I have it! The wine comes from one of those small vineyards around Beychevelle. I remember now. The Beychevelle district, and the river and the little harbour that has silted up so the wine ships can no longer use it. Beychevelle ... could it actually be a Beychevelle itself? No, I don't think so. Not quite. But it is somewhere very close. Château Talbot? Could it be Talbot? Yes, it could. Wait one moment.'

He sipped the wine again, and out of the side of my eye I noticed Mike Schofield and how he was leaning farther and farther forward over the table, his mouth slightly open, his small eyes fixed upon Richard Pratt.

'No. I was wrong. It is not a Talbot. A Talbot comes forward to you just a little quicker than this one, the fruit is nearer the surface. If it is a '34, which I believe it is, then it couldn't be Talbot. Well, well. Let me think. It is not a Beychevelle and it is not a Talbot, and yet – yet it is so close to both of them, so close, that the vineyard must be almost in between. Now, which could that be?'

Adds to dramatic tension – sense of hushed awe.

He hesitated, and we waited, watching his face. Everyone, even Mike's wife, was watching him now. I heard the maid put down the dish of vegetables on the sideboard behind me, gently, so as not to disturb the silence.

'Ah!' he cried. 'I have it! Yes, I think I have it!'

For the last time, he sipped the wine. Then, still holding the glass up near his mouth, he turned to Mike and he smiled, a slow, silky smile, and he said, 'You know what this is? This is the little Château Branaire-Ducru.'

Roald Dahl, 'Taste'

→ In the second paragraph Pratt comes to his first positive conclusion about the wine. In the process he keeps repeating words and phrases. How does this make him sound convincing?

→ Are you beginning to believe that he is going to guess the wine correctly by the end of this paragraph?

→ What is the dramatic significance of Pratt's response to Louise striking a match to light a cigarette?

→ How does she react to his bullying?

→ The narrator suggests that Pratt is mocking his host to some extent. Can you find any evidence of this in the paragraph beginning: 'He paused again'? Do you think that Mike deserves to be mocked?

→ What is the effect of him saying: 'Now we are closing in!'?

→ The narrator describes him carrying out further tests on the wine in the paragraph beginning: 'Again he paused', and calls it 'a repulsive sight'. How does Dahl make Pratt seem repulsive by his use of language? How does this add to the build-up towards the climax?

→ How does Pratt create an even stronger feeling in the next paragraph that he is going to win?

➡   What is the effect of the description of Mike's posture?

➡   What is the dramatic effect of re-introducing the maid in the paragraph beginning: 'He hesitated'?

This story could be used in questions focusing on the following topics:
➡   stories focusing on a wager
➡   the exploration of male/female relationships
➡   the theme of deceit
➡   the creation of suspense
➡   the creation of atmosphere and drama.

Coursework suggestions

Apart from question 1, all of these questions can be answered by using stories from Unit 8 as well as this unit.

1 Write an essay showing the different treatments of the device of a wager, in 'Man from the South' and 'Taste'.
2 Compare Roald Dahl's approaches to the presentation of relationships between men and women in 'Lamb to the Slaughter', 'Taste' and 'Neck'.
3 Discuss Roald Dahl's treatment of the theme of deceit in two or more of these stories.
4 Write an essay showing how Roald Dahl creates suspense in two or more stories, and discuss the importance of suspense in the stories.
5 Show how Roald Dahl creates atmosphere and drama in two or more stories.

Speaking and Listening: Drama-Focused Activity

The activity is to continue the story 'Taste'. Five students, two female and three male, should work together on developing the dramatic situation on which the story ends, and carry it forward to some sort of resolution. A storyline needs to be worked out, and each character's role and response to the crisis needs to be sketched in. There is no need to actually produce a written script to be learnt (though this is a possibility if time allows); the story can be improvised, as long as each student knows roughly how they are going to react and what is going to happen. There is obviously a range of possibilities for conflict, between Mike and his wife and/or between Louise and her mother, in their conflicting reponses to the main conflict between Mike Schofield and Richard Pratt.

When you write a coursework piece on prose fiction, it is important that you show that you have your own views on the text, rather than someone else's opinion, whether they are from your teacher or from a revision or study-aid guide to the text. Your teacher/moderator is very likely to have read the study guide anyway and can recognise second-hand opinions and other people's style of writing. You must show you've read the text closely and can support your views by detailed reference and quotation. It's important too, that you comment on the way the writer has presented characters, on how the story is structured and organised and also on its key ideas and themes. Above all, don't just re-tell or summarise the story in your own words.

Spelling: the 'i' before 'e' rule

As was suggested in Unit 1, the best way to improve your spelling is to keep a systematic record of the correct spellings of all the words you spell incorrectly in your written work, and test yourself on them regularly.

However, there are *some* spelling rules that are worth remembering if you are uncertain of the spelling of words to which the rules apply.

The rule that most people know is the rule that goes 'i before e except after c'. Unfortunately, apart from the fact that there are some exceptions to the rule, the actual rule itself is more complicated than just 'i before e except after c', making it probably the most difficult rule of all to apply.

This *is* the rule:
1 'I' before 'e', except after 'c', **when the 'ie' or 'ei' sound is 'ee'.**
2 When the 'ei' or 'ie' sound is the short 'e' (as in 'leisure'), 'a' (as in 'weight') or 'i' (as in 'height') the reverse is the case. Thus:
   'brief' is spelt 'ie' because the sound is 'ee' but it does *not* come after 'c';

'ceiling' is spelt 'ei' because the sound is 'ee' but it *does* come after 'c';
'neighbour' is spelt 'ei' because the sound is not 'ee'.

3 The exceptions to the rule are: seize, weir, weird, protein, caffeine.

➔ As a test of whether the rule is worth trying to apply, fill in 'ie' or 'ei'
in the following words:

dec--t	ch--f	fr--ght
c--ling	for--gn	forf--t
gr--f	shr--k	bel--ve

Reading a play by Shakespeare and producing an analytical response to it are requirements of all the GCSE specifications. Shakespeare features in the AQA specifications as coursework. The play chosen for study here is *Macbeth*, and an approach to tackling the requirement in a limited time span is suggested in this unit and the next.

The onus will be on you to read the play in your own time. If you can get hold of a performance of the play on CD, and listen to it while you are reading the play, this will aid your understanding.

The best way to bring the play to life *as* a play is to see it in performance. If this is not possible, the next best way is to watch a good film version of it. This is the approach taken in this unit.

Perhaps the most atmospheric film version of the play is Roman Polanski's *Macbeth*, made in 1971, and issued on Columbia Tristar video, number CVR 20668. This can be watched in various ways:

A scene from Polanski's *Macbeth*

→ straight through, without interruptions
→ episode by episode, pausing for brief explanations
→ episode by episode, pausing for fuller discussion
→ reading the scene summary that follows, bit by bit, before watching each episode, as an aid to your understanding of the action. It should be noted that parts of scenes, and some complete scenes, are missed out in the film, and occasionally the order of episodes is changed.

Introduction

First, here is a brief introduction to the play. It was written in 1606 and is a tragedy. Like all of Shakespeare's major tragedies (such as *Hamlet*, *Othello* and *King Lear*), it centres on a nobleman who is in many respects an admirable person, but who finds himself in a situation that tests his strength and virtue beyond its limits. Macbeth is a leading nobleman in the land of Scotland at the time when it was a self-governing country, ruled by its own kings. He is a fearless military leader, and is so highly regarded by the King of Scotland that he is rewarded, in the opening scene of the play, with the title Thane of Cawdor, after the owner of that title is found guilty of treason and sent to be executed. Just before receiving the news of his elevation to this exalted title, Macbeth has encountered three witches who possess prophetic powers and who prophesy that not only will he become Thane of Cawdor, but also King. When the first prophecy is immediately fulfilled, and King Duncan then announces that he will spend the next night at Macbeth's castle, the temptation to ensure the speedy completion of the witches' predictions is born. It is from this that the tragedy grows.

Plot summary

Act I, Scene 1

Three witches meet on a heath, and an atmosphere of malevolence is created. They speak of meeting with Macbeth on the heath.

Act I, Scene 2

News is brought to King Duncan of the battle between the Scottish King's army, led by Macbeth and Banquo, and an invading force from Norway. The Norwegian army has been defeated, and Macbeth's bravery has played a major part in the Scottish victory. As a result of this, King Duncan announces that Macbeth will be rewarded with the title Thane of Cawdor, after the arrest of the current Thane, who had treacherously sided with Norway.

Act I, Scene 3

The three evil witches confront Macbeth and Banquo as they return from the battle, and prophesy Macbeth's elevation to the titles of Thane of Cawdor and then King, but they also say that it will be Banquo's heirs who will be kings after Macbeth. Macbeth is startled by these predictions.

Two noblemen arrive with the news of the fulfilment of the first part of the witches' prophecy, and Macbeth begins to fear his own ambitious nature once the possibility of ultimate power is suddenly within his grasp.

Act I, Scene 4

King Duncan informs Macbeth, now formally recognised as Thane of Cawdor, that Malcolm, the King's eldest son, will inherit the throne. Macbeth realises that he will have to find a way to 'o'erleap' Malcolm if he is to fulfil his 'black and deep desires'.

Act I, Scene 5

Lady Macbeth, receiving her husband's news by letter, fears that Macbeth lacks the necessary ruthlessness to gain the throne by foul means. Further news, that the King will be spending the night at Macbeth's castle, excites her murderous ambitions. When Macbeth arrives, she begins to tempt him to murder the King.

Act I, Scene 6

Duncan arrives and is greeted warmly by Lady Macbeth. He is surprised by Macbeth's absence.

Act I, Scene 7

Macbeth, alone, contemplates the assassination of the King. His 'vaulting ambition' is weighed against the practical and moral arguments against murdering Duncan. He expresses his doubts to his wife, who mocks his unmanly cowardice and unfolds a plan to get Duncan's guards drunk, steal into the King's chamber and stab him, and accuse the guards of the murder. Macbeth is persuaded.

Act II, Scene 1

Macbeth meets Banquo and pretends he has given no thought to the witches' predictions; but alone, in a state of restless agitation, he imagines that he sees a bloody dagger in the air above his head, leading him towards the King's chamber.

Act II, Scene 2

Having carried out Lady Macbeth's plan, and stabbed Duncan and the guards, Macbeth is riddled with guilt, imagining a voice saying, 'Macbeth shall sleep no more'. Lady Macbeth tells him to wash his hands, attempting to reassure him that: 'A little water clears us of this deed'. In his panic Macbeth came away from the chamber with bloody daggers in his hands, which she has to take back because Macbeth is too horrified by what he has done to return to the chamber of death. Someone is knocking at the door.

Act II, Scene 3

The tension is briefly relaxed as a drunken porter takes his time to open the door, offering comic reflections on human frailty. Macduff and Lennox, two other leading noblemen, are at the door. Macduff is greeted by Macbeth, and then goes up to the King's chamber and makes the discovery of the murder of Duncan.

Macbeth puts on a convincing performance of shocked ignorance, rushes into the chamber, and claims, when he comes back out, to have killed Duncan's guards, assuming they were the murderers. Malcolm and Donaldbain, the dead King's sons, decide to flee the country, in fear of meeting the same fate as their father if they stay.

Act II, Scene 4

Malcolm and Donaldbain's flight has aroused suspicion that they were behind the murder of Duncan. Macbeth has been named as King.

Act III, Scene 1

Banquo privately suspects Macbeth of the murder. Macbeth requests Banquo's presence that night at supper, and mentions rumours that Malcolm and Donaldbain are in England and Ireland, openly making accusations against Macbeth.

Macbeth, in soliloquy, speaks of his fears about Banquo and the witches' prophecy that it would be Banquo's rather than his own sons who would form a dynasty. He secures the services of two bitter and desperate men to murder Banquo and Fleance, Banquo's son, while they are out riding that afternoon.

Act III, Scene 2

Macbeth speaks darkly to his wife of his fears and the mental torture induced by guilt over the murder of Duncan. He speaks mysteriously of a deed of darkness that will be performed before nightfall. Despite his feelings of guilt and self-disgust, he is now taking the initiative to safeguard his position, and is sinking deeper into evil.

Act III, Scene 3

Banquo is killed by the hired murderers, but Fleance escapes.

Act III, Scene 4

Macbeth hears from one of the hired killers of the murder of Banquo, but the news of Fleance's escape only increases his anguish.

The guests are all seated at table for the evening's banquet. Macbeth is invited to take the last empty seat. He cannot find one, however, and suddenly realises, to his stark horror, that the seat he has been offered is filled with the gashed and bloody figure of Banquo. His seemingly insane ramblings, addressed to Banquo's ghost that only he can see, are explained away by Lady Macbeth as a childhood infirmity that will soon pass. The ghost fades, and Macbeth seems to recover, but then it returns, and the banquet is called off by Lady Macbeth.

The ghost again disappears, but Macbeth is convinced that 'blood will have blood'. The absence of Macduff at the banquet is a further worry. Macbeth decides to return to the 'weird sisters', for another glimpse into the future.

Act III, Scene 5

The witches meet again, and speak of Macbeth's imminent visit to 'meet his destiny'.

Act III, Scene 6

Suspicions of Macbeth are now rife, and are voiced by Lennox, another leading nobleman. Malcolm, Duncan's son, now in England, is plotting a civil war to overthrow Macbeth, who is now openly being called a 'tyrant'. Macbeth is also making preparations for war, and Macduff, in secret consultation with Macbeth's enemies, has refused to join Macbeth's side.

Act IV, Scene 1

The witches are preparing for the visit of Macbeth by casting spells over a cauldron. Macbeth arrives, and a series of prophetic apparitions appear before him. The first warns him to 'beware Macduff', but the second and third seem reassuring: he cannot be killed by anyone 'of woman born', and he will not be defeated until Birnam Wood moves to the hill of Dunsinane. The final vision is of a procession of eight kings, with Banquo appearing last with a mocking smile.

News is brought of Macduff's flight to England. Macbeth's heart hardens at the news, and he resolves to have Macduff's wife and babies murdered, to wipe out his line, as he had failed to wipe out Banquo's.

Act IV, Scene 2

Lady Macduff is angry and distraught at her husband's abandonment of his family. Her eldest son bravely and wittily stands up for his father in the face of his mother's bitterness. The hired killers arrive, stab the child, and chase the fleeing Lady Macduff.

Act IV, Scene 3

Macduff and Malcolm, the dead King Duncan's son, now at the King of England's palace, talk of the tyranny set in train by Macbeth, as 'Each new morn/New widows howl, new orphans cry'. Malcolm longs to 'tread upon the tyrant's head'. He then pretends that he would become an even more evil tyrant than Macbeth if he were to become king; in the process he describes the qualities of an ideal ruler, which he claims to lack. The King of England, Edward the Confessor, is described, presenting a portrait of the noble and virtuous ruler.

Ross, another Scottish nobleman, brings news of the full extent of the tyranny that reigns in Scotland, where 'sighs and groans and shrieks' daily rend the air. He speaks of rumours of an impending civil war in Scotland to overthrow 'the tyrant' Macbeth, and asks Malcolm and Macduff to return to Scotland to join the rebel army. He then informs Macduff of the murder of his wife and children. Macduff vows revenge.

Act V, Scene 1

Lady Macbeth has gone mad, and wanders round the castle talking to herself and rubbing her hands constantly, trying to clear imaginary blood from them. She hints at the cause of her obsession – her involvement in the murders of Duncan, Banquo and Macduff's wife.

Act V, Scene 2

The rebel forces, led by Malcolm, Macduff and Malcolm's Uncle Siward, are massed near Dunsinane Castle, which Macbeth is fortifying to withstand a siege. Macbeth's control over his own forces is growing steadily weaker.

Act V, Scene 3

Macbeth remains defiant, emboldened by the recollection of the witches' promises that he could be killed only when Birnam Wood comes to the castle where he now is, and by a man not born of woman. News of an enemy army of ten thousand approaching causes Macbeth merely to give the order: 'Hang those that talk of fear'. His inner feelings are bordering on despair, however: he knows that he is hated by everyone, and his life has lost all meaning. The doctor brings news of his wife's mental illness, and he longs for not only her, but the country to be cured of its sickness.

Act V, Scene 4

Malcolm gives the order that boughs be cut from the trees in Birnam Wood, which the rebel army has now reached, so that his troops can carry them to conceal their numbers.

Act V, Scene 5

Macbeth remains confident that Dunsinane can withstand a siege. The cries of women are heard, and Macbeth reveals that he has become completely insensitive to 'horrors'. He is told that Lady Macbeth is dead, and the news provokes an outburst of the deepest despair: he feels now that human life is worthless and meaningless. News is brought that Birnam Wood is on the move. Macbeth's confidence is shaken; all that is left to him now is to die bravely.

Act V, Scene 6

Final preparations are made by Malcolm for the imminent battle.

Act V, Scene 7

The battle is raging, and Macbeth is confronted by Young Siward, whom he kills, again feeling invulnerable because of the witches' prediction that he cannot be killed by 'man that's of a woman born'. Macduff appears, bent on personal revenge for the murder of his wife. Siward reveals that the castle has been breached, and victory for the rebels is now close.

Act V, Scene 8

Macduff confronts Macbeth, who defiantly tells him of the 'charmed life' the witches' prophecy promises him. Macduff reveals that he was 'ripped' from his mother's body by a Caesarean operation, and therefore not 'born' in the natural way. Macbeth's last hope is gone, but he has sufficient pride left to fight to the death rather than surrender.

Act V, Scene 9

Macduff brings in the head of Macbeth, and Malcolm is hailed as the new King of Scotland. Malcolm pronounces that everyone who fled the tyranny of Macbeth's rule should be welcomed home to Scotland, and all the agents of Macbeth should be punished. Everyone is invited to attend the coronation of the new King.

Performing a scene

When you have watched the film and discussed the issues it raises, you might attempt a performance of one of the scenes. A good one to act out is Act V, Scene 5, as it is particularly dramatic and emotionally charged.

The person playing Macbeth will need to study his speeches carefully, and work out how to convey the different feelings expressed in the scene.

Reading the play

In preparation for the next unit, you should read the play at home, so that you have a full enough understanding of it to be able to explore sections of it in depth, with an awareness of how the sections chosen for detailed study fit into the development of the play as a whole.

Shakespeare's language

Perhaps the major stumbling block to the appreciation of Shakespeare is the difficulty of actually understanding the words he uses. The language used by the characters in Shakespeare's plays seems so different from the language spoken today that people often refer to it as 'old English'.

In fact, it isn't. There *is* a form of English that language experts refer to as 'Old English'. It was spoken 800 years before Shakespeare, and is also known as Anglo-Saxon English, pre-dating the Norman conquest of 1066. It is almost completely unrecognisable as English at all. By the time of the poet Geoffrey Chaucer, in the fourteenth century, a new form of English had developed, that linguists refer to as Middle English. This is more obviously a form of English, but it still seems alien when you first encounter it, and has to be learnt.

Compared even with Middle English, let alone Old English, Shakespeare's language is *comparatively* easy to understand, once you have got used to it. Here is a brief extract from *Macbeth*:

> If thou speaks't false,
> Upon the next tree shalt thou hang alive,
> Till famine cling thee. If thy speech be sooth,
> I care not if thou dost for me as much.

There are 31 words in this extract.

→   How many of them are modern words?
→   Underline all the words that are not modern.
→   What do you notice about these words?

As you will no doubt have recognised, one of the archaic words is 'thou' (used three times), another is 'thee', and another is 'thy'. Two of the 'thous' are followed by words that are not quite modern. This is, in fact, one of the main reasons why Shakespeare's English seems so different from modern English, and why people think of it as 'old English'. In fact, the language of Shakespeare is referred to as *Early Modern English*, as distinct from Old English and Middle English. Once you've got to grips with the 'thees', 'thous' and 'thys' (which are simply archaic forms of 'you' and 'your') and the verb forms which go with them – 'thou *speakest*' (instead of 'you speak', 'thou *dost*' (instead of 'you do'), etc. – then it really isn't very different from modern English.

The other main differences are also illustrated in this extract. A comparatively small proportion of Shakespeare's words have disappeared from the English language over the intervening four centuries ('sooth' in this extract, for example), and others have gradually changed their meaning over the centuries (like 'cling'). Such words should be explained in the notes in your text. Most of the words, however, have retained their spelling and meaning, unlike Chaucer's words from two centuries before Shakespeare.

Shakespeare's verse

Another of the difficulties that people experience with Shakespeare is that his plays are written in verse (or poetry). This makes them seem all the more remote, in comparison with a modern play.

Writing plays in verse form was a convention of Shakespeare's time. It makes the language seem much grander and, of course, poetic, which people in Shakespeare's day thought fitting for plays about kings and queens and the nobility.

There is a form and rhythmic pattern to Shakespeare's verse. It is called **iambic pentameter** verse. If we look at a line from *Macbeth* we can see how it works:

Till famine cling thee. If thy speech be sooth.

→ How many separate syllables are there in this line?
→ Which of the syllables receive stress when you speak them out loud?

You may have decided that the stressed syllables are the second ('fa-' of 'famine'), the fourth ('cling'), the eighth ('speech') and the tenth ('sooth'). This illustrates the basic pattern. The lines are generally of ten syllables, and there is a pattern of stresses: generally an unstressed syllable followed by a stressed syllable, repeated five times. The rhythmic (or metrical) pattern of unstressed syllable followed by stressed syllable is called an **iamb,** hence the name **iambic pentameter,** meaning a metre of five iambs ('pent' meaning 'five'). Shakespeare does not stick rigidly to this pattern, which would quickly make it seem unduly artificial and wooden, but it provides an overall rhythmic flow to the language, which is part of its power.

Spelling: the prefix rule

There is a simple way of remembering how to spell words that begin with a prefix like 'un-', 'mis-', 'ir-' 'dis-', etc.

Write the prefix, then add the *complete* word that goes with it, e.g., *un*natural, mi*s*spell, i*r*relevant, di*s*satisfied.

To check your understanding of this rule, write down the *opposite* of the following words:

appear	necessary
legal	regular
moral	mature
logical	rational

SHAKESPEARE'S *MACBETH* (2): DETAILED ANALYSIS

In this unit, we shall focus on the central theme of *Macbeth*. In the previous unit, it was pointed out that *Macbeth* is an example of the genre of drama called 'tragedy'. All Shakespeare's major tragedies have aspects in common. In all of them, the character after whom the play is named is a man of noble birth who is confronted with a situation that tests him to the limits and ultimately brings about his destruction and that of those nearest to him.

➡   What do you think *is* the central theme of *Macbeth*?

➡   What causes Macbeth to contemplate murdering the king to achieve ultimate power?

➡   What causes him to lose all moral scruples and become a tyrant?

➡   Do you think that *Macbeth*, which was written at the turn of the seventeenth century, has any relevance to the world at the turn of the twenty-first century?

The coursework suggestions at the end of this unit will focus on these issues.

We shall now look in more detail at ten key passages, tracing Macbeth's descent into tyranny and despair, and attempt to analyse the way Shakespeare captures the growth of his ambition and the emotions that accompany it.

1   Macbeth, having heard the witches' prophecies in Act I, Scene 3, has just been informed of the fulfilment of the first of them. He expresses his private reactions to the news.

> (Aside) This supernatural soliciting
> Cannot be ill; cannot be good: – if ill,
> Why hath it given me earnest of success,
> Commencing in a truth? I am Thane of Cawdor.
> If good, why do I yield to that suggestion
> Whose horrid image doth unfix my hair,
> And make my seated heart knock at my ribs
> Against the use of nature? Present fears
> Are less than horrible imaginings.
> My thought, whose murder yet is but fantastical,

Shakes so my single state of man, that function
Is smothered in surmise, and nothing is,
But what is not.

➔ What does Macbeth mean by saying that the witches' predictions 'cannot be ill, cannot be good'?

➔ What are the 'horrible imaginings' to which he refers?

➔ How would you describe Macbeth's state of mind? How is it conveyed by Shakespeare's use of language?

2 Lady Macbeth reads her husband's letter, in Act 1, Scene 5, informing her of the witches' predictions and the fulfilment of the first of them. The news of King Duncan's arrival at their palace fosters her murderous fantasies. Macbeth arrives and greets her.

MACBETH: My dearest love,
    Duncan comes here to-night.
LADY MACBETH: And when goes hence?
MACBETH: To-morrow, as he purposes.
LADY MACBETH: O never,
    Shall sun that morrow see.
    Your face, my Thane, is as a book, where men
    May read strange matters: to beguile the time,
    Look like the time, bear welcome in your eye,
    Your hand, your tongue: look like th' innocent flower,
    But be the serpent under 't. He that's coming,
    Must be provided for: and you shall put
    This night's great business into my dispatch,
    Which shall to all our nights, and days to come,
    Give solely sovereign sway, and masterdom.
MACBETH: We will speak further.
LADY MACBETH: Only look up clear:
    To alter favour, ever is to fear:
    Leave all the rest to me.

➔ What is Lady Macbeth proposing?

➔ What does her use of language show about her character?

➔ How does Macbeth respond?

3 Macbeth, alone, in Act 1, Scene 7, agonises over the temptation to commit the ultimate act of betrayal by murdering Duncan to gain absolute power. Lady Macbeth enters and begins goading him to ignore the voice of conscience.

MACBETH: He's here in double trust:
First, as I am his kinsman and his subject,
Strong both against the deed; then, as his host,
Who should against his murderer shut the door,
Not bear the knife myself. Besides, this Duncan
Hath borne his faculties so meek, hath been
So clear in his great office, that his virtues
Will plead like angels, trumpet-tongued, against
The deep damnation of his taking-off;
And pity, like a naked new-born babe,
Striding the blast, or heaven's cherubin, horsed
Upon the sightless couriers of the air,
Shall blow the horrid deed in every eye,
That tears shall drown the wind. I have no spur
To prick the sides of my intent, but only
Vaulting ambition, which o'erleaps itself
And falls on th' other –
Enter Lady Macbeth.
How now? What news?

LADY MACBETH: He has almost supp'd: why have you left the chamber?

MACBETH: Hath he ask'd for me?

LADY MACBETH: Know you not, he has?

MACBETH: We will proceed no further in this business:
He hath honour'd me of late, and I have bought
Golden opinions from all sorts of people,
Which would be worn now in their newest gloss,
Not cast aside so soon.

LADY MACBETH: Was the hope drunk,
Wherein you dress'd yourself? Hath it slept since?
And wakes it now to look so green, and pale,
At what it did so freely? From this time,
Such I account thy love. Art thou afear'd

> To be the same in thine own act, and valour,
> As thou art in desire? Wouldst thou have that
> Which thou esteem'st the ornament of life,
> And live a coward in thine own esteem?

MACBETH: Pr'ythee, peace.
> I dare do all that may become a man;
> Who dares do more is none.

LADY MACBETH: What beast was 't then
> That made you break this enterprise to me?
> When you durst do it, then you were a man;
> And to be more than what you were, you would
> Be so much more the man. Nor time nor place
> Did then adhere, and yet you would make both:
> They have made themselves, and that their fitness now
> Does unmake you. I have given suck, and know
> How tender 't is to love the babe that milks me:
> I would, while it was smiling in my face,
> Have plucked my nipple from his boneless gums,
> And dash'd the brains out, had I so sworn as you
> Have done to this.

MACBETH: If we should fail –

LADY MACBETH: We fail?
> But screw your courage to the sticking-place
> And we'll not fail.

→   In the opening soliloquy, what does Macbeth mean by saying: 'He's here in double trust'? Why does this trouble him?

→   What does he fear will be the consequences for himself if he murders Duncan?

→   Try to explain how the similes about 'angels', 'naked new-born babe' and 'Heaven's cherubim', and the metaphor in the last four lines of the soliloquy, help to convey Macbeth's emotions.

→   What does the soliloquy show about his character?

→   What do you think Macbeth means by his second speech after Lady Macbeth's entry ('We will proceed . . .')?

➜   How does Lady Macbeth try to persuade him to keep to the plan of
     murdering Duncan?

➜   Is her appeal effective? Comment on the power of her language.

4 Having murdered Duncan, Macbeth, in Act II, Scene 2, is filled with a
     sense of horror at what he has done, and Lady Macbeth attempts to
     reassure him.

> *Knocking within*
> MACBETH: Whence is that knocking?
>   How is 't with me, when every noise appals me?
>   What hands are here? Ha! they pluck out mine eyes.
>   Will all great Neptune's ocean wash this blood
>   Clean from my hand? No, this my hand will rather
>   The multitudinous seas incarnadine,
>   Making the green one red.
> *Re-enter* LADY MACBETH.
> LADY MACBETH: My hands are of your colour; but I shame
>   To wear a heart so white. (*Knock*) I hear a knocking
>   At the south entry: retire we to our chamber.
>   A little water clears us of this deed:
>   How easy is it then! Your constancy
>   Hath left you unattended. (*Knock*) Hark! more knocking,
>   Get on your night-gown, lest occasion call us,
>   And show us to be watchers. Be not lost
>   So poorly in your thoughts.
> MACBETH: To know my deed, 't were best not know myself.
> *Knock*
>   Wake Duncan with thy knocking: I would thou couldst!

➜   Try to explain and comment on the effectiveness of Macbeth's image
     of the 'multitudinous seas'.

➜   How is the difference between Macbeth's and Lady Macbeth's reac-
     tions to the murder of Duncan highlighted by what they say about
     washing hands? What is ironic about this in the light of what happens
     later in the play?

➜   What do Macbeth's last two lines reveal about his attitude to what he
     has done?

5 Macbeth is established as king, but is not at peace in his mind. In this soliloquy in Act III, Scene 1, he expresses his anxiety about Banquo.

To be thus is nothing,
But to be safely thus. – Our fears in Banquo
Stick deep, and in his royalty of nature
Reigns that which would be feared. 'T is much he dares;
And, to that dauntless temper of his mind,
He hath a wisdom that doth guide his valour
To act in safety. There is none but he
Whose being I do fear; and under him
My genius is rebuked, as, it is said,
Mark Antony's was by Caesar. He chid the sisters
When first they put the name of King upon me,
And bade them speak to him; then, prophet-like,
They hailed him father to a line of kings.
Upon my head they placed a fruitless crown,
And put a barren sceptre in my gripe,
Thence to be wrenched with an unlineal hand,
No son of mine succeeding. If 't be so,
For Banquo's issue have I filed my mind;
For them the gracious Duncan have I murdered;
Put rancours in the vessel of my peace
Only for them; and mine eternal jewel
Given to the common enemy of man,
To make them kings, the seed of Banquo kings!
Rather than so, come, Fate, into the list,
And champion me to th' utterance!

➜ Why do you think Macbeth fears Banquo?

➜ Why does the witches' prophecy relating to Banquo prey on Macbeth's mind?

➜ What does Macbeth feel he has done to himself by murdering Duncan? You should try to show how his uses of imagery convey his anguish.

6 Having hired murderers to kill Banquo and Fleance, in Act III, Scene 2, Macbeth speaks ominously and mysteriously to his wife.

> MACBETH: O! full of scorpions is my mind, dear wife!
> Thou know'st that Banquo and his Fleance lives.
> LADY MACBETH: But in them nature's copy's not eterne.
> MACBETH: There's comfort yet; they are assailable:
> Then be thou jocund. Ere the bat hath flown
> His cloistered flight; ere to black Hecate's summons
> The shard-borne beetle, with his drowsy hums,
> Hath rung night's yawning peal, there shall be done
> A deed of dreadful note.
> LADY MACBETH: What's to be done?
> MACBETH: Be innocent of the knowledge, dearest chuck,
> Till thou applaud the deed. Come, seeling Night,
> Scarf up the tender eye of pitiful day,
> And, with thy bloody and invisible hand,
> Cancel, and tear to pieces, that great bond
> Which keeps me pale! Light thickens; and the crow
> Makes wing to the rooky wood;
> Good things of day begin to droop and drowse,
> Whiles night's black agents to their preys do rouse.
> Thou marvellest at my words: but hold thee still,
> Things bad begun make strong themselves by ill.
> So, prithee go with me.

→ How does Shakespeare capture the sense of a mind increasingly in the grip of evil thoughts and deeds in the images and figures of sound in Macbeth's speeches?

→ What change do you notice in the way Macbeth speaks to his wife?

7 The ghost of the murdered Banquo has appeared to Macbeth at the banquet in Act III, Scene 4, and the guests have been told to depart. Macbeth and Lady Macbeth are left alone.

MACBETH: It will have blood, they say, blood will have blood:
Stones have been known to move, and trees to speak;
Augurs, and understood relations, have
By maggot-pies and choughs, and rooks, brought forth
The secret'st man of blood. What is the night?
LADY MACBETH: Almost at odds with morning, which is which.
MACBETH: How say'st thou, that Macduff denies his person
At our great bidding?
LADY MACBETH: Did you send to him, Sir?
MACBETH: I hear it by the way; but I will send.
There's not a one of them, but in his house
I keep a servant fee'd. I will tomorrow
(And betimes I will) to the weird sisters:
More shall they speak; for now I am bent to know,
By the worst means, the worst. For mine own good
All causes shall give way: I am in blood
Stepped in so far, that, should I wade no more,
Returning were as tedious as go o'er.
Strange things I have in head, that will to hand,
Which must be acted, ere they may be scanned.
LADY MACBETH: You lack the season of all natures, sleep.
MACBETH: Come, we'll to sleep. My strange and self-abuse
Is the initiate fear, that wants hard use:
We are yet but young in deed.

→ How do you explain Macbeth's reactions to the ghostly apparition?
→ How is he keeping a check on what the leading noblemen are thinking?
→ Has Macbeth any semblance of conscience left? What is the significance of the image of wading in blood?
→ What are the implications of the final speech, in terms of his future conduct?

8 Macbeth has just met with the witches again, in Act IV, Scene 1, and been warned to 'beware Macduff'. He is now informed by Lennox of Macduff's flight to England. His thoughts are revealed in this aside.

> MACBETH: (*Aside*) Time, thou anticipat'st my dread exploits:
> The flighty purpose never is o'ertook,
> Unless the deed go with it. From this moment
> The very firstlings of my heart shall be
> The firstlings of my hand. And even now,
> To crown my thoughts with acts, be it thought and done:
> The castle of Macduff I will surprise,
> Seize upon Fife; give to th' edge o' th' sword
> His wife, his babes, and all unfortunate souls
> That trace him in his line. No boasting, like a fool;
> This deed I'll do, before this purpose cool.

➜   In what ways has Macbeth's behaviour changed since the banquet scene?

➜   What is particularly horrible about his plan to take revenge against Macduff?

9 The plans for a civil war to overthrow Macbeth are well advanced.

> MALCOLM: Let us seek out some desolate shade, and there
> Weep our sad bosoms empty.
> MADCUFF: Let us rather
> Hold fast the mortal sword: and like good men,
> Bestride our down-fall'n birthdom: each new morn,
> New widows howl, new orphans cry, new sorrows
> Strike heaven on the face, that it resounds
> As if it felt with Scotland, and yell'd out
> Like syllable of dolour.

• • •

MALCOLM: I think our country sinks beneath the yoke,
    It weeps, it bleeds, and each new day a gash
    Is added to her wounds. I think withal,
    There would be hands uplifted in my right:
    And here from gracious England have I offer
    Of goodly thousands.

• • •

MACDUFF: Not in the legions
    Of horrid Hell, can come a devil more damn'd
    In evils, to top Macbeth.

➜   Why is Macbeth resorting to the methods described by Macduff?
➜   What is the effect of his tyrannical rule?

10 Macbeth and his followers are preparing for the siege of Dunsinane, in
Act V, Scene 3. A servant comes in with disturbing news of the strength
of the army from England, which is advancing on the castle.

Enter a SERVANT
MACBETH: The devil damn thee black, thou cream-faced loon!
    Where gott'st thou that goose look?
SERVANT: There is ten thousand –
MACBETH: Geese, villain?
SERVANT: Soldiers, sir.
MACBETH: Go, prick thy face, and over-red thy fear,
    Thou lily-livered boy. What soldiers, patch?
    Death of thy soul! Those linen cheeks of thine
    Are counsellors to fear. What soldiers, whey-face?
SERVANT: The English force, so please you.
MACBETH: Take thy face hence. (*Exit* SERVANT) – Seyton! – I am sick at heart,
    When I behold – Seyton I say! – This push
    Will cheer me ever, or disseat me now.
    I have lived long enough: my way of life
    Is fall'n into the sere, the yellow leaf;
    And that which should accompany old age,

As honour, love, obedience, troops of friends,
I must not look to have; but, in their stead,
Curses, not loud but deep, mouth-honour, breath,
Which the poor heart would fain deny, and dare not.

➡ How would you describe Macbeth's mood, and the way he talks to the servant? Explain how his language and imagery reveal his mood and behaviour.

➡ How does his mood change after the servant's exit? What conclusions has he come to about the way he has treated his subjects? Try to explain the significance of the 'yellow leaf' image.

Act V, Scene 5

The final section chosen for detailed discussion is a complete scene, Act V, Scene 5. This is a scene of changing moods, with Macbeth again the focus. It would be a good scene to present in performance if anyone is willing to take the part of Macbeth and do a little advance work on his speeches. Here is the scene.

Dunsinane. Within the castle.

Enter, with drum and colours, MACBETH, SEYTON, *and* SOLDIERS.

MACBETH: Hang out our banners on the outward walls;
   The cry is still, 'They come!' Our castle's strength
   Will laugh a siege to scorn; here let them lie,
   Till famine and the ague eat them up.
   Were thy not forc'd with those that should be ours,
   We might have met them dareful, beard to beard,
   And beat them backward home. (*A cry within, of women*) What is that noise?

SEYTON: It is the cry of women, my good lord.

Exit

MACBETH: I have almost forgot the taste of fears.
   The time has been, my senses would have cooled
   To hear a night-shriek; and my fell of hair
   Would, at a dismal treatise, rouse and stir,
   As life were in 't. I have supped full with horrors:
   Direness, familiar to my slaughterous thoughts,
   Cannot once start me.

Re-enter SEYTON.

                                        Wherefore was that cry?

SEYTON: The queen, my lord, is dead.

MACBETH: She should have died hereafter:

    There would have been a time for such a word.

    Tomorrow, and tomorrow, and tomorrow,

    Creeps in this petty pace from day to day,

    To the last syllable of recorded time;

    And all our yesterdays have lighted fools

    The way to dusty death. Out, out, brief candle!

    Life's but a walking shadow, a poor player

    That struts and frets his hour upon the stage,

    And then is heard no more: it is a tale

    Told by an idiot, full of sound and fury,

    Signifying nothing.

Enter a MESSENGER

    Thou com'st to use thy tongue; thy story quickly.

MESSENGER: Gracious my lord,

    I should report that which I say I saw,

    But know not how to do 't.

MACBETH: Well, say, sir.

MESSENGER: As I did stand my watch upon the hill,

    I looked toward Birnam, and anon, methought,

    The wood began to move.

MACBETH: Liar and slave!

MESSENGER: Let me endure your wrath, if 't be not so.

    Within this three mile may you see it coming;

    I say, a moving grove.

MACBETH: If thou speak'st false,

    Upon the next tree shalt thou hang alive,

    Till famine cling thee: if thy speech be sooth,

    I care not if thou dost for me as much.

    I pull in resolution, and begin

    To doubt th' equivocation of the fiend,

    That lies like truth: 'Fear not, till Birnam wood

    Do come to Dunsinane'; and now a wood

Comes toward Dunsinane. Arm, arm, and out!
If this which he avouches does appear,
There is nor flying hence, nor tarrying here.
I 'gin to be aweary of the sun,
And wish th' estate o' th' world were now undone.
Ring the alarum bell! Blow, wind! come, wrack!
At least we'll die with harness on our back.

Exeunt

→ What is Macbeth's mood in his first speech? How is it revealed through his use of language?

→ In Macbeth's second speech, what is he revealing about the effects of his tyrannous rule on his personal life?

→ How does Macbeth's mood change in the speech that follows the news of his wife's death? Discuss the effectiveness of the sequence of metaphors in conveying his feelings about life now.

→ Do you feel any sympathy towards Macbeth in this speech?

→ How does he react to the messenger's news? Pick out and discuss the effectiveness of phrases that capture his feelings particularly strongly.

→ Do you think the last two lines of the scene show him in a better light?

Writing an essay on *Macbeth*

If you decide to write an essay for your Shakespeare coursework, there are certain guidelines that you should bear in mind.

There are formal requirements that govern the writing of an essay on any subject and these are explained in Unit 15. The structure of your essay must follow this pattern:

> a general introduction to the essay topic
> a series of paragraphs developing different aspects or sections of the topic
> a final general concluding paragraph.

In an essay on a literary work, it is necessary to develop an argument by means of a series of points, backed up by references to the text. The purpose of these textual references is to provide evidence for the points you are making – to prove them. They can take the form of either references to incidents or speeches from the text, expressed in your own words, or direct quotations from the text. You may then need to add some further comment on the textual evidence.

Here is an example. You are tracing the growth of Macbeth's descent into tyranny and are discussing his decision to wipe out Macduff and his whole family, in Act IV, Scene 2. This is an illustration of how to make a point and back it up by indirect reference to the text rather than by direct quotation.

The news of Macduff's flight to England stings Macbeth into even greater ruthlessness, as he abandons any moral considerations whatever, and decides to arrange the slaughter of Macduff's wife and children and all his lineage, without allowing time for any scruples to deflect his murderous purpose.

Here is another example, this time using direct quotations from the text. You are discussing the moment in Act I, Scene 7, when, after the arrival of Duncan at his castle, Macbeth agonises over his wife's insistence that he should seize the opportunity to kill the King while he is under his roof.

Macbeth is afraid of the consequences for his immortal soul if, as 'his kinsman and his subject', he kills the King who 'hath been / So clear in his great offices'. Macbeth imagines that Duncan's virtues

> Will plead, like angels trumpet-tongued
> Against the deep damnation of his taking-off.

The simile of 'angels' suggests that Duncan's 'virtues' will speak directly to heaven with a loud and persuasive voice, and bring about Macbeth's 'damnation' to hell. The alliteration in the phrase 'deep damnation' adds to the sense of Macbeth's horror at the thought. He reasons further:

> ... I have no spur
> to prick the sides of my intent, but only
> Vaulting ambition, which o'erleaps itself
> And falls on th' other.

Macbeth is using the metaphor of horse riding to suggest that the only 'spur' he has to kill Duncan is his own 'vaulting ambition'. This suggests that Macbeth is well aware of the danger of his ambitious nature, and he is afraid that, like a horse out of control, it will bring about his destruction.

Several points need to be made about the use of quotations here:

1 The remarks that follow the quotations offer *comments on them, not just a paraphrase of them*. There is no point in simply rewriting the quotations in your own words.
2 Notice the way the quotations are set out in lines of verse, as in the text.
    → If a quotation begins within a line of verse, the incomplete line is preceded by three dots. Quotations of two full lines or more should begin on a new line, and be written out as lines of verse as in the text of the play.
    → Quotations of less than 2 lines can be fitted in as part of your sentence, as in the first line of the analysis above.
    → If a short quotation runs over into a second verse line, a forward slash should be placed between the last word of one line and the first word of the other, which should begin with a capital letter.

3 Comments on Shakespeare's use of language and imagery should always refer to the effect and significance of the words and phrases he uses.

4 Whenever you quote directly from the text, you must always make sure that you make the **context** of the quotation clear: explain who speaks to whom and in what situation.

Here is an exercise to test your understanding of how to use quotations. Turn to Act V, Scene 3, and make a statement about the effects on Macbeth's own mental state of his ruthless pursuit of ambition, using this quotation:

> I have lived long enough: my way of life
> Is fall'n into the sere, the yellow leaf.

(V, 3, lines 22–3)

As with any essay, you must make sure you write in developed and self-contained paragraphs. Each paragraph should deal with a new stage of the argument, and the points you make should be adequately developed, over several sentences, with textual reference and quotation, as illustrated above.

Coursework suggestions

→ Write an essay on the effects of the ruthless pursuit of ambition, as shown in *Macbeth*. You should discuss the effects on Macbeth himself, Lady Macbeth, other characters in the play, and the country as a whole.

→ Write an essay on the portrayal of Lady Macbeth, showing her dramatic significance to the play as a whole.

→ Write an essay on Act V, Scene 5 of *Macbeth*, showing its dramatic importance in the play as a whole. You should analyse the effectiveness of the language and imagery of the scene in capturing mood and feeling. You must make sure that you discuss the scene in terms of types of language and imagery and their effects.

→ Write a critique of Roman Polanski's film version of *Macbeth*. You might focus on scenes that were particularly well presented, with reference to the written text. You might also discuss sections of the film that you found less effective, in terms of the written text.

Speaking and Listening: Drama-Focused Activity

A drama-focused activity based on *Macbeth* could involve individual students taking on the roles of characters in the play in different activities. If preferred, this could be assessed as an Extended Individual Contribution.

The student being assessed could take the following roles.

1   Lady Macbeth talking to a member of her family about the possibilities arising from Macbeth's letter in Act I, Scene 4: her plan for the murder of King Duncan, and the chances of getting away with it; her fears about Macbeth's willingness to go ahead with the murder; and her dreams of what it would be like to be Queen of Scotland.

2   A student taking the role of Macbeth could be hot-seated by someone he trusts about the situation he is in at the end of Act V, Scene 3. He must give an honest account of his feelings about the prospect of victory and his own security; his feelings about his wife's mental condition: how he feels about his life now, and whether he regrets murdering Duncan to become King.

3   A student taking the role of Malcolm after he has fled to England at the end of Act II, Scene 3, could be hot-seated and asked the reasons for his flight, and his hopes for a return to Scotland as part of an invasion force to overthrow Macbeth.

 **EXAMINER'S TIPS**

What was said about your coursework response to prose fiction remains true when you are writing about Shakespeare, but in addition to the tips about giving your own views on characterisation, use of language and themes (all supported by detailed reference to the text, of course), your examiners want you to show them that you realise that Shakespeare wrote plays to be performed in the theatre. He wasn't just writing stories about interesting characters. The implication of this for your coursework is that you should, at the very least, show how the play would appeal to an audience. Better candidates can write about specific features of the text and show how it would be effective as drama. They always try to answer the question 'What would be the effect of this feature in the theatre?'. Remember, Shakespeare was an actor as well as a dramatist!

Punctuation and sentence structure

Write out the following passage, correcting all the mistakes.

A TRIP IN THE COUNTRY

We set off at ten thirty am. I had a nap for an hour, I awoke to the sound of twittering swallows. We were driving along country lanes lined with huge oak trees. Which were shedding their leaves onto the road. The cool, fresh, morning was exhilarating. On the left of us as we passed through a small village, cows were being herded for milking. With the farmer, a small well-built man following behind with a pipe in his mouth and a stick in his hand.

MEDIA: FILM, TELEVISION AND ADVERTISING

This unit focuses on both written coursework and preparation for the terminal exams. The sections on film and television are designed to provide guidance and suggestions for the AQA A media coursework requirement. The final section, on advertising, as well as providing further material for coursework, also offers advice and practice exercises for tackling texts of the kind that might feature in the media section of the AQA B and B (Mature) pre-release booklets, and as an unseen exercise in the AQA A examination.

Writing a film review

As a coursework piece, you may wish to write a review of a film of your own choice. The best approach to this might be to watch a film at the cinema or on television/video/DVD, with a checklist of aspects of film reviewing in mind while you are watching. Here is a possible checklist:

➡   Give the title of the film and the director's name, and an idea of what *kind* of film it is (thriller, romance, comedy etc.).

➡   Give a *basic* outline of the plot, without going into too much detail.

➡   Write about the main characters and the actors who play them, commenting on how good their performances are.

➡   Make a personal evaluation of how good the film is. You could try to answer such questions as:
  - Is the pace and interest maintained, or are some sections weak, too long, drawn-out, etc.?
  - Does the story hang together, or does it lose realism, and if so, at what point in the film does this begin to happen?
  - Are there any particularly brilliant episodes? If so, explain them and analyse what is particularly powerful, exciting, funny, etc. about them.

➡   Make comparisons with other films on the same theme, or in the same genre, or by the same director.

➡   Discuss other aspects of the film, such as:
  - the screenplay (script and dialogue)
  - the camera work
  - special effects
  - use of music.

A Crash Course in Hatred

Matthew Bond – Films of the Week

Changing Lanes

Director: Roger Michell

Certificate: 15

Time: 1hr 39mins

★★★★○

Had Brian De Palma not made such a mess of Tom Wolfe's Eighties best-seller *The Bonfire Of The Vanities*, there probably wouldn't be room for another film beginning with a car accident anywhere near New York's Franklin D. Roosevelt Drive.

But he did, leaving a veritable cinema superhighway of space for Roger Michell's *Changing Lanes*, which addresses many of the same issues – race, wealth, dodgy ethics – but is infinitely better than De Palma's effort, and never resorts to the terrifying spectacle of Melanie Griffith in her underwear.

In *The Bonfire Of The Vanities*, a slim Tom Hanks played Sherman McCoy, a young New York banker with a neurotic wife and a pneumatic mistress. But his high-maintenance lifestyle was turned upside-down when his car collided with a young black mugger in The Bronx.

In *Changing Lanes*, Ben Affleck plays Gavin Banek, a young Wall Street lawyer who has an ambitious wife (Amanda Peet) and an on-off relationship with an attractive colleague at work (Toni Collette). His life is about to be turned upside-down too.

Driving to court one morning and distracted by the impending case, he makes a mess of changing lanes on the FDR and collides with a rust-bucket driven by the equally distracted Doyle Gipson (Samuel L. Jackson), a recovering alcoholic and insurance salesman who is late for the crucial custody hearing to determine the future of his two young sons.

Despite the rush, Gipson wants to play it by the book and swap insurance details properly. Banek, however, is an arrogant young man in a hurry. He offers Gipson a blank cheque and when that is refused he just drives off, leaving Gipson stranded, angry and very late.

But – oh, cruel hand of fate – Banek also leaves behind the vital document that proves that his law firm won control of a $100 million charity fund legally, if not entirely ethically. Without it, he and his father-in-law boss (Sydney Pollack) are well and truly in the Wall Street mire.

With the court giving him until the end of the working day to produce the document, Banek desperately needs to find the man he abandoned on the freeway. The only problem is, having arrived late for the hearing and lost joint custody of his sons, Gipson isn't just angry, he's mad as hell.

British director Roger Michell, the man who brought us *Notting Hill*, quickly establishes all this with energy and style before steering us through a tense and potentially lethal game of spiralling revenge.

Suddenly *Changing Lanes* is no longer reminiscent of *The Bonfire Of The Vanities* but *Run Lola Run*, the strange but popular German thriller which retold the same basic story several times (Lola has 20 minutes to raise 100,000 Deutschmarks or something terrible happens) but varied the outcome of specific events. Some things, you see, are in our control but others – as Banek and Gipson duly discover – are not.

But don't be put off. Michell may have art-house aspirations but this is a commercial Hollywood movie with a brisk beginning, an absorbing middle and a slightly disappointing, sentimental end.

Affleck's emoting is still one of the most painful sights in modern cinema (one of these days he'll squeeze out a tear) but he's perfectly cast as the yuppie lawyer still just about in touch with his conscience. Jackson, too, is good as the former lush who has made a low-key success of his new sober life – until Banek drives it off the road.

But what really makes this a superior evening out and compensates for the odd jarring moment is the quality of Chap Taylor's screenplay and the standard of Michell's supporting cast. The ever-watchable William Hurt turns up in a tiny role as Gipson's sponsor at Alcoholics Anonymous; Richard Jenkins is a sinister, smiling treat as the computer creep who bankrupts Gipson with a few clicks of his mouse; while Kim Staunton, as Gipson's estranged wife, comes impressively close to making that ending work. One of my top ten films of the year.

The Mail on Sunday, **3 November 2002**

➡ Make your final judgment on the film, its strengths and weaknesses, and indicate the kind of audience you think it might appeal to.

Apart from the first and the last, there is no need to take the points in any particular order in your review. You can include two or more together in the same section, as the specimen review on page 154 should illustrate.

You might find it useful to highlight the sections of the review that deal with particular aspects of film reviewing from the checklist above. Ideally, this should be done on a photocopy of the review, with different coloured highlighter pens.

You may also find it useful to study other reviews of recent films in newspapers and magazines as further guidance.

Coursework suggestion

➡ Watch a full-length film at the cinema or on television, video or DVD, and write a review of it, along the lines suggested and illustrated above. The total length of your review should be about 500 words.

➡ Write a comparison of two films in the same genre. You should make use of the film review suggestions above to compare the plots, characters, acting, pace, realism etc., in the two films, and attempt to make an evaluation of the effectiveness of each film.

Soap operas

Soap operas are the most popular form of drama in Britain. British and Australian 'soaps' command daily audiences of millions. The objective of this section is to compare British and Australian soap operas, and to take an objective look at particular soap opera episodes.

Discussion of British and Australian 'soaps'

Discuss each of these differences between soap operas dealing with life in Britain and those set in Australia. You should give examples from soap operas that you watch.

➡ Social mix, age range and variety of the characters.
➡ Realism of the characters.
➡ Use of stereotypes.

➜ Emotional range of the story lines and situations.
➜ Treatment of relationships.
➜ Exploration of controversial issues.
➜ Use of comic situations and characters.
➜ Range of settings.
➜ Pace of plot development/rapidity of scene changes.
➜ Use of 'cliff-hanger' episode endings.
➜ Quality of the acting.

Episodes from soap operas

Perhaps the best way to analyse soap operas is to watch episodes on video. You could choose one episode from both a British and an Australian 'soap' and discuss and compare them.

Barbara Windsor as Peggy Mitchell in *Eastenders*

You might consider these questions:

➜ How many different conflict situations were presented in each episode?
➜ How many times and why did each episode switch from one story-line to another? Did the scene switches add to or detract from your enjoyment? Why?
➜ How true-to-life did you consider the situations depicted to be? Try to give examples.
➜ Did you find yourself sympathising or empathising with any of the characters? What was it about the situation that the character was dealing with that caused you to experience this response?
➜ Did you feel angry or irritated by the behaviour of any of the characters? Why?
➜ How good did you think the acting was?
➜ Did you gain any insights into human life and behaviour from either of the episodes you watched?
➜ If you watch either of the 'soaps' regularly, take one of the story-lines in each of the episodes you watched and try to analyse what makes it, over the whole period since it was first introduced, interesting and entertaining.

→ Of all the soap operas currently shown on British television, which do you think is best? Why?

Coursework suggestions

→ Choose a social issue, such as adultery, marital cruelty, alcohol or drug abuse, unemployment, which is dealt with in more than one soap opera. Write about the way it is treated in the different 'soaps', referring to the characters involved and the extent to which we are encouraged to sympathise with them; the attitudes of other members of the community who are not directly involved; the degree of depth in which the issue is explored, and the moral stance, if any, that the programme encourages us to take. Give your own view of the characters and situation.

→ Write a comparison between British and Australian soap operas, using the discussion suggestions on pages 155–156 as a guide.

→ Write a comparison between a single episode of a British soap opera and a single episode of an Australian soap opera, using the questions above as a guide.

Advertising

Questions on the language and presentation of advertisements can be set as media coursework writing assignments for AQA A, and an advertisement may be set as the media text for the AQA B and B (Mature) examinations. The final section of this unit is devoted to the study of advertising.

Appeals to drives and desires

There are several basic human desires and urges that advertising companies draw on when designing their advertisements. The most common ones are:

→ identification with a fashionable 'elite'
→ wealth, status and greed
→ glamour, sex appeal and the desire to feel youthful
→ health fears
→ domestic comfort and security
→ maternal feelings
→ fear of non-conformity and the urge for acceptance and popularity.

Logo, slogans and images

In order to make their appeals, newspaper and magazine ads invariably carry a brand-name **logo**, and eye-catching **slogan** and a **visual image**. These are the elements that attract the reader's attention, and persuade them to read the text, or **copy**, which forms an additional part of most advertisements.

Other important typographical features to consider when analysing an advertisement are the uses of **bold print**, **capitalisation** and different **typefaces**, **colour**, the **placing** of the various elements and the **layout** of the copy on the page, and the **balance** of the space devoted to pictures, slogans and copy.

Advertising language

Some advertisements rely entirely on an arresting or enticing picture to create their effect. Most, however, use copy as well, and often quite a substantial proportion of an advertisement is taken up with information and claims about the product.

There is a distinct language of advertising. These are some of its common features:

Imperatives: verbs commanding you to do things, like 'treat yourself', 'act now'.

Superlatives and exaggeration: words which claim that the product is the 'softest', 'best', etc., or which claim it is 'unique', 'a major breakthrough', etc.

Language making unprovable claims, like saying that the product 'costs less' or is 'a much better way' to do something, without saying *what* it costs less than or is better than.

Pseudo-scientific language, designed to sound impressive, like 'thanks to a unique ratifying complex'.

Enticing words, like 'magic' and 'bargain', and especially adjectives, like 'beautiful, 'exquisite' and 'luxurious', which make the product sound desirable or special.

Neologisms: words invented by advertisers, like 'tangy', 'flaky', 'cookability' and 'innervigoration', to create a sense of uniqueness.

Imagery: metaphors and personification used to add colour and vitality to the copy.

'Sound' devices, like alliteration, assonance and rhyme, to make slogans and copy stand out.

Repetition: key words and phrases are repeated to punch the message home.

Listing: lists of nouns or adjectives, to make the copy seem more emphatic and punchy.

Language using humour and puns: wordplay and 'double entendre' (sexual double meanings) to add spice to the copy.

Personal pronouns, especially 'you', to appeal directly to the readers and make them feel special.

Colloquial language: using a chatty style, with phrases and clichés common in ordinary speech, and contractions ('we've', 'you'll') to create an informal, direct feel.

Abbreviated sentence structures: leaving out grammatical elements from sentences, especially subjects, to keep sentences short and striking; beginning sentences with the conjunctions 'and' and 'but', to create a feeling of informality and closeness to spoken language.

Sample analysis of an advertisement

Study 'The Footprints Diamond Eternity Ring' advertisement on page 161, and go through the different features of advertising listed above. Make brief notes, identifying as many of these features in the advertisement as you can, and any other other features that you can think of, with examples.

Now study the following sample analysis of this advertisement, before going on to prepare for an examination or coursework analysis of (an) advertisement(s) of your own. The original advertisement was in four colours: blue, gold, white and black, and the significance of the colours is mentioned in the analysis.

The purpose of this advertisement is to entice people to buy an eternity ring by focusing the visual image and the copy on the words inscribed on the inside of the ring, which are taken from a love poem. It relies, therefore, on the potential buyer's sentimental response to the words of the poem, and the urge to present something glamorous as an expression of love and devotion.

The ring is made to seem special and highly desirable by the use of various advertising devices. The product name is highlighted at the top of the advertisement in elegant script and layout. The key words of the product name, 'Footprints Diamond', are set right across the page in large capitals, which immediately attracts the eye. The initial letters of each of these words ('F' and 'S') have an elegant flourish, which makes them stand out even more, and blend in with the movement of waves approaching a seashore in the background picture. The other words of the product name ('The...eternity ring') are presented in much smaller capitals and carefully placed to create a harmonious overall effect.

The introductory words at the top of the advertisement are capitalised in black on a gold strip, which makes them blend with the gold of the visual images. The emphasis here is on suggesting that the product is remarkably good value, with the words 'Only £98.00' followed by an asterisk and an exclamation mark.

The main image is of the ring itself, shown in its gold and white colours, and tilted upwards to display most of the words on the inside, since these are the major selling point of the product. The print design on the outside of the ring is also highlighted by the touches of black on the white footprints. The diamond is emphasised by showing it sparkling.

The background to the advertisement is a scene of a calm sea and shoreline, in hazy blue. This is designed to suggest tranquil beauty, and to link in with the product name and design and the extract from the poem inside the ring. Against this dark, indistinct background, the gold and diamond ring is made to stand out all the more radiantly.

The two lines of copy underneath the main image, which are also in gold, describe the words inscribed inside the ring, in rather inflated, sentimental language: 'Inspirational words of comfort and hope', and this style of exaggeration is continued in the description of the ring itself as a 'masterpiece'.

The passages from the poem inscribed on the ring are quoted below the statement in gold lettering, in old-fashioned calligraphy, suggesting timeless elegance. Below this, part of the visual image containing the words is shown again, in box form, to emphasise how they are 'beautifully inscribed', as the words below the visual image tell us, and the word 'inspirational' is repeated, to further press the point home.

To the left and right of this dual quotation of the poem are four blocks of copy,

each of them set out on the page in a rounded way, to suggest the shape of a ring, and to add further to the visual elegance of the advertisement. The two blocks on the left provide a detailed description of the ring. Enticing adjectives, like 'enchanting', 'heart-warming', 'breathtaking', 'dazzling', and adverbs like 'radiantly' and 'beautifully' are used to make the product seem as desirable as possible. The description of 'a single trail of delicate footprints gracefully encircling the design' is intended to create a poetic atmosphere in keeping with the nature of the product.

The two blocks of copy on the right explain the payment options. Even here the language is sentimental and enticing, with phrases like 'To bring the wonder of The Footprints Diamond Eternity Ring into your life', and the additional enticement of 'a copy of this uplifting verse for you to treasure forevermore'. The use of the personal pronouns 'you' and 'your' appeals directly to the potential purchaser so that (s)he is made to feel special.

The reservation form at the bottom of the advertisement repeats the phrase 'the remarkable issue price of just £98.00', used in the payment options section, so that the idea that the product is outstandingly good value for money is reinforced. The section headed 'Our Pledge of Complete Satisfaction' again uses language suggesting that the product is something truly special and desirable, with the impressive-sounding claim that 'Brooks and Bentley takes pride in offering works of uncompromisingly high standards of quality, created with care and dedication by skilled craftsmen', making it sound as if the offer is too good to resist.

Examination practice

Media texts are set in each AQA specification as a Reading response in the terminal examination. In AQA A the text(s) will be on your examination paper, while in AQA B and B (Mature) they will be pre-released. In either case you might be set an advertisement to analyse.

As exam practice you might attempt the following question:

→ Write a detailed analysis of the Micro Power Cycle advertisement on page 163. You should write about:
  – the target audience
  – the pictures, layout and presentational devices
  – the uses of language and the claims made for the product.

Share your new baby, instantly

hp digital photography.

Shoot.

When it's this easy, why not?

With its exclusive HP Instant Share technology, your classically styled 3.3 megapixel HP Photosmart 720 digital camera can be instructed to automatically share your pride and joy in seconds. Simply place the camera in its dedicated docking station* and, at the touch of a button, you can send shots via e-mail to 12 pre-assigned destinations. Or print, or download, as you like. It also boasts 12x zoom† and 30-second video clip with audio.

invent

The HP Photosmart 720 digital camera is available at Jessops, John Lewis and all good stockists. £299 (rrp). **Visit www.hp.com/uk/create** *Sold separately. †3x optical, 4x digital. ©Hewlett-Packard 2002.

3.45pm Goooooaaa!

life is what you take it

only 88mm x 55mm x 11mm

Make the most of every day with Exilim and capture real life as it happens. Once you've tried it, you'll find it as essential as your mobile, wallet and keys. Not only is it the world's smallest 2 megapixel digital camera but it's also packed with BESTSHOT function, movie playback and 1 second start-up time. So now you can expect the unexpected.

In stores now

digital vision by
CASIO.

www.exilim.co.uk

The Casio digital camera range includes everything from 3 and 4 megapixel compacts to wrist cameras.
Available from selected Dixons, Jessops, House Of Fraser, Debenhams, Cecil Jacobs stores and Casio@Carnaby (32 Carnaby street, London. 020 7437 1441).
Plus all other good digital camera retailers. For further details on Exilim and other digital cameras by Casio please call 020 8450 9131 or visit www.exilim.co.uk

Coursework suggestions

Media analysis is also a coursework requirement of AQA A. It is assessed for Writing, in the triplet 'analyse, review, comment'.

Here are some suggestions for media coursework on advertising:

→ Write detailed analyses of two contrasting advertisements, taking account of all the aspects of newspaper and magazine advertising discussed in this unit.

→ Study the two advertisements for digital cameras on pages 164 and 165. Find two more advertisements for other brands of digital camera, and write an analysis of the different approaches taken in the different advertisements.

→ Find a range of advertisements for different makes of the same kind of product, such as clothes, cars, food, mobile phones, and write a detailed analysis of the similarities and differences in the approaches and devices used for selling the products in the various advertisements.

You should aim to write at least 400 words.

Television commercials

To study TV commercials you will need a video of an evening's commercials for the class to study.

Taking them one by one, discuss:

→ the relevance of the visual images and spoken text to the product
→ the visual effects
→ the drives and desires that the advert is appealing to
→ the uses of language
→ the use of music
→ the use of humour
→ the use of famous actors or celebrities
→ the overall effectiveness of the advert
→ the target audience at which it is aimed.

Coursework sugestion

→ Watch, and preferably record, two or more TV commercials for similar products, and write an analysis of them, showing the approach taken to advertising each product, along the lines suggested above, and discuss their relative effectiveness.

You should aim to write at least 400 words.

Spelling rule: adding suffixes to words ending in a silent 'e'

Another spelling rule worth learning is the suffix rule governing words ending with a silent 'e' (like 'hope', 'safe', 'manage').

The rule

When you add a suffix beginning with a *consonant* (like '-less', '-ly', '-ment') the 'e' is kept.

When you add a suffix beginning with a vowel or 'y' (like '-ing', '-able', '-y') the 'e' is dropped.

e.g.

hop*e* + less	hop~~e~~ + ing
sincer*e* + ly	subtl~~e~~ + y
arrang*e* + ment	arrang~~e~~ + ing
complet*e* + ly	complet~~e~~ + ing

There are exceptions, of course, such as: argument, truly, awful, duly, wholly, saleable, rateable.

Exercise

Make words by adding the bracketed suffixes to the words below:

care (-less, -ing)
improve (-ment, -ing)
laze (-y, -ing)

like (-ly, -able)
argue (-ment, -ing)
hope (-ful, -ing)

Media analysis is continued in this unit, focusing this time on extracts from newspapers and magazines. Both the media coursework requirement for AQA A and the examination media requirements of each AQA specification are covered, and the majority of the material in this unit is relevant to both coursework and exam preparation. In the terminal exams for each AQA specification, responses to media texts appear in the same section of Paper I as a response to an unseen non-fiction text. In AQA A all the texts are unseen, and in AQA B and B (Mature) the media texts are pre-released.

In this unit we will look at newspaper and magazine texts in terms of the national Assessment Objectives for Reading, and the types of questions that are likely to be set on them in the media section of the exams.

We will look first at newspapers.

Before going on to explore and analyse a set of newspaper articles, it would be useful to consider the *range* of newspapers in Britain. As most people are at least vaguely aware, there is a world of difference between a newspaper like *The Sun* and a newspaper like *The Times*.

➡   How would you describe the difference?

There are, in fact, special terms for the general *types* of newspaper in Britain. Papers like the *Sun* are called **tabloids**. All that the term actually means is that they are comparatively small in size.

➡   What are the names of the other tabloid daily and Sunday newspapers?

The other category, covering newspapers like *The Times*, is **broadsheets**. They are so called because they are bigger and broader than the tabloids.

➡   What are the other broadsheets?

In fact, as you may already have decided, there are two broad categories of tabloids. The *Mail* and the *Express* are often referred to as 'middle-brow' papers, as distinct from the 'high-brow' broadsheets and the other tabloids (which are sometimes disparagingly referred to as the 'gutter press'). Even here, a distinction can be drawn: *The Star*, *The Sun* and *The Daily Mirror* do deal with world news to a certain extent; the same cannot really be said of *The Sport*, which perhaps should not be called a newspaper at all!

Analysing different newspapers' treatment of a news story

The break-up of the hippie convoy

This section looks at the style, presentation, balance and bias of British newspapers. It can be treated as preparation for AQA A coursework, but its main purpose is to show how the Assessment Objectives for Reading apply to examination Reading questions, and to prepare you for the media analysis exercise in the terminal exams for each AQA specification.

The articles that follow all deal with events which took place in June 1986, in Hampshire, England. A so-called 'hippie convoy', attempting to camp near

Stonehenge at the time of the summer solstice, was forcefully broken up and dispersed by police.

The background to these events is described in the first article. This is a report that appeared in a weekly newspaper.

1

Police 'victory' over hippies

For almost three weeks British newspapers and television screens have been full of reports, commentaries and even 'research' articles on a rather unusual subject – the struggle between a group of homeless and aimless people denoted in the press here by the vague term 'hippies', and the British authorities.

The reason for the confrontation was the intention by representatives of this group to hold their traditional song festival in the Stonehenge area, where there is a concentration of structures dating back to the Neolithic era.

The hippies have been organising such festivals every year since 1977. Last year, however, the attempts to organise it came up against a ban by the authorities. On arriving there the hippies were met by the police and bloody clashes ensued.

The same thing happened this year as well. Driven out of Stonehenge, the homeless people, many of them with small children, tried to set up camp on vacant land belonging to a local farmer.

A few days later, however, the Supreme Court issued an edict prohibiting them from staying there and the hippies, under pressure from the law and order forces, ended up on the road once again.

About a week ago they made yet another attempt to set up camp – this time on a disused airfield near the village of Stoney Cross in Hampshire. Nor on this occasion, however, did they manage to hold out for longer than a week.

At dawn on June 9 about 500 policemen arrived in special vehicles, surrounded the camp and once and for all broke up the hippies' refuge. Reporting the successful completion of 'Operation Dawn', as the police raid is bombastically named in official documents, the newspapers wrote that as result of it, 42 persons were arrested and the rest were 'dispersed' and 'sent home' – to homes which they simply do not have.

Of course, the government can ban and even break up song festivals set up by the hippies. But the root of the problem lies elsewhere.

The hippies are first and foremost homeless and deprived people who can find no place for themselves in contemporary British society, and the more unemployment grows and the other social problems intensify, as is happening at present, the more frequently will arise similar types of conflicts reflecting the overall sick state of contemporary Western society.

The second extract was written by a columnist in a Sunday newspaper.

2

NO HIPPY ENDING THEN

HOME SECRETARY Douglas Hurd describes the hippy 'peace convoy' as 'a band of medieval brigands'.

But in the Middle Ages brigands did not have half so cushy a time as these bums, beggars, vandals, and thieves, with whom grovelling TV personalities like Frank Bough and Desmond Morris, both of whom should know better, choose to sympathise.

Medieval brigands would swiftly have found themselves set upon by the vassals and hounds of baron landlords, or by royal servants or by local freemen. They would have found their lives to be not only nasty and brutish, but decidedly short.

What is more, they would not have been followed around by clerks from the exchequer dishing out substantial sums of cash each Thursday to enable them to carry on marauding through the countryside.

The hippies claim, with arrant humbug, to be living 'an alternative life style'. The claim would be marginally less fraudulent if they had found an alternative to the dole we so foolishly give them, and they so eagerly take.

The third extract was written by a columnist in a provincial newspaper.

3

THE HIPPY saga has gone on since my comments last week, and part of the lovely New Forest has been spoiled by this scruffy bunch of layabouts. All at our expense, of course.

We continue to dole out state benefits to law-breakers (one newspaper even reported that the social security employs special staff to wander round the country servicing these vagabonds).

I wonder if the state is equally careful about ensuring that hippies are up to date with their taxes, road fund licences and MoT testing of their raggle-taggle vehicles?

TALKING about the hippies, television news one night showed a wild-eyed, tangle-haired harpie spit at a policeman seeing them off the New Forest site: 'Have you got a home to go to?' – followed by a companion bawling 'We haven't, we haven't a home'.

The policeman resisted the provocation. He did not reply. So I will reply for him.

'Yes, ducks, I do have a home which I pay for, care for, and look after. I keep it clean, pay my way, and don't offend my neighbours. I don't doss down on anybody else's land and I don't leave it looking like a tip. How about you?'

The fourth extract is another daily newspaper report.

4

SO WHERE DOES HE GO NOW?

Innocent on the road of rejection

HUNCHED against the wind in the security of a borrowed blanket, the child stumbled across the land that had briefly been his home.

The boy looked bewildered against the background of the three unmoved policemen.

Confusion

The man with him, a ragged symbol of the hippies, plunged his hands into the empty pockets of his tattered jeans and the stones on the ground bit into his feet. His bedding hung over his arm.

The child burrowed deeper into the blanket and stared back with innocent confusion at the towering, impassive policemen. Little emotion flickered from their eyes.

The only friendship, the only token of parting affection, the only hint of kindness to a child came from a free-running dog. An old Labrador sniffed the child amiably and licked gently.

The Child and The Man With Nowhere to Go looked at one another with despair. He plunged his hands even more deeply into his pockets – and the three of them set off together.

A confused child, a ragged, hope-crushed man and a friendly old dog.

All on the Road of Rejection.

We shall now look in detail at the four articles, with several objectives in mind:

→ to recognise the difference between fact and opinion
→ to identify purpose and audience
→ to identify and analyse features of journalistic language and methods of persuasion
→ to identify bias in the use of language and to recognise the way news can be slanted
→ to consider the effects of presentational devices.

You must have noticed, just by reading the articles, that the attitudes towards the 'hippies' and the police taken by the various writers are poles apart. We are now going to identify how the writers have presented their particular viewpoints.

Assessment Objective (ii) for Reading requires the ability to 'distinguish between fact and opinion'. Let us begin with this essential distinction.

Fact and opinion

One of the distinguishing and perhaps disquieting features of newspaper journalism is the way that writers *slant* their stories to fit in with the social and political viewpoint of the newspaper in general. One of the ways they do this is to present opinions masquerading as facts. It is important to be able to recognise when this is happening.

➡   How would you define the difference between a fact and an opinion?

Perhaps the simplest way of distinguishing between fact and opinion would be to say that if a statement is incontestable and verifiable it is a fact; if it could be reasonably challenged or disagreed with it is an opinion.

➡   Look at two statements describing a person called John:

John is 42 years old.

John is old.

Assuming that the information about John's age is correct, the first statement must be a fact. What about the second?

➡   Now look at these two statements. Are they fact or opinion?

The theatre is an old listed building, dating from the late seventeenth century, and is therefore safe from the threat of destruction from planners who want to build a fly-over through the area.

The ugly old theatre is an eyesore, and ought to be knocked down.

The description of the theatre as 'old' in the first sentence could be regarded as a fact, since no one would be likely to regard a building that has been standing for over three hundred years as anything other than 'old'. The statement about it being 'safe' must also be factual, since listed buildings cannot be knocked down. However, in this case, an *attitude* towards the preservation of the building is implied in the words chosen to describe it: *'safe from the threat of destruction'*. An opinion about the facts is *implied*, therefore, by the use of *loaded language*.

Now let us look at the *first* of the 'hippies' articles and see how far it is factual.

In the opening sentence the so-called 'hippies' are described as 'homeless and aimless'.

➡️   Is this a factual statement?

The article goes on to describe how they made various attempts to set up camp, and were moved on each time. It is reasonable to assume, therefore, that they do not have a settled home.

But what about 'aimless?'

Is it not possible that the aim of some of them is to live a life free from the ties of a settled home and job? If so, they cannot be 'aimless'. This part of the statement, therefore, although it is presented as if it is a fact, is actually an opinion.

The next six paragraphs explain the events leading up to 'Operation Dawn'. The information is verifiable and therefore, as long as it isn't invented (which is another common aspect of journalism!), it is factual.

An opinion about the police raid is clearly given in the seventh paragraph, in the phrase 'as the police raid is bombastically named', and an opinion about it is *implied* in the phrase that ends the paragraph: '– to homes which they simply do not have'.

The description of the 'hippies' in the last paragraph as 'deprived people who can find no place for themselves in contemporary British society' is *presented* as a fact, but many people would view them less charitably. It is therefore an opinion masquerading as a fact. The article ends with a comment on the whole episode in terms of what it reveals about 'contemporary Western Society'.

Discussion or writing exercise

➡️   Re-read the third article. Analyse it in terms of fact and opinion.

It is possible that in your exam a question may specifically ask you to give examples of fact and opinion. Let us sum up what we have discovered from the above analysis. As well as presenting straightforward fact and opinion, a writer may:
- present opinion as fact
- imply opinions in statements that are essentially factual.

If you can find examples of these more subtle uses of fact and opinion you will get extra credit. It would be a good idea to mention them in an answer to a more general question about the persuasiveness of a piece of writing.

We will now look in general terms at some further key elements in media analysis. You should then be ready to attempt an analysis of all four 'hippy convoy' articles, to see in detail how journalists attempt to influence our views of a news item by their uses of language, presentation and selection.

Purpose and audience

The term 'purpose' means the reason for producing a piece of writing. It could be to persuade you in favour of an idea, or against it; to amuse or entertain you; to shock you; to inform you about a topic, and so on.

The 'audience' means the kind of people at whom the author is targeting his/her work. It could be targeted at people of a particular political or social viewpoint, people of a particular age group or gender, a particular interest group, people with a particular level of sophistication, etc.

You can gauge the author's purpose and target audience by the *way* s/he writes, the attitude s/he expresses, the tone s/he adopts and the subject matter of the piece of writing.

Journalistic language

Newspaper writing has its own particular style of writing, sometimes referred to as 'journalese'. Tabloid journalists in particular employ a distinctive language and style. Here is a checklist of common features of tabloid journalism:

→ **puns,** used especially in headlines

→ **alliteration,** used especially in headlines, to catch the reader's attention and add punch

→ **'loaded'** words: expressions that convey a strong impression of support or condemnation

→ **emotive** words, conveying strong positive or negative emotions

→ words that **sensationalise** events, like 'scandal', 'shock', 'torment', 'battle'

→ derisory **'slang',** to vilify hate figures

→ **colloquial** language and informal tone, to make the reader feel more personally involved and on a wavelength with the writer

→ **coined** words like 'sexpert', to deride the target through humour

→ **'tabloidese' words:** short words that are generally used only in tabloid newspapers, and are designed to sound tough, and give an exaggerated impression of events, for example: 'axed' instead of 'made redundant'; 'quit' instead of 'resigned'; 'slam' or 'blast' instead of 'criticise'; 'clash' instead of 'disagreement'.

Structure and presentation

Assessment Objective (v) for Reading requires you to show that you can 'understand and evaluate how writers use linguistic, structural and presentational devices to achieve their effects'. The section on journalistic language, above, dealt with language use in terms of newspaper journalism. The previous chapter explained what 'structural and presentational devices' means in terms of advertisements, in the section headed 'Logo, slogans and images' on page 158. It would be worth looking at this section before you go on.

'Structural and presentational devices' have a special terminology and set of common features relating to newspapers and magazines. The term 'linguistic devices' relates to grammatical structure as well as choices of language. Here is a further checklist of devices you might consider in analysing newspaper and magazine journalism:

→ Main headline: much bigger and bolder in tabloids

→ Strapline: the headline that appears *above* the main headline; it provides extra information or explanation of the main headline

→ Sub-headline: appears *below* the main headline and elaborates it

→ Caption: the words that appear underneath a picture

→ Sub-headings, or bolded quotations, that break up the text

➡ Differences in print size

➡ Pictures dramatising or supporting the story

➡ Layout of text and pictures on the page

➡ Use of italics, underlining and emboldening, to make key passages and statements stand out

➡ Use of colour

➡ Use of unconventional grammatical features, especially leaving out the subject of a sentence, and beginning sentences with the conjunction 'and' or 'but'

➡ Paragraphs: generally short, often a single sentence in tabloids, to break up the text and make it look snappy

➡ Omission of commas and use of dashes in tabloids, to create a more informal and chatty impression.

Detailed analysis of the 'hippie convoy' articles

The four articles on pages 170 to 172 can now be explored in detail, using the questions that follow. By looking at the language and presentation of these pieces, you will learn about the use of *bias* in journalism.

The analysis could be written as an AQA A media coursework submission, or the articles could be discussed and dissected in class, as preparation for the media reading response examination task in each AQA specification.

In either case, a good approach might be to begin by allowing yourself time to think about the questions, perhaps highlighting words and phrases that are relevant to them on a photocopy of each article, and jotting down notes in the margin. Before beginning, you might find it useful to study the checklist of journalistic language on page 176.

1 Police 'victory' over hippies

➡ What do you notice about the headline?

➡ What is the effect of specifying the places where the 'hippies' attempted to camp?

➡ Pick out and discuss phrases in the last paragraph that indicate where the writer's sympathies lie in the conflict.

2 No hippie ending then

➡ What is the significant feature of the headline?

→   How does the writer show his/her bias by the language and tone of the article?

3 Untitled piece

→   What do you notice about the language and tone of the piece?

→   What conclusions might you draw about the writer's political stance?

4 So where does he go now?

→   What is the effect of the headline and the sub-heading?

→   How would you describe the tone of this article: angry, compassionate, scornful, despairing?

→   Look at the descriptions of the man, the child and the policeman. How does the reporter show on which side his sympathies lie by his use of language?

→   What effect is created by the paragraph about the dog, and how is it created?

→   How do sentence and paragraph structure add to the overall effect in the last two paragraphs?

→   Articles 3 and 4 both make use of an incident between an individual policeman and some 'hippies'. Compare the uses they make of the incident they describe.

→   What conclusions would you draw about the purpose and target audience of each of the articles?

Newspaper editorials

The editorial comment section of British newspapers presents the views of the editorial board on two or three of the issues taken up in the day's news stories. They give a particularly clear insight into the attitudes, values and style of the paper.

Here are three editorials published on 1st November 2002, dealing with a derisory remark made by a government minister at the Department for Culture, Media and Sport about the entries for the Turner Prize, an annual competition for the most outstanding exhibition by a British artist under 50.

Read them, and highlight phrases that reveal the writers' attitudes, then illustrate the features of the style, tone and syntax of each.

The Artless Minister

If anybody else but Kim Howells had described the Turner Prize shortlist as 'cold, mechanical, conceptual bullshit', the silent majority might well have murmured assent. This tawdry annual circus demeans the great artist after whom it is named and the great institution that runs it. The prize no longer arouses indignation, merely derision.

Whether Mr Howells is right about the Turner, however, is not the point. As a junior minister at the Department for Culture, Media and Sport, he is one of the few people in the country who is not entitled to air his opinions about art. Even if the Turner Prize were paid for by the tax-payer, rather than sponsored by Channel 4, as it is, Mr Howells would still be trampling all over the principle on which state subsidies for the arts have been based ever since Keynes created the Arts Council in 1946: that the Government be kept at 'arm's length' from decisions about how the subsidies should be spent.

Indeed, it would be better to abandon state sponsorship altogether than to allow governments to control culture ... Having studied art in the 1960s, Mr Howells owes allegiance to Henry Moore, Jackson Pollock and Francis Bacon – all of whom would have been damned by the culture ministers of their day ...

© *The Telegraph*, 1 November 2002

Sun Says
BRUSH OFF

THE Arts Minister is a brave man.

Kim Howells brands as "bullshit" the entries for the modern art Turner Prize.

He's right: Modern art is pretentious and meaningless, a con trick perpetrated on people with more money than sense.

They should hang a picture of Kim Howells in every gallery ...

He's priceless – a politician who's not afraid to say what he feels.

© *The Sun*, 1 November 2002

STRIKING A CHORD

QUESTION: what is the connection between the latest baffling display of modern art and a sticky lump of chewing gum stuck to the bottom of your shoe?

ANSWER: yesterday, they both revealed Ministers at their most appealing.

Take the chap who said what he thinks. So appalled was Culture Minister Kim Howells by this year's Turner Prize exhibition that he denounced the show as 'conceptual bull****'.

As a former art student himself, Mr Howells is well aware that fashionable opinion will react with disdain. No matter. By pointing out – with a spontaneous honesty rare in a politician – that the emperor has no clothes, he has done a public service and shown up the Turner's tedious annual attempt to shock.

Then we come to that old warhorse, Deputy Prime Minister John Prescott, whose plan for £50 spot fines to tackle the curse of dropped chewing gum – not to mention his proposed purge on graffiti artists – promises a small but welcome contribution to our quality of life.

For once, Ministers must be congratulated for striking a chord and talking common sense. What a pity it doesn't happen more often.

© *The Daily Mail*, 1 November 2002

Examination practice

As examination practice you might attempt the following question:

Read the three newspaper editorials on Kim Howells and the Turner Prize, and answer the following questions:

→   What are the main points being made about the Turner Prize entries and the minister's remarks about them, in *The Telegraph* editorial?

→   What differences in viewpoint do you find between *The Telegraph* editorial and the other two?

→   Compare the three editorials in their uses of language, tone and syntax.

Analysing a magazine article

The article 'Majorca: the place to be seen' on page 182, is a travel piece from the magazine *Bella*.

Read the article and briefly jot down your thoughts about the target audience, the purpose, the style and tone, and the methods used by the writer to persuade you that Majorca is a desirable place to go on holiday.

Majorca: the place to be seen

Busy beaches and high-rise hotels – if that's all that comes to mind when you think of Majorca, then we'll let you in on a secret. You've been had! Because not only have the Douglases, Claudia Schiffer and Michael Schumacher bought houses there, but its capital, Palma, is one sophisticated, buzzy little place. Add to that four-season sunshine, a flight time of just over two hours and you couldn't have a destination that's more 'now'! Prepare to be seduced ...

RUB SHOULDERS WITH THE RICH AND FAMOUS ON OUR FAVOURITE HOLIDAY ISLE

WHERE IS IT?

Majorca is the largest of the Balearic Islands, which lie east of Spain. Palma, capital of the Balearics, is on Majorca's south coast.

WHERE TO STAY?

Palma is packed with places to suit all pockets. For something traditional, head for the old town, where houses and palaces have been converted into hotels. Towards the marina are the larger chains, many with harbour views. If you hanker after beaches, there are lots within a short drive.

JUST AROUND THE CORNER

Hop aboard the Tren de Soller scenic railway for the perfect day out from Palma. This old-fashioned locomotive, which looks like something from an Agatha Christie film, cuts cross-country from the capital to the 'star-studded' north coast. After a breathtaking hour or so through mountains and valleys you reach Soller, where you can treat yourself to a ride on an original 1920s San Francisco tram down to the port. Just as popular here is walking. An hour through valleys of olive and orange trees will take you to the picture-postcard village of Fornalutx.

While you're on the north coast, if you fancy seeing how the rich and famous holiday, explore the beautiful stretch from Valldemossa to Port d'Andtrax. Catherine and Michael live in the former, while Claudia Schiffer and Michael Schumacher are practically neighbours in the latter. Boris Becker and Annie Lennox also have homes nearby.

TOP NOSH

- For a traditional Majorcan night, the Meson Ca'n Pedro, at Genova, on the outskirts of Palma, can't be beaten. Full of local people, this large restaurant is alive with chatter and great fun.
- Tapas is a must. La Boveda on Boteria has a good choice.
- For a quick snack and star treatment, head for the Cine Café, Plaça Del Mercat, where you can sit in a 'director's chair' bearing your favourite star's name.

NIGHT ON THE TILES

Dress up and head for Abaco, on Saint Juan in central Palma. Saying too much would spoil it, but just imagine stepping on to a lavish film set. A cocktail will set you back £9–£10, but it's worth every penny to wander round this unusual converted house with terrace – and watch heads turn as people try to work out if you're famous!

This is also your opportunity to have a go at salsa. Arrive fashionably late – venues like Azzuro, opposite the marina, don't get going until 11pm.

Just as entertaining, though, is sitting in a pavement café watching locals promenade.

SLUSHY MOMENTS

- Take the coastal path from the top of the bay at Soller to see the sun set over the Med.
- In Palma a horse-and-carriage ride under the stars can be quite something.

TIME IT RIGHT

Spring and autumn are ideal – warm, but not scorchingly so. Winter is definitely an option, too, when you can leave behind your scarf and gloves and enjoy an average temperature of 14°–15°C in December and January.

YOUR HOLIDAY

Flights with Air Europa start at £118 return including taxes. Call 0870 240 1501. Rooms at the marina-side Melia Victoria hotel start at around £55 pppn, including accommodation and breakfast. Call 00 34 971 732 542.

BEST SIGHTS

The Old City

Get lost! It may sound like odd advice, but just wandering through this ancient area, with its Moorish influence and intriguing narrow lanes is a simple but unmissable experience.

The Cathedral

Start your exploration here. This 500-year-in-the-making Gothic masterpiece towers over the harbour. Look out for the fancy wrought-iron work that Catalan artist Gaudi added earlier this century. The Baroque, Gothic rooms and treasury are also impressive. For the best view, stand across the lake in the adjacent Par de la Mar and enjoy its full reflection. At night, when the cathedral's lit up, it's even more of a treat.

Arab Baths

The tranquil garden of lemon and orange trees is a great place for a picnic and it also houses one of the few remaining relics of Arab rule. So this is how people used to socialise before pubs came into their own! Don't take your towel, tough, as the baths themselves are just ruins now.

Bellver Tower

For truly fantastic views of the bay head three kilometres west of the centre to this striking fortress.

Joan Miró Foundation

Whether you're a fan of this surrealist painter's work or a first-timer, the treat here is not just the exhibition and the 17th-century manor house he lived in, but being able to step into the studio, which is exactly as he left it, it can't help but inspire.

© *Bella* magazine, issue 44, 5 November 2002

Here is a specimen analysis of the section of text beginning: 'Busy beaches and high-rise hotels'.

Alliteration is used in the first phrase, to grab the reader's attention. In the second line the use of a dash makes the article seem informal, and the reader is drawn in by being addressed with the personal pronoun 'you' in the fourth line, followed by the enticing phrase, 'we'll let you in on a secret'. The colloquial style and tone is designed to involve the reader and put her/him at ease. The style is maintained in the next sentence: 'You've been had!', this time using a slang phrase as a short, snappy sentence, ending with an exclamation mark. This comes as a shock to the reader, and definitely creates the desire to read on. The next sentence uses non-standard grammar, beginning with the conjunction 'because', again creating a sense of easy informality. It goes on to list the celebrities who have bought houses in Majorca, giving a clear indication of the target audience: people who enjoy reading gossip about the rich and famous. The phrase 'not only' is designed to suggest 'as if this isn't enough ... there's more!', and the sentence continues with a description of the capital city as 'one sophisticated, buzzy little place'. The phrase is brash and modern-sounding, and designed to appeal to a young audience. The mention of 'four-season sunshine' and the short flight time are also designed to make Majorca sound appealing to young people. The next sentence uses a modern colloquial style again, in the phrase: 'you couldn't have a destination that's more "now"'! The final direct address to the reader: 'Prepare to be seduced', followed by three dots, almost impels you to read on.

In the exam practice exercise that follows, there is no need to go through the text analysing it sentence by sentence, as the specimen analysis does. This was done just to give you an example of the way to make points about the text. What you should try to do is pick out quotes that illustrate a good range of points relating to a question, and write your answer after drawing up a list of features you are going to mention, with illustrations of each drawn from different points in the text.

Examination practice

Read the article 'Majorca, the place to be seen' and answer the following questions:

→   List two facts and two opinions in the section headed: 'Just around the corner'.

➔ Comment on the layout and presentation of the article.

➔ What clues have you found as to the target audience of the article?

➔ Comment on the language, style and tone of the article, showing how the writer attempts to persuade you of the attractions of Majorca.

Another exercise, linking the Majorca article with an extract from a non-fiction text, will be found on page 225.

Coursework suggestions

➔ Write a detailed comparison of the four 'hippy convoy' articles, bringing out the differences in viewpoint, presentation and style.

➔ Write a comparative analysis of the ways a news story of your choice is reported in four different newspapers on the same day.

➔ Analyse a selection of newspaper front pages chosen on the same day. You should compare and contrast different types of newspapers, in terms of choice and range of front page items, presentational features and use of pictures, language, syntax and paragraphing.

➔ Write a comparison of an offical match-day programme and a football fanzine of the same club, published in the same month. You should compare the style, tone and attitudes adopted in a range of features and match reports.

EXAMINER'S TIPS

Whether you are writing about a media text as part of your coursework or in an examination, your examiner will expect you to put forward your ideas and opinions as clearly as you can. S/he will also be looking to see whether you have paid close attention to the way that language is used in the text and, of course, quoted evidence to support your views. Because media texts can also communicate their meaning using other ways in addition to language, you should also be prepared to comment in some detail on these aspects of the texts you are working with.

Punctuation and sentence structure

One of the activities that takes place before a newspaper goes on sale is proof-reading. People are employed to check the accuracy of the English in the articles chosen for publication, although this does not always seem to be done with football programmes. You have the job of proofreading the manager's notes for a programme of a Division One football club. The extract that follows is taken, unaltered, from an actual football programme. On a copy, correct all the inaccuracies in the use of commas and full stops.

FROM THE BOSS

Good afternoon ladies and gentlemen and welcome to today's very important game against Black Country rivals Wolverhampton Wanderers.

My notes for the Reading game dwelt on the unexplainable result against Colchester, fortunately our performances since then haven't been influenced by that experience. Tuesday's victory over Reading was particularly pleasing, it was our first game at the Hawthorns since we entertained Colchester and it is a tribute to the players that they took the game by the scruff of the neck and converted the pressure into an early goal. We could have scored five or six, but in the end it was a bit of a nail biter as Reading came back at us, however the lads showed excellent discipline and obviously everyone was very pleased for Andy Hunt who scored a superb hat-trick.

Albion News, 15 September 1996

WRITING TO INFORM, EXPLAIN OR DESCRIBE

The National Curriculum GCSE requirement of writing that seeks to inform, explain or describe is dealt with differently in the AQA A specification compared with the two B specifications. In AQA A it appears as an examination exercise; in AQA B and B (Mature) it features as coursework.

In reality, the distinctions between the four Writing 'triplets' (the other three being 'imagine, explore, entertain', 'argue, persuade, advise' and 'analyse, review, comment') are far from clear cut. For example, there is considerable overlap between writing tasks that involve *commenting* on an issue, *arguing* about an issue, or *explaining/describing a point of view* on an issue. As far as it is possible distinctions will be drawn between the types of writing represented by each of the categories in each of the triplets, but where there is overlap this will be mentioned in the units dealing with each triplet, and cross-referencing between units will be used to avoid repetition.

As regards the type or *genre* of writing you may be asked to produce, you could be asked to write your answer in the form of an essay, letter, etc. in response to *any* of the categories of writing that figure in the terminal examinations.

It is quite likely that one or more of the exam Writing questions will not specify a genre of writing, but simply ask you to 'write' a response to the question topic. Most of the questions *will* specify a genre of writing, though, the likeliest being:

→ essay
→ magazine or newspaper article
→ letter
→ speech.

The study texts in this unit include an illustration of a magazine article and an essay. Article writing is the genre that is explored fully in this unit; essay, speech and letter writing are dealt with in detail in Unit 15.

Since this unit deals with a triplet of categories of writing that appears as coursework in specification A and as an examination exercise in specification B and B (Mature), a distinction is drawn between coursework and examination tasks. The material that focuses particularly on coursework is, however, of direct relevance to exam preparation as well.

Writing to inform/explain

Establishing a clear distinction between writing to inform and writing to explain is particularly difficult. Look at these two possible exam questions:

➔   Write an *informative* article about a sport or hobby that interests you.

➔   Write an article that *explains* your interest in a sport or hobby.

What is the difference between them?

The first focuses on providing *information* about the sport or hobby *itself*; the second involves giving an *explanation* of *why* you are interested in it.

However, now look at this question:

➔   Write an article about one of your sporting interests or hobbies, giving your reasons for taking it up, and *commenting* on the benefits you have gained from it.

How does it differ from the second question above? Would it be possible to write the same answer for both?

To complicate distinctions further, because of its *wording*, this last question would be set in a different triplet of writing categories altogether, that of writing to 'analyse, review, comment'.

In reality, it should be obvious how you should tackle any question, whatever the category.

On pages 189–190 is an exam answer to a question that comes under the category 'explain'.

Write about a sport or hobby in which you participate, and explain how your interest in it developed.

giving up tennis and taking up squash
how I felt about it at first.
how my game developed
injuring Dave
squash league
handicap tournament.

At the age of fourteen I took up squash as my main sport. Before that I'd played tennis, but the tennis court was quite a long way from my home, so a game of tennis took up most of an evening — unless of course it was rained off!

A school friend called Dave played squash at the David Lloyd club, which was a short bus ride from my house, ~~so I thought I'd give it a go~~ and he invited me to come and try it. I thought I'd give it a go.

After a couple of games I felt like giving it up. Squash is a very fast game, and you've got to be pretty fit to play it. I wasn't. The court is shaped rather like a tennis court, but it's smaller, and enclosed by walls and a ceiling. There's no net, so you're hitting a very small hard rubber ball against the walls for forty minutes. This means that you're ~~running almost non-stop~~ dashing backwards and forwards and sideways almost non-stop. The better you get at it, the longer the rallies go on — so you can imagine how tired you get!

At first I thought I'd never be any good at it. Dave could beat me without trying. But I enjoyed dashing around, and I really started to feel fit. Once I'd started learning to play little drop shots just above the 'tin' ~~(the section of wall below the bottom line)~~ (the out-of-bounds section at the bottom of the front wall), and 'boasts' off the side wall into the front wall, and smashes and lobs into the back corners, I was away!

One day though, I found out what a dangerous game it can be. Dave and I were playing one evening, and he hit a shot towards the centre of the court. ~~I swung my racquet at it and he was too close to me.~~ I launched myself at it and swung my racquet -straight into his right eye! I was terrified! I thought I'd blinded him! ~~There was blood. The court.~~ The court was splattered with blood, and we had to call an ambulance! Luckily, he only needed to have stitches. I promised him I'd have a lesson with the club professional about ~~argue~~ racquet control before we played again!

There was a happy ending to the saga. I learnt how to control my racquet swing, and followed the lesson up with three more. Surprisingly enough, my game got worse! But after a while I got to grips with the new techniques he'd taught me, and now I have a better control over my game all round.

I joined the squash league, which made it more interesting, because I could play people of the same standard as me, but with totally different styles of play. Some of the older players seemed to be able to dominate the court with hardly moving, and that I've learnt a lot about positioning from playing them.

My best experience so far was playing in the club ~~tournament~~ handicap tournament. The handicap is supposed to make it possible for a poor player to beat a really good one. My handicap was pretty high! I lost in the first round, and went into the loser's plate competition. Then I kept winning. I played six games in six days, including two on the Saturday. The final was on the Sunday, and I won it. The plate was actually a useless glass mug, but I felt very proud going up to collect it, and being applauded by lots of club members. At the end of that week I felt capable of running two marathons!

I hope to go on improving, and moving up the leagues. Who knows, maybe ^gradually I'll eventually win the club handicap outright, and get a proper trophy ~~insted~~ instead of a stupid mug!

Now re-read the answer paragraph by paragraph, and answer the following questions on the content and style of the piece.

→ In the *first* paragraph, why does the writer mention tennis when the piece is about squash?

→ Why do you think he uses a dash and an exclamation mark at the end of the paragraph?

→ What is the effect of writing 'I wasn't' as a sentence on its own, in the *third* paragraph?

→ Why does he go on to inform the reader of the differences between a squash and a tennis court in the third pararaph? Is this information necessary?

→ At the end of this paragraph he addresses the reader directly as 'you'. What is the effect of doing this?

→ Why does he use brackets in the *fourth* paragraph?

→ What do you notice about the final sentence of this paragraph, in contrast with the sentence that precedes it?

→ The *fifth* paragraph is about injuring someone on a squash court. How is this relevant to a piece about how his interest in the sport developed?

→ Do you think this paragraph adds to the interest of the piece for the reader? Why?

→ What do you notice about the variation of sentence length in this paragraph? Does it add to the effectiveness of the writing?

→ What is the purpose and effect of the sentence: 'Surprisingly enough, my game got worse', in the *sixth* paragraph?

→ The third sentence of this paragraph begins with the conjunction 'But'. In what way does this break the standard rules of grammar? Do you think it is acceptable in a piece of writing like this? What is the effect of 'breaking' the rule?

→ What effect do you think the writer was trying to achieve by the last sentence of the *penultimate* paragraph?

→ Is the final sentence of the whole piece a good way to finish it off? Why?

→ Throughout the piece the writer uses contractions (I'll, wasn't, it's etc.) Is this a good idea, rather than using the more formal 'I will', etc.? What difference to the tone of the writing does it make?

→ Try to work out the reasons for the crossings out and added words in this piece.

Now try to write a summary list, or brainstorm as a group, the features of this exam answer that might be worth remembering if you have to produce a piece of *personal* writing to 'inform, explain or describe'.

Examination practice

➜ Write about a sport or hobby in which you participate, and explain how your interest in it developed.

If this is to be a genuine exam practice, you should allow yourself no more than 45 minutes to write your answer.

Writing an article

At least one of the three or four questions set in the AQA A terminal examination Paper 2, section B (writing to inform, explain, describe) is likely to require you to write an article for a newspaper or magazine. As a coursework topic for AQA B and B (Mature) Personal Writing: Non-Fiction (inform, explain, describe) you could choose to write a feature article for a magazine.

If you decide to write an article for coursework, greater elaboration and attention to presentation would be expected than would be reasonable to expect of an exam answer. However, even in the exam you would be expected to take account of presentation. How should you present an article in the exam?

It depends to some extent on whether the task set involves writing a magazine article or a newspaper article. Magazine articles tend to be more elaborate than newspaper articles.

A typical broadsheet newspaper article is set out in columns, without breaking up the text. In a tabloid article the columns are generally broken up with emboldened sub-headings or juicy quotations from the body of the article.

An article written in response to an exam question should *look* like an article. You should at least divide the page of your exam booklet up into two columns, and break up the text in one of the two ways mentioned above. It should not take up too much time, and you will gain marks for effective presentation.

The next section should help you to think of other ways of making your writing suitable for a magazine format.

A coursework article

The article on pages 194 to 195 was written by a college student. It is an example of a piece of writing that encompasses more than one writing category.

It can be treated as a sample response to the following suggestion for AQA B and B (Mature) coursework: Personal Writing: Non-Fiction (inform, explain, describe):

Write an article for a quality magazine which is an informal account of a topic of interest to the writer.

The analysis below of the way the article is written and presented should be useful as practice in analysing media texts for the terminal exams in each AQA specification.

➜   What *kind* of article is it?
➜   Is it meant to be taken seriously?
➜   How many of the sub-sections contain information about tea and tea drinking?

As you may have decided, there *is* a fair amount of information about tea in this article, but it is presented in a light-hearted, tongue-in-cheek way. It would probably be classified as a light *feature* article, suitable for a quality magazine that takes occasional articles designed to provide information in an informal, entertaining way.

Let us look first at the presentation:

➜   What is notable about the title?
➜   What is the connection of the drawings to the text? What do you notice about the placing of the drawings?
➜   What other presentation features are used?

Now we will look at the content and style of the article:

➜   In the first column, some of the 'sentences' break the rules of formal grammar. Which ones? What is the effect of this informal style of writing?

Feeling sluggish? Then it's time you had a nice cup of tea.

There is a whole lot more to drinking tea than simply pouring it out and gulping it back. Tea is a central part of the British way of life. So central, that when someone asks, "Do you want a cuppa?", nobody has to verify what substance the cup will contain. Instinctively we know that it will be the result of the infusion of boiling water poured over a selection of dried, crumbled leaves of a plant that was picked some several thousand miles away. Strange? Yes, but strangely enough, we British do take our tea drinking seriously. Or do we?

TEA SPEAK - COLLOQUIALLY.

A cup of tea is commonly known in friendly circles as 'a cuppa', (or a mugga) London's cockneys use rhyming slang, as in 'Rosy Lea', though their version is not as weak and insipid as its fairground, fortune-telling namesake, who feigns knowledgeable insight into your future by staring into the soggy tea leaves at the bottom of your spent teacup! The term 'Cha' comes from the old colonial days when 'char wallers' served tea to their 'Mem Sahibs' in India, to cool their thick British blood on hot sultry afternoons. Northerners drink 'a brew', and let a pot of tea 'mash(brew)' Southerners 'brew' a pot of tea and drink a cuppa.

WHERE TO DRINK TEA.

The act of drinking tea socially has played an important part in our heritage for centuries. It can be 'taken', elegantly, in that epitome of etiquette 'The Ritz', or as humbly as in the plastic cupped variety imbibed on the factory floor. A family picnic on the beach, at the height of the sweltering summer, would never be the same without mother's obligatory cup of tea! Thank God for 'Mr Thermo'! In simplicity, tea can be taken, slurped, sipped or supped anywhere.

TEDIOUSLY TASTEFUL TEA TECHNIQUE ...

To make proper tea follow this proper procedure. Pour cold water into a vessel, especially made for boiling water, called 'a kettle'. For each person partaking tea, place one spoonful of tea leaves, and one extra spoonful, into a vessel appropriately called 'a teapot'. When the water in the vessel called a kettle' has boiled, pour it over the leaves in the vessel called 'a teapot'. Leave to infuse for approximately five minutes. Meanwhile, place a china vessel, called 'a cup', on a flat china object, called 'a saucer', and place a silver stick, called 'a spoon', on the saucer. Pour the infused liquid, from the vessel called 'a teapot', into a vessel called 'a cup'. Add some 'juice of a cow' called 'milk' and, if required to sweeten, the product of the cane plant called sugar. Stir with the object called 'a spoon', and sip gently!

... OR, TEA IN A TICK.

Throw a teabag into a mug, fill with boiling water, splash in some milk, add a spoonful or two of sugar, stir well and drink in huge satisfying gulps.

DESERVING DRINKERS.

Always offer the plumber, gasman, decorator, carpet-layer, copious cups of the strong, liberally sugared variety. Loose leafed Earl Grey just

ACCOMPANIMENTS, or, befitting companions to specialist teas. One should drink: Darjeeling - to accompany a pungent Indian takeaway. Camomile - definitely on the lawn. China - speaks for itself. Earl Grey - when the aristocracy drop in. Lapsang-Souchong - learn the language first, or you might not be drinking what you think you are!

doesn't raise the interest of the thirsty digger-driver who is decimating your daffs to

replace the sewerage pipes! The humble tea bag, for some reason, tastes best when the pungent aroma of damp earth and brick-dust abounds! Ply the D.I.Y. enthusiast with tea and your home could be a safer place to live for all concerned

TEA SERVICE.

When we serve tea in china cups it tends to be only on polite occasions usually it's in a mug. The British household should have a good selection of one or more of the following:
● a mug bearing the name of a member of the family that everybody uses.
● a mug bearing the name of nobody in the family which nobody uses. (A good bargain at the time!)
● at least one 'yukky'

yellow mug with the name of a popular chocolate bar adorning it, that supported last year's Easter egg.
● an assortment of chipped, cracked, stained and handle-less varieties, used for whatever substance requires a vessel at the time.
● half a set of relatively useable mugs obtained free with petrol tokens.
● a set of fine bone china mugs, only bought into commission when Granny calls, or that posh lady from the W.I. drops in for the 'jumble' and pleads, 'Don't stand on ceremony for me!' Or, for the workmen directly outside your front gate, in case the Jones' are watching your generosity!

WHO MAKES TEA?

The wife or mother of the family makes for the kettle before anyone else can, therefore, she makes the tea. It is her prerogative, unless it is Sunday morning, when the man of the house should go downstairs, collect the newspaper from the mat, put out the cat, and bring a cup of tea back to his wife. Ahh, there's nothing quite like that Sunday morning 'cuppa'.

TOTAL

Val Clarke-Allen

➡ How would you describe the *tone* in which the information about the terminology relating to tea is presented, in the first sub-section of column two? Pick out a phrase or statement that illustrates the tone particularly vividly.

➡ What stylistic device is used in the last sentence of the sub-section: 'Where to drink tea'? What does the use of the device add to the effect of the paragraph?

➡ What stylistic device is used in the next sub-heading, in column three? Is it effective, in terms of the tone and style of the article as a whole?

➡ Is this section really providing information about tea making? What is the point of it?

➡ Why does the next sub-section begin with three dots?

➡ What is the difference between the language and style of this sub-section and the previous one? Why do you think the author made this change in the style of writing?

➡ Pick out a particularly descriptive phrase in the sub-section 'Deserving Drinkers', and comment on the use of language.

➡ What is notable about the sub-heading 'Tea Service'? Why does this sub-section contain bullet points? What is the purpose of this sub-section?

➡ Do you think the last sentence of the article is a good way to end it?

➡ Why do you think the insert is placed across three columns, instead of simply being added to the bottom of the fourth column?

Writing to describe

Descriptive writing is clearly different from informative or explanatory writing. When you are describing something, your purpose is to create pictures in words, so that the reader can imagine the person or scene or situation you are describing. You are trying to convey a visual impression as vividly as possible.

The probability is that you will be describing a personal experience if you choose to write a descriptive piece in the terminal examinations (AQA A) or for coursework (AQA B and B (Mature)).

Here is an example of a descriptive essay, in response to the following title:

Write an essay describing the scene at a busy airport, port or railway station.

A descriptive essay
Birmingham New Street Station on a Saturday Afternoon.

Random notes
escalator
barrier with arrivals and deps. board
queues at ticket windows
magazine stall
bar – 4 drunks shouting and singing
crowd of football supporters pile down escalator
platform – people milling about
             – tramp lying on bench
train arrives – couple caress

Plan

Intro:	personal introduction
	station entrance
	crowds of people
Para. 2:	electric arr. and dep. board
	magazine stall
	tea bar
Para. 3:	bar
Para. 4:	platform: tramp
	arrival of 1st train
Para. 5:	my train arrives

It is six o'clock on a Saturday evening in mid-October, and I have just got out of my uncle's car on the forecourt of New Street Station, Birmingham. I allow the escalator slowly to draw me down into the station itself. I am in no hurry; my train does not leave for forty-five minutes. I have time to relax and observe.

   As the escalator descends, a man rushes by, brushing my knee with the suitcase in his left hand. A woman in a fur coat also scurries past, a startled-looking poodle under her arm and an exasperated expression on her face. At the bottom she totters awkwardly towards the barrier, her poodle yapping and struggling in her grasp. Other people step past purposefully, while others again, like me, allow the machinery to usurp the function of their legs. I step off, onto the huge open area housing all the many amenities of a major modern railway station: bar, restaurant, coffee stall, book stall, telephone booths, ticket office, information office and platform entrances.

The first feature to attract my attention, however, is the massive electric arrivals and departures board. I stand watching it in fascination for a couple of minutes as it clicks up its messages: '11.05 from Edinburgh 40 minutes late', then '14.52 from Reading at platform 5'. A bell jingles over the tannoy and a metallic voice pronounces semi-audibly about 'the train now standing on platform 5'. I saunter over to the books, magazines and sweets counter and stand in line to purchase a means to while away the hours ahead. Then I wander over to the far side of the station entrance to buy some coffee. A couple of children are flicking orange juice at one another and shrieking with delight. At the counter an old lady in a dirty, shapeless brown coat is haggling over the price of coffee with the woman behind the counter, who is saying, in a tone of weary irritation, 'Look, I don't decide on the price. You don't have to have it.' Here, everything is plastic: the cups, cutlery, sauce bottles, sandwich wrappers; even the contents look as if they are made of the same ubiquitous material. The coffee is tasteless. I feel a sudden urge for a proper drink.

The bar is crowded. At a table over the far side sit four men. They are already drunk. They sing lugubrious snatches of song, and one of them shouts an incoherent remark at the girl who moves around the tables collecting glasses, while the others laugh raucously. She ignores them. I stand next to a group of pin-stripe suited men who swap jokes in fruity accents. The beer is as tasteless as the coffee. I tire of the crush and the din in the bar.

Moving through the milling throng, I queue to buy my ticket. A young woman wearing jeans and anorak pushes to the front. She looks distraught. 'Do you mind if I get my ticket first? My train leaves in two minutes,' she says to a little balding man at the front of the queue. He grudgingly steps back for her and a woman in front of me mutters irritably to her husband, who says nothing. It is now ten minutes before my train is due and as I walk towards the barrier I hear a commotion on the escalator. A couple of dozen youths in blue and white scarves, one of them blowing a whistle and all of them shouting, are clanging down the escalator, jostling the other passengers, who cower against the rail. They break into a discordant song, repeatedly inviting certain unnamed 'bums' to 'go home'. People scuttle out of their way as they go marauding aimlessly around.

I queue at the barrier and the ticket collector cheerily tells me to go to platform seven. On the platform there are scores of people. My eyes light on a youngish man, his dark suit in tatters, who lies asleep on a bench, a wine bottle beneath him. A train

arrives. It disgorges its passengers and amongst the throngs who hustle with anxious expressions to get a window seat a girl wearing a bobble hat steps down and stares around her. She suddenly darts forward and into the arms of a young man. She grabs off her hat and shakes out her long, auburn hair, and my heart warms at the look of rapture on her face.

Soon my own train arrives and no sooner am I settled in than the train is swallowed into a tunnel and leaving New Street Station and its multifarious cross-section of humanity behind. I am not sorry to depart.

You will notice from the 'random notes' and 'plan' that this piece was organised into a series of paragraphs, each with a distinct focus. This is a requirement of any essay. A fuller explanation of the essay genre will be found in the next unit, on pages 204 to 213.

Whatever the genre of writing you are engaged in, you will need to brainstorm your ideas before you start writing, and organise them into a logical paragraph sequence.

It would be useful to look at some of the ways in which language is used in this essay to bring the scene to life. You might highlight words, phrases or sentences in response to the following analytical exercise, and be prepared to explain why you have chosen them.

➡ What is the point of the first paragraph?

➡ Pick out some vivid descriptive phrases in the second paragraph. What makes them vivid?

➡ Identify the verbs in the third paragraph. Does the choice of verbs add to the atmosphere of the description?

➡ How is the sense of development between paragraphs created in the last sentence of the third paragraph?

➡ Look at the sentence structure of the fourth paragraph. What do you notice about it? Does it add to the atmosphere of the paragraph?

➡ Identify the adjectives and adverbs in the fourth paragraph. Are they effective in bringing the description to life?

➡ How is a link beween the fourth and fifth paragraphs established?

➡ In the fifth paragraph, how does the choice of adjectives and verbs create a contrast in atmosphere between the description of the queue and the arrival of the football fans on the escalator?

➡ The sentence lengths vary considerably in the sixth paragraph. What is the effect of the variation in syntax?

→   Can you picture the incident involving the young couple? Which words particularly bring this brief incident to life?

→   Do you think the last paragraph is effective as a conclusion? Why?

A few other points are worth making about this essay:

1. It is written in the present tense. There is nothing wrong with this, but it is risky. There is a good chance that if you begin a descriptive piece in the present tense, you will slip at some point into the past, and possibly back and forth between present and past. This will spoil the effect of your writing to some extent. It is safter to start in the past and stay there!

2. There are seven paragraphs in the essay, which is two more than the plan indicates. What happened was that some aspects of the description needed fuller treatment than was anticipated at the planning stage, and other ideas surfaced while writing, so that the plan was, to some extent, abandoned. There is nothing wrong with this. The purpose of a plan is to develop an overall structure for your piece of writing. There is no need to stick to it rigidly.

3. The description is not a reconstruction of the actual events of a single visit to Birmingham New Street Station. Memories from several visits were dredged up at the random note-making stage and, in the case of the description of the drunks and the waitress in the bar in paragraph four, this was actually a recollection of a scene in Swindon Railway Station. The sleeping 'wino' in paragraph six was borrowed from a London tube station.

An autobiographical piece written by a student, this time a description of a traumatic experience that occurred when she was 13, can be found in Unit 2, on page 14. You might spend a little time reading this piece and trying to work out how she has created a sense of atmosphere and drama by her use of language.

Examination practice

→   Write a feature article about an event that you found particularly unusual and interesting.

If this is to be a genuine exam practice, you should allow yourself no more than 45 minutes to write your answer.

Coursework suggestions (inform, explain, describe)

→   Write an account of a personal experience, or somebody else's experience, of the paranormal, and comment on the significance of the experience.

→   Write an account of an experience from your childhood that stood out in some way, explaining what effect it had on you.

→   Write a magazine article on the theme of race relations in Britain.

→   Describe your feelings and explain your point of view on the conditions experienced by the developing world's poor.

→   Write an article for a magazine describing a place that had a particularly strong impact on you, and explain how and why it has stayed in your memory.

→   Write a description of a concert that you attended, capturing the atmosphere of the event and describing the performance, your own reactions and those of other members of the audience.

→   Choose a controversial issue that interests you, and write two speeches presenting opposing viewpoints on the issue.

→   Research the lives of two or three infamous tyrants, and write an essay or a feature article giving an account of their lives and describing their impact on the lives of the people in the countries they ruled, or on the world.

→   Write an account of the life of a person you particularly admire, describing him/her and explaining what you find exceptional about him/her.

EXAMINER'S TIPS

As we've said before, your examiner will be looking for evidence that you've planned and structured your answer carefully and that you've written accurately, with few or no mistakes in your spelling, punctuation and grammar. In addition, s/he'll be keen to see whether your answer would actually do the job it was intended to. The question will always have indicated who you are writing for (audience), why you are writing (purpose) and the type of writing required (genre). So, you've got to make sure that the language you chose and the tone you use will be effective for the audience, purpose and genre of your task. The closer you get to what is appropriate, the higher your mark.

Spelling: the '-ful' rule

This is a simple rule to remember and apply. When a word is turned into an adjective by adding the suffix '-ful', there is *always* only one 'l' on '-ful.' Thus:

care + ful	– careful
pocket + ful	– pocketful
wonder + ful	– wonderful
spoon + ful	– spoonful
beauty + ful	– beauti_ful
skill + ful	– sk_il_ful
mouth + ful	– mouthful

WRITING TO ARGUE, PERSUADE, ADVISE AND ANALYSE, REVIEW, COMMENT

The Writing triplet 'argue, persuade, advise' appears in the terminal examinations of each AQA specification. The triplet 'analyse, review, comment' appears as media coursework in AQA A, and in the terminal examinations of AQA B and B (Mature).

The categories of writing overlap to a considerable extent, and the kind of language you use is unlikely to differ very much whichever of the categories a question appears in, except perhaps in the case of persuasive writing.

The differences between the categories can be summed up as follows:

Writing to argue involves presenting a case in favour of something you believe in. Your argument will rely mainly on logic, and the use of factual evidence to back it up. You may be asked to present arguments for *and* against something, but it is more likely that the question will ask you to argue on one side only. In the latter case, you can still mention an opposing point of view, but only to show why you believe it is wrong, or why your argument outweighs it. You can use persuasive language to sway the reader in favour of your point of view.

Writing to persuade also needs to be logical, but it is likely to be written in a more personal way, and may appeal more directly to the reader's emotions. Especially in the case of a speech, a range of rhetorical devices designed to sway the audience's emotions may be used.

Writing to advise is addressed directly to an individual or group, presenting a series of suggestions about a topic or issue, using an imperative style, telling the reader what to do or think.

Writing to analyse also involves expressing a viewpoint on something in a logical way. However, it is more concerned with showing that there are two sides to an issue rather than arguing a case for one side, or trying to persuade someone to do or believe in something.

Writing to review tends to involve an assessment of your own experience, attitudes, ambitions and so on, and questions in this category are likely to be focused on your personal life.

Writing to comment involves expressing your personal opinions about something. All the other categories in this unit involve comment to some extent.

This unit focuses on three of the writing genres you might be required to use: essay writing, letter writing and speech writing, and explores the techniques involved in writing to argue, persuade, analyse and comment.

Writing an essay

The essay is the standard form of academic writing. It is quite likely that the argument question in your exam will be set in the form of an essay.

An essay is a specific genre of writing, with its own rules. You must be aware of these rules, and how to structure an essay according to them. We shall start with the basics.

➡   What is an essay?
➡   What is a paragraph?

There is, as you may have concluded, a formal pattern which any essay on any topic must follow. There are three components:

> introduction
> main paragraphs
> conclusion

We shall look at each of these in a generalised way, and then study an essay that was written to argue a case.

Essay structure

The introduction

➡   Why is it necessary to write an introduction to an essay?

If you start by exploring the subject of the essay without introducing the question and the approach you are going to take to it, then you are leaving the reader to work this out for him/herself. The main purpose of the introduction, therefore, is to explain the focus of your essay.

The introduction does not need to be long. A concise statement in a couple of sentences is all that is usually necessary.

The main paragraphs

These form the body of the essay. Each paragraph must concentrate on one aspect of the subject. This aspect must be **developed**. This means that a paragraph must consist of several sentences.

→   What is wrong with a one-sentence paragraph?
→   How long should a main paragraph be?

Just to make it clear what the **theme** of a paragraph is going to be will take a sentence. You will need more than one further sentence to *develop* the topic. It would be almost impossible to develop a topic fully in less than a third of a page. It should be obvious, then, that very short paragraphs of one or two sentences are unsatisfactory. All you can do in a sentence or two is to *state* an idea. You cannot develop it in such a short space.

The main paragraphs, therefore, must develop a series of perhaps three or four topics/themes/aspects of the question, at reasonable length. In an argument essay it is a good idea to establish a link between one paragraph and the next, to create a sense of a developing argument. It is a good idea in any examination Writing exercise to re-read each paragraph before starting on the next. This will help to keep your ideas coherent.

The conclusion

The object of the concluding paragraph is to round off the essay in a satisfactory way, so that it is not left hanging.

One way of doing this is to summarise what you have said in the essay. This is not, however, a particularly good way to end an essay. If the points you have made in the essay are clear, they should not need restating at the end.

Perhaps the best way to round off an essay is to think of an idea that ties in with the subject of the essay as a whole, and end with a sentence that sums up the whole argument or experience you have been writing about.

In the next section you will study an argument essay, from the planning stage onwards.

Writing an argument essay

Here is an example of an argument essay. Read the essay and discuss the aspects of argument writing and essay technique brought out in the questions that follow it.

Write an essay arguing a case for or against the view that cars are more a curse than a blessing in the world of the twenty-first century.

Notes:
convenience
reorganised public transport system
using up world's scarce oil
noise pollution
greenhouse effect
ozone layer
accidents
motorways – pollution of environment
        – destroy countryside
air pollution – carbon monoxide, especially Tokyo and Los Angeles
destruction of towns – flyovers and bypasses
        – motorways go right into cities
intro – origins of car
    – are cars a blessing?
effects on people – adds to isolation
        – stress: traffic jams/rushing through traffic
conclusion: – could cars be done away with?
      – effect on unemployment

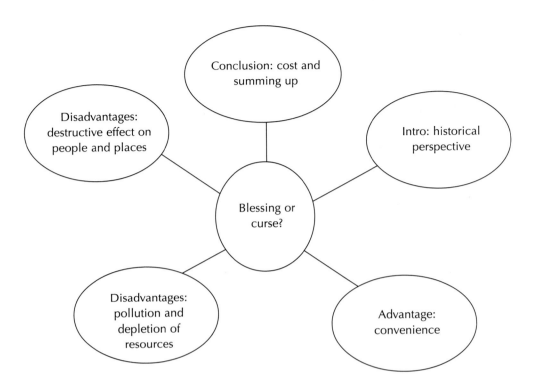

In 1885 a German, Carl Benz, produced the first petrol-driven vehicle, which proved to be the forerunner of the modern car. Few people in those days realised what a monster had been spawned. If they had foreseen the extent to which the automobile has come to dominate life in the Western world a century later, would they have looked on Herr Benz's achievement with approval?

To many people at the end of the twentieth century, a car has come to seem an indispensable part of daily life. The extent to which I myself have become dependent on my car is highlighted whenever it breaks down and I have to use buses. By the time I have walked to the bus stop, which is some distance from my house, and waited for twenty minutes in the pouring rain for a bus which leaves me with a twenty-minute walk the other end, the car does indeed seem a blessing. In a town like Bournemouth, the public transport system is so run-down that cars tend to be the only comfortable and efficient mode of travel. Does this have to be the case?

Many people feel that the days of the car are numbered, that the world's reserves of oil will be exhausted within a generation, and the petrol-driven car will have to be phased off the roads. What will happen then? The answer which many have suggested, a full-scale reorganisation of the public transport sysstem, shows that the car is not necessarily such an indispensable asset as we tend to assume. If everyone used buses instead of cars, then public transport could be run efficiently, with a regular, rapid network of routes in every town and city in the country, and with no traffic jams! There could be express buses, stopping only at major points along the route, even within cities. However, cars are fast and efficient, except in rush hours, so what, apart from slowing down the depletion of oil reserves, would mankind gain from the loss of the motor car? Is it really a curse?

You have only to travel to Tokyo or Los Angeles to realise the appalling effects of cars on the environment. Traffic police in Tokyo have to wear masks and carry oxygen, or they would collapse because the air is so polluted with carbon monoxide from cars. Cars produce other, more insidious types of pollution. Perhaps the most deadly threat facing mankind is the global warming resulting from the Greenhouse Effect and the destruction of the ozone layer. Cars are considered by scientists to be the major contributors to this potential catastrophe. On a less cataclysmic scale, noise pollution, caused by the ceaseless roar of engines and honking of horns, is a further cause of stress in major cities. Actual death from these causes at the moment, however, is rare. The car is, nevertheless, a major killer.

One of the principal causes of premature death in the Western world is from car accidents. Thousands of people are killed on the roads every year in Britain. Thousands more are injured and maimed, which results not only in indescribable suffering, but also in a serious drain on the resources of the National Health Service, with precious space in hospital wards taken up, for months or years, by the car's victims. Not only human life is destroyed by the ubiquitous car. Towns and cities are ruthlessly knocked about to build flyovers and bypasses which destroy the character of our urban areas; motorways destroy the peace and beauty of the countryside.

Clearly the car has come to dominate human life to an unhealthy extent. Can the monster be killed off, without too much pain? Car workers will say 'no'. Unemployment would soar if the motor industry folded up. But is the saving of jobs a strong enough reason for the destruction of human life and the environment? With an efficient public transport system, the only real blessings of the car – speed and convenience – would be rendered insignificant, and the death of the private car would make the world altogether safer and less stressful.

Discussion of the essay

→ What is the point of mentioning Carl Benz in the first paragraph?
→ What has the second paragraph got to do with arguing that the car is a curse?

→ How does the third paragraph lead on from the second? How does it lead into the fourth?

→ Is the argument against private cars in the fourth paragraph made powerfully? You should look at both the ideas themselves and the uses of language to express them.

→ What is the difference in focus between the fourth and fifth paragraphs?

→ Is the final paragraph effective as a conclusion?

It should be pointed out that you could not possibly write an essay of this length in 45 minutes. However, it illustrates all the essential aspects of essay writing that you need to consider.

Planning an argument essay

As it is essential to structure an essay into a series of paragraphs, it is important to *think the structure through* before you begin writing. Unless you decide on the *topic* of each paragraph before you write an essay, you are likely to end up with an unstructured essay with undeveloped or single-sentence paragraphs. It is, therefore, a good idea to *write a plan first*.

The few minutes you spend thinking of ideas for your essay, and arranging them into a paragraph plan, is time well spent. It is certainly not time wasted, because if you have not thought it out before you start, you will have to keep stopping to think about the structure of your essay while you are writing it.

There is no particular need to have a clear idea of the paragraph scheme for your essay at the brainstorming stage. Once you've finished brainstorming your ideas, you can then organise them into a plan. There is no need to feel that you *have* to follow your plan. It is purely for your benefit. New ideas can be added to your spider diagram after you have begun writing the essay.

If you *do* think of new ideas as you go along, however, you may come up against the eternal bugbear of examinations: time. Trying to develop every idea that occurs to you can result in you running out of time before you have managed to follow through your prepared structure fully. Therefore, it is essential to *pace* yourself. Good ideas may have to be discarded if time is getting short; other ideas, which you would have liked to develop, may have to be stated much more briefly than they might be. The final sentence of paragraph five of the sample essay, for instance, glosses very briefly over two ideas that could have been embellished and made more compelling with examples. This would have been at the expense of a proper conclusion, however, which is more important.

When ideas are flowing freely, self-discipline is required! No illustration of a single idea should take too much of your writing time and, even more crucially, you should *never* include ideas just because you have thought of them. Your essay must have direction, and every idea must be clearly relevant to the theme of the paragraph in which it appears.

How the argument is built up

Let us now look at the content of the essay on cars, to see how the paragraph structure works.

The introductory paragraph gives a clue as to the viewpoint to be taken in the essay, by setting it in the context of the whole period of the motor car's existence, leading to a **rhetorical question** in the last sentence of the introduction. A rhetorical question is one in which the answer is implied in the way the question is posed. This leads us directly into the second paragraph.

The second paragraph appears to be arguing that cars *are* a blessing. The idea that cars are often the only convenient way of travelling is expressed in terms of the writer's personal experience. This is a good way of making the argument seem down-to-earth. Making some reference to the opposing point of view in an argument essay is, in fact, a good idea, as long as you soon go on to focus on why you *disagree* with it. It shows that you are aware that there are two ways of looking at the issue, and can be a good way of *building up* to your central argument. A bald statement of your attitude to the discussion topic, at the beginning of the essay, tends to pre-empt the argument.

The second paragraph again ends with a question, as does the third. The questions are then answered in the paragraph that follows. This is a simple and effective way to achieve **links** between paragraphs, and create a sense of a developing argument. It is not a good idea to end *every* paragraph with a question, however; it will begin to seem rather artificial if you do. It *is* a good idea to try to establish links between all the paragraphs somehow, though. In this essay the fourth paragraph is linked to the fifth by a **bridge** sentence, introducing the theme of the destructive effect of cars, which is the focus of the following paragraph, with the use of a **connective**: 'nevertheless'. The concluding paragraph begins with the word 'Clearly', linking it with the argument built up in the whole essay, and suggesting that it has been proved.

In terms of the development of the argument in this essay, the pivotal paragraph is the third. It provides a solution to the problem of the inconvenience of other modes of transport in comparison with cars, which was argued and illustrated in the second paragraph, and provides the basis on which to build the arguments developed in the fourth and fifth paragraphs, which get to grips with the issue of cars being a curse. Without the third paragraph the argument would be much less convincing.

Paragraphs four and five deal with different kinds of problems caused by the use of private cars: the fourth with the environmental effects of car use, and the fifth with the ways cars destroy people and places. If you look at the first sentence of each of paragraph four and five you will see how to **state the theme** of the paragraph. This is called the **topic sentence**. It is a good device to try and use, since it clarifies for the examiner (and for you!) which aspect of the topic you are going to be dealing with in that paragraph.

The concluding paragraph of the essay makes brief reference to another argument in favour of private cars continuing to be built, but only in order to ridicule it with another rhetorical question. This leads into the final decisive statement of the essay. It is a good idea to try to say something interesting in the conclusion, rather than just briefly summing up what you have already said, as long as you don't spend too long trying to think of a good way to round off the essay.

The uses of language

The style of writing of this essay is essentially formal. The syntax and punctuation are entirely conventional and there are no contractions, like 'there's' and 'wouldn't', and no colloquialisms. Connectives are used, like 'however', 'so' and 'nevertheless', to provide links between ideas, and questions are used, as discussed above. In the fourth paragraph, where the essay deals with the dangers that the continuing use of private cars poses, it begins to seem more like a piece of persuasive writing. Emotive language is employed, with words like 'appalling', 'deadly', 'catastrophe', and the writing becomes more descriptive, with the use of onomatopoeia in the phrases 'ceaseless roar' and 'honking of horns' adding colour to the writing. Another device more associated with imaginative or persuasive writing, that of repetition, is used in the second and third sentences of the fifth paragraph, which both begin with 'Thousands'. Finally, the argument is given a satisfying sense of finality in the second sentence of the final paragraph by a repetition of the metaphor of the car as a 'monster', previously used at the very beginning of the essay.

One final point is worth making. The information about 'thousands' of people being killed on the roads in Britain each year is rather vague. This does not negate its effectiveness. You are not being assessed on the accuracy of the information you present in your argument, and you will not gain a lower mark than someone who produces precise statistics. You cannot be expected to have detailed knowledge of the subject you are asked to write about in the examination; what you are being assessed on is the accuracy and effectiveness of your use of language, and your ability to write interestingly and convincingly for the specified audience and purpose.

Group Speaking and Listening

The topic dealt with in the argument essay might prove the stimulus for a Speaking and Listening: Group Interaction assessment, covering the skill area 'discuss, argue, persuade'.

Possible discussion topics might be: 'The future of the car' or 'Transport in the twenty-first century'.

Examination practice

Write an answer to this question:

➡ Write an essay arguing for or against the suggestion that prisons should be made harsher, and convicted criminals should be given longer sentences.

You are advised to spend about 40 minutes on your answer.

Writing to persuade

When you are writing an argument, you are trying to persuade the reader to accept your point of view. Most of the points made about the argument essay on cars are also likely to apply to a question requiring persuasive writing.

It is possible, however, to identify some features of style and language that might be called 'techniques of persuasion', and which you might consider attempting to use in a persuasive piece, depending on the nature of the task. Here are some techniques of persuasion:

➜   emotive language, appealing directly to the reader's emotions

➜   expressive, colourful language, especially alliteration and similes

➜   colloquial, everyday language, to put the reader at ease

➜   addressing the reader directly as 'you' to involve him/her more in what you are saying

➜   rhetorical questions, involving the reader, and drawing him/her into agreement with you

➜   repetition, hammering the point home in a forceful or emotional way

➜   tripling: also referred to as 'speaking in threes', this involves making three related assertions, using a repeated phrase in each, building up to a climax of intensity, for example, 'We've taken the West Wing, we've shaken the White House, and here in Georgia tonight we're shaking the world'

➜   listing of words and phrases, separated by commas, to add intensity and forcefulness

➜   creating a sense of a personal 'voice', so that the reader can relate to you on a human level

➜   manipulation of tone, such as a mocking, scornful, sarcastic, bitter or angry tone, to add to the emotional impact

➜   short sentences, adding force and 'punch' to the writing.

Writing a speech

The techniques listed above may be particularly relevant to an exercise requiring you to write a speech.

On pages 214–215 is part of a speech by Tony Blair, delivered at the first Labour Party Conference after Labour came to power in the General Election of 1997.

Read the speech, and try to identify as many of the techniques of persuasion listed as you can.

Fourteen years ago, our party was written off as history. This year we made history. And let our first thanks be to the British people. You kept faith with us. And we will keep faith with you. Thank you to the party organization, the volunteers, the professionals who fashioned the finest political fighting machine our country has ever known.

Ours was not a victory of politicians but of people. The people took their trust, and gave it to us. I want them to say, this week as they watch us here in Brighton, 'We did the right thing.' I want the British people to be as proud of having elected us as we are to serve them. We won because we are new Labour, because we had the courage to change ourselves, and the discipline to take hard decisions, whilst remaining united.

But I want to do more than keep our promises. I sense the British people demand more of us, too. People ask me the highlight of the election. Mine was driving from home to Buckingham Palace, along streets we had driven hundreds of times, past soulless buildings and sullen faces on their way to work. This drive was so different. As we turned into Gower Street, people watching our journey on TV came pouring out of the doorways, waving and shouting and clapping, with an energy and excitement that went beyond anything I imagined would happen.

They were liberated. Theirs were the smiles of tolerant, broad-minded, outward-looking, compassionate people and suddenly they learnt that they were in the majority after all. As one woman put it to me: 'We've got our Government back.' And with them I could sense confidence returning to the British people, compassion to the British soul, unity to the British nation, and that all three would give us new-found strength.

You see, the people were yearning for change in their country at a time when they could see we had had the guts to modernize our party. The two came together.

. . .

Even today in Britain we lead the world, in design, pharmaceuticals, financial services, telecommunications. We have the world's first language, English. Britain today is an exciting, inspiring place to be. And it can be much more, if we face the challenge of a world around us today that has its finger on the fast-forward button; where every part of the picture of our life is changing, changing constantly.

So today I say to the British people the chains of mediocrity have broken, the tired days are behind us, we are free to excel once more. We are free to build that model twenty-first-century nation, to become that beacon to the world.

It's pretty simple, the type of country I want. It's a country where our children are proud and happy to grow up, feeling good not just about themselves, but about the community around them.

I don't want them living in a country where some of them go to school hungry, unable to learn beause their parents can't afford to feed them; where they can see drugs being traded at school gates; where gangs of teenagers hang around street corners, doing nothing but spitting and swearing and abusing passers-by.

I don't want them brought up in a country where the only way pensioners can get long-term care is by selling their home, where people who fought to keep that country free are now faced every winter with the struggle for survival, skimping and saving, cold and alone, waiting for death to take them.

And I will not rest until that country is gone, until all our children live in a Britain where no child goes hungry, the young are employed, and the old are cherished and valued to the end of their days.

Examination practice

➜ A poll is being held for people to vote for their choice of the greatest Briton in history. You have been asked to give a speech to persuade people to vote for your choice of the greatest Briton. Write the speech.

You are advised to spend about 40 minutes on your answer.

Writing a letter

A letter is very likely to be the genre of writing required for at least one of the Writing questions in the terminal examinations. You may be asked to write a letter to a friend, in which case you dispense with the formalities of letter layout. It is more likely, though, that the audience for your letter will be an organisation, such as a local newspaper or a school Board of Governors, in which case you will be expected to set the letter out according to the conventions of a formal business letter.

Layout of a formal letter

A formal letter should be set out as follows:

Your address
Street
Town
County and postcode
Date

Business address
Name or position of individual (e.g. The Editor)
Name of business/organisation
Street
Town
County and postcode

Summary of subject of letter
Re: (subject of letter)

Greeting
Dear Sir/Madam (or name, if known),

Opening paragraph, explaining the subject of the letter.

Main paragraphs, presenting your suggestions, etc.

Closing paragraph, stating action requested.

Closing salutation
Yours faithfully/sincerely

Signature

Name

Points to note

1 It is no longer considered necessary to use punctuation in addresses. (It is obviously less confusing to leave it out.)

2 It is likewise unnecessary to indent your address. If you do, then the date should be in line with the beginning of the address. It is definitely wrong to indent the business address.

3 The accepted rule about the greeting is that you use the name of the person you are writing to if you know it. Otherwise you use 'Sir' or 'Madam' and 'Sir/Madam', if you are unaware of their gender.

4 The body of the letter should be paragraphed and written in formal English (e.g., using 'you are' instead of 'you're'). The first paragraph should briefly state the topic of your letter. The final paragraph should politely indicate the action you expect.

5 The closing salutation should be 'sincerely' if you know the person you are writing to, or if you are greeting them by name, and 'faithfully' if not.

Writing a letter to analyse and comment

Here is a specimen question covering the categories analyse and comment.

➔   The council-run concert hall in your local area is almost a century old, and in need of major refurbishment. The options are to spend a great deal of public money to keep it open, or to demolish it and offer the space to developers. Write a **letter** to the leader of the council analysing and commenting on the options.

Write down your ideas for an answer to this question, in summary form, with the following structure: an opening paragraph, three main paragraphs analysing and commenting on different ways of looking at the issue, and a concluding paragraph offering your suggestions.

Here is an outline answer to the question:

Para. 1: Explain the subject and purpose of the letter.

Para. 2: Analyse some of the facilities that are lacking in the area, and other amenities that are run down.
Comment on how the sale of the concert hall site would raise money for such much-needed improvements.

Para. 3: Analyse the importance of the concert hall in the town's history.

Analyse your pesonal experience of seeing major concerts there, and the pleasure you gained from the experiences.

Comment on the effect the loss of the concert hall would have on the town's cultural life.

Para. 4: Analyse the possible uses that might be made of the site if the concert hall was demolished, e.g. another shopping centre, a multi-storey car park.

Comment on the difference this would make to the character of the town.

Para. 5: Conclude with recognition that the council cannot afford to continue to spend large sums of money on the upkeep of the concert hall.

End with suggesting that a private buyer should be sought, who would keep it open as a concert venue.

As this summary response to the question should have shown, writing to 'analyse, review or comment' is more concerned with presenting a balanced perspective on an issue than is writing to 'argue, persuade or advise'. The former triplet, unlike the latter, does not necessarily require you to come to a final conclusion on an issue, though it is quite likely that you will. You are likely to make use of connectors like 'on the other hand', 'and yet' and 'however', rather than 'therefore' and 'clearly', and your answer will almost certainly be less biased and assertive.

Examination practice

Write an answer to this question:

→ Write a letter to your local newspaper, analysing the benefits and drawbacks of the invention of television.

You are advised to spend about 40 minutes on your answer.

EXAMINER'S TIPS

Examiners are always impressed by candidates who can structure and organise their answers clearly. Nowhere is this more important than when you are writing to argue forcefully or persuade sensitively. Examiners look for the signs that indicate you are linking your arguments together coherently. These can range from simple signals like *firstly, secondly* to the more sophisticated *furthermore, in addition, taking all this together*. There are a whole host of these linking signals in English (*accordingly, as a result, similarly, alternatively* are a very small sample), but used carefully they can result in a boost in your marks.

Spelling: the '-y' to '-ie' rule

Most words ending in 'y' drop the 'y' and replace it with 'ie' when an 's' is added.

The rule

Words ending in a vowel plus 'y' just add an 's':

donkey	– donkeys	valley	– valleys
repay	– repays	journey	– journeys

Words ending in a consonant plus 'y' change the 'y' to 'ie':

marry	– marries	tragedy	– tragedies
deny	– denies	party	– parties
enquiry	– enquiries	country	– countries

NON-FICTION TEXTS

The study of a non-fiction text or texts is among the requirements for GCSE English. In each AQA specification it features as part of the terminal examination, linked with a media text or texts.

You are likely to have to answer a question or questions on an extract from a work of literary non-fiction, such as a travel book or an autobiography. In both specifications the text is unseen. It will appear on your exam paper along with a question or questions on a media text or texts. This will also be unseen in the case of specification A, but pre-released in specification B and B (Mature).

The questions are likely to be multi-part. At least one of the questions set for the AQA A exam is likely to require you to *compare* the non-fiction text with media material; in the AQA B and B (Mature) exams you are likely to be set separate questions on the two varieties of texts.

We will begin by looking at an extract from a travel book, and consider how to set about answering questions that relate only to this extract. We will then look at how to compare it with a media travel piece.

Travel writing

The extract is taken from a book by the American writer Bill Bryson, called *Neither Here Nor There*, recording his experiences on a several-month-long tour round Europe. The final city he visited on his trip was Istanbul, the capital of Turkey, a city which he had previously visited nearly twenty years before. He has just arrived there by air. These are his impressions.

NEITHER HERE NOR THERE

Things did not start well. I had made a reservation at the Sheraton through the company's internal reservation system in Sofia, but the hotel turned out to be miles away from the Golden Horn and old town. The room was clean and passably swank, but the television didn't work, and when I went to the bathroom to wash my hands and face, the pipes juddered and banged like something from a poltergeist movie and then, with a series of gasps, issued a steady brown soup. I let the water run for

ten minutes, but it never cleared or even thinned. For this I was paying $150 a night.

I sat on the toilet, watching the water run, thinking what an odd thing tourism is. You fly off to a strange land, eagerly abandoning all the comforts of home, and then expend vast quantities of time and money in a largely futile effort to recapture the comforts that you wouldn't have lost if you hadn't left home in the first place.

Sighing, I smeared a little of the brown water around my face, then went out to see Istanbul. It is the noisiest, dirtiest, busiest city I've ever seen. Everywhere there is noise – car horns tooting, sirens shrilling, people shouting, muezzins wailing, ferries on the Bosphorus sounding their booming horns. Everywhere, too, there is ceaseless activity – people pushing carts, carrying trays of food or coffee, humping huge and ungainly loads (I saw one guy with a sofa on his back), people every five feet selling something: lottery tickets, wristwatches, cigarettes, replica perfumes.

Every few paces people come up to you wanting to shine your shoes, sell you postcards or guidebooks, lead you to their brother's carpet shop or otherwise induce you to part with some trifling sum of money. Along the Galata Bridge, swarming with pedestrians, beggars and load bearers, amateur fishermen stood pulling the most poisoned-looking fish I ever hope to see from the oily waters below. At the end of the bridge two guys were crossing the street to Sirkeci Station, threading their way through the traffic leading brown bears on leashes. No one gave them a second glance. Istanbul is, in short, one of those great and exhilarating cities where almost anything seems possible.

The one truly unbearable thing in the city is the Turkish pop music. It is inescapable. It assaults you from every restaurant doorway, from every lemonade stand, from every passing cab. If you can imagine a man having a vasectomy without anaesthetic to a background accompaniment of frantic sitar-playing, you will have some idea of what popular Turkish music is like.

I wandered around for a couple of hours, impressed by the tumult, amazed that in one place there could be so much activity. I walked past the Blue Mosque and Aya Sofia, peeling postcard salesmen from my sleeve as I went, and tried to go to Topkapi, but it was closed. I headed instead for what I thought was the national archaeological museum, but somehow missed it and found myself presently at the entrance to a large, inviting and miraculously tranquil park, the Gülhane. It was full of cool shade and happy families. There was a free zoo, evidently much loved by children, and somewhere a café playing Turkish torture music, but softly enough to be tolerable.

At the bottom of a gently sloping central avenue, the park ended in a sudden and stunning view of the Bosphorus, glittery and blue. I took a seat at an open-air taverna, ordered a Coke and gazed across the water to the white houses gleaming on the brown hillside of Üsküdar two miles across the strait. Distant cars glinted in the hot sunshine and ferries plied doggedly back and forth across the Bosphorus and on out to the distant Princes' Islands, adrift in a bluish haze. It was beautiful and a perfect place to stop.

Bill Bryson, *Neither Here Nor There*

Preparing the text

In none of the specifications will you have had the chance to study the non-fiction text before the examination. The exam paper lasts for 1¾ hours, but it also contains a writing exercise, so the advice in each specification is to devote one hour to preparing and answering the questions on the non-fiction and media texts. This means, in practice, that you will have less than half an hour to write about the non-fiction text, and very little time to prepare it.

It is essential therefore, that your preparation is closely focused on the question(s) you are being asked. You will probably *have* to read it through once, to get an overall sense of what it is about, before you start working on it. Then you will need to read through it again, highlighting phrases that you think you can comfortably discuss in terms of effective use of language, the writer's attitudes, or whatever the question asks you to write about. There is no point highlighting *every* interesting use of language etc., because there simply won't be time to mention many. You should concentrate on making a *variety* of points. You will be wasting your time if you give more than one example of a simile or a use of onomatopoeia, for example, because whichever language feature you are illustrating, you've got to go on to say something about its effectiveness, which all takes time!

Here is a possible question on the Bill Bryson text:

➡   Read the extract from Bill Bryson's *Neither Here Nor There* and answer the following questions:
  (a) Write about Bryson's reactions to Istanbul on his arrival, and how his attitude changes.
  (b) Show how he uses language to capture the atmosphere of the city and to entertain the reader.

Now spend five minutes marking in pencil, or a highlighter pen if you have a photocopy of the extract, the most useful quotations you can find to cover the various aspects of the question.

When you come to write your answer in the exam, there is no particular need to take each point separately, as long as you deal with everything that you are being asked to write about.

Here is the first part of the extract again, this time with words and phrases highlighted, and marked with the word 'reaction' in the left-hand margin and 'lang.' (short for 'language') in the right-hand margin. You will probably not have time when you are highlighting your text to identify the kinds of reaction and language; you can leave this for when you are writing your answer.

Things did not start well. I had made a reservation at the Sheraton through the company's internal reservation system in Sofia, but the hotel turned out to be miles away from the Golden Horn and old town. The room was clean and passably swank,

reaction   but the television didn't work, and when I went to the bathroom to wash my hands and face, the pipes juddered and banged like something from a poltergeist movie and *lang.* then, with a series of gasps, issued a steady brown soup. I let the water run for ten *lang.*
reaction   minutes, but it never cleared or even thinned. For this I was paying $150 a night.

I sat on the toilet, watching the water run, thinking what an odd thing tourism is. You fly off to a strange land, eagerly abandoning all the comforts of home, and then expend vast quantities of time and money in a largely futile effort to recapture the comforts that you wouldn't have lost if you hadn't left home in the first place.

reaction

Sighing, I smeared a little of the brown water around my face, then went out to see Istanbul. It is the noisiest, dirtiest, busiest city I've ever seen. Everywhere there is noise

reaction

– car horns tooting, sirens shrilling, people shouting, muezzins wailing, ferries on the *lang.* Bosphorus sounding their booming horns. Everywhere, too, there is ceaseless activity – people pushing carts, carrying trays of food or coffee, humping huge and ungainly

reaction

loads (I saw one guy with a sofa on his back), people every five feet selling something: lottery tickets, wristwatches, cigarettes, replica perfumes.

Every few paces people come up to you wanting to shine your shoes, sell you post-cards or guidebooks, lead you to their brother's carpet shop or otherwise induce you to part with some trifling sum of money. Along the Galata Bridge, swarming with *lang.* pedestrians, beggars and load bearers, amateur fishermen stood pulling the most

reaction

poisoned-looking fish I ever hope to see from the oily waters below. At the end of the bridge two guys were crossing the street to Sirkeci Station, threading their way through the traffic leading brown bears on leashes. No one gave them a second

reaction

glance. Istanbul is, in short, one of those great and exhilarating cities where almost anything seems possible.

A specimen examination answer

Here is an example of a complete response to the question. As you read it, notice how the remarks about Bryson's reactions to the city are linked to analysis of his uses of language. Notice also how quotations from the text are blended into the discussion of it.

The last paragraph of the answer refers to changes in the type of language used in the final part of the extract, compared with the earlier part. This section fulfils the last part of GCSE Reading Assessment Objective (v): comment on ways language varies and changes.

Bill Bryson finds Instanbul crowded and suffocating on first arrival. He is disgusted by the facilities in his hotel, and creates a sense of how hopelessly run down it is in a series of images. He describes how 'the pipes juddered and banged like something from a poltergeist movie'. The use of onomatopoeic verbs and the vivid and amusing simile in this description capture a sense of how loud and annoying the sound

was. When he does get some water, it is described as 'brown soup', the metaphor suggesting it is thick and disgusting.

When he goes out into the streets he is struck by the noise and dirt. He captures the noise in a series of precise verbs such as 'shrilling' and 'wailing'. He reaches the Galata Bridge and becomes aware of the extent of the pollution, describing the fishermen's catch as 'the most poisoned-looking fish I ever hope to see'. He finds the music, which is 'inescapable', particularly maddening. This is captured in the comic alliterated metaphor: 'Turkish torture music'. He does, however, find the city exciting, summing it up as 'one of those great and exhilarating cities where almost anything seems possible'.

When he reaches the park his attitude changes, and this is reflected in the language. He suddenly feels at peace, captured in the phrase describing the park as 'miraculously tranquil'. His use of language is quite different in this section, the sibilance in the phrase 'a sudden and stunning view of the Bosphorus' adding to the sense of his wonder at the magnificence of the scene.

Questions linking non-fiction and media texts

In the AQA A examination there may be at least one task requiring comparison of a non-fiction text and a media text. This is likely to involve analysing the language used in the two texts.

On pages 182–183 you will find a magazine feature article entitled 'Majorca: the place to be seen'. As practice in answering a question linking non-fiction and media pieces, you might read the article and try answering this question:

➡ Consider the differences in audience and purpose between 'Majorca: the place to be seen' and the extract from *Neither Here Nor There*. Your answer should focus on the content, language and tone of the two pieces.

Autobiographical writing

The following extract is taken from a book called *The Road to Wigan Pier* by George Orwell. Orwell is travelling by train through Northern England in the 1930s, and he records his thoughts as he passes through an industrial slum area and on into the countryside.

THE ROAD TO WIGAN PIER

The train bore me away, through the monstrous scenery of slag-heaps, chimneys, piled scrap-iron, foul canals, paths of cindery mud criss-crossed by the prints of clogs. This was March, but the weather had been horribly cold and everywhere there were mounds of blackened snow. As we moved slowly through the outskirts of the town we passed row after row of little grey slum houses running at right angles to the embankment. At the back of one of the houses a young woman was kneeling on the stones, poking a stick up the leaden waste-pipe which ran from the sink inside and which I suppose was blocked. I had time to see everything about her – her sacking apron, her clumsy clogs, her arms reddened by the cold. She looked up as the train passed, and I was almost near enough to catch her eye. She had a round pale face, the usual exhausted face of the slum girl who is twenty-five and looks forty, thanks to miscarriages and drudgery; and it wore, for the second in which I saw it, the most desolate, hopeless expression I have ever seen. It struck me then that we are mistaken when we say that 'It isn't the same for them as it would be for us', and that people bred in the slums can imagine nothing but the slums. For what I saw in her face was not the ignorant suffering of an animal. She knew well enough what was happening to her – understood as well as I did how dreadful a destiny it was to be kneeling there in the bitter cold, on the slimy stones of a slum backyard, poking a stick up a foul drain pipe.

But quite soon the train drew away into open country, and that seemed quite strange, almost unnatural, as though the open country had been a kind of park; for in the industrial areas one always feels that the smoke and filth must go on for ever and that no part of the earth's surface can escape them. In a crowded, dirty little country like ours one takes defilement almost for granted. Slag-heaps and chimneys seem a more normal, probable landscape than grass and trees, and even in the depths of the country when you drive your fork into the ground you can half expect to lever up a broken bottle or a rusty can. But out here the snow was untrodden and lay so deep that only the tops of the stone boundary-walls were showing, winding over the hills like black paths. I remembered that D. H. Lawrence, writing of this same landscape or another near by, said that the snow-covered hills rippled away into the distance 'like muscle'. It was not the simile that would have occurred to me. To my eye the snow and the black walls were more like a white dress with black piping running through it.

Although the snow was hardly broken the sun was shining brightly, and behind the shut windows of the carriage it seemed warm. According to the almanac this was spring, and a few of the birds seemed to believe it. For the first time in my life, in a bare patch beside the line, I saw rooks treading. They did it on the ground and not, as I should have expected, in a tree. The manner of courtship was curious. The female stood with her beak open and the male walked round her and appeared to be feeding her. I had hardly been in the train half an hour, but it seemed a very long way from the Brookers' back-kitchen to the empty slopes of snow, the bright sunshine, and the big gleaming birds.

George Orwell, *The Road to Wigan Pier*

When you have read the extract, highlight words and phrases in preparation for answering the following question:

➜ How does Orwell manage to convey, through his choice of language:
   – the grimness of life in industrial slum areas
   – the change in his mood and feelings when he passes into the countryside.

You will probably have noticed a considerable difference between the subject matter and the language of the first paragraph compared with the last two. Although Orwell makes very little use of images and figures of sound in the first paragraph, the language is nevertheless powerful and persuasive. If you found the description of the slum girl moving, you should highlight words and phrases that are particularly expressive, and in your answer you should try to identify the *type* of language and stylistic device used.

When you move on to the last two paragraphs, you should look for words and phrases that illustrate a different type of language and mood, and try to explain the purpose and effect of this section.

Now write your answer. You should limit yourself to thirty minutes for this exercise.

As a final brief exercise on non-fiction texts, you might discuss how the differences in purpose between the George Orwell and Bill Bryson extracts are revealed in the language they use.

EXAMINER'S TIPS

When you are answering questions on non-fiction texts (or, indeed, on any texts in an examination) one of the keys to success is to answer the question that the examiner has asked. This sounds simple, but many candidates fail to do so. For instance, if the question asks you to write about the uses of fact and opinion in a text, don't just list some of the facts and some of the opinions. You wouldn't then be writing about what *use* the writer made of these facts and opinions and an examiner wouldn't be able to give you many marks. Always do what the question asks you to do, as marks are only available for relevant answers.

Spelling test

Write out this passage, correcting all the spelling mistakes.

I was beggining to think I would never find a job, when I saw an advertisement in the local paper for a secetary at a solicitor's office in Newcastle. I begun writting a letter, and my father asked me what I was doing. He proberly thought I was planing to leave home, and he started an argument.

'I hope you no what your doing,' he said. 'Their isn't a lot of point in going to live miles away just for the sake of it.'

He must of thought I was tired of living with him. He was right. Their was know doubt that are relationship was becomming impossible.

I was thrilled when I recieved a letter offering me an interview. Soon I would be independant at last. I brought myself a new skirt to celebrate.

POETRY FROM DIFFERENT CULTURES AND TRADITIONS

In each AQA specification poetry analysis is an examination task. The source material for AQA A is the AQA anthology section on 'different cultures', and for AQA B and B (Mature) it is a collection of poems in a pre-released booklet. The anthology contains 16 poems in two 'clusters' and you will be expected to study them all. The pre-released booklet is likely to contain about 8–10 poems.

In terms of lesson time, this may be the most demanding part of the course. It is important to be clear about how the examination requirements work in each specification.

The AQA anthology divides the 'different culture and traditions' poems into two clusters of 8 poems each, with no obvious distinguishing characteristics between them. The AQA A examination on this anthology gives a choice of two questions. Each question requires students to write on two poems, one named and the other chosen by the student. It is highly likely that the named poem will be from one of the clusters for one question, and the other cluster for the other. The chosen poem can be from either cluster. It is therefore essential to study all the poems in one of the clusters in some detail. Since it is extremely likely that students will be able, if they wish, to write about two poems from the same cluster, it would be reasonable to study the other cluster of poems less fully, rather than trying to hurry through all sixteen poems with the same degree, or lack, of thoroughness.

There is no option but to study all the pre-released poems for AQA B and B (Mature) with more or less equal thoroughness, since there is only one question in the poetry section of the examination in this specification, and it will be set on a named pre-released poem and an unseen poem printed on the exam paper.

The poems chosen in this unit for discussion of how to analyse, prepare and write about poems from different cultures and traditions are both taken from the first cluster in the AQA Anthology. In each specification the questions are likely to involve comparing the two poems in some way, and are certain to require you to focus on the meaning/ideas/themes of the poems, the uses of language, and the verse structure.

The essentials of poetry analysis

The GCSE Assessment Objectives for Writing that apply particularly to poetry are numbers (i), (iv) and (v).

The essential requirement of number (i) is 'making appropriate references to texts and developing and sustaining interpretations of them'. As with all analysis of literary texts, it is of paramount importance that you back up every point you make in your answer by referring to details from the poems, either in your own words or by direct quotation. This is what is meant by 'making appropriate references to texts'. Methods of doing this will be illustrated later in the unit. The effectiveness of your interpretations will hinge on your ability to discuss different aspects of the poems based on textual reference.

The essential detail of Assessment Objective (iv), in terms of poetry, is the requirement to 'make cross-references'. The nature of the question will ensure that you do this by referring to details in one poem, and comparing them with details in the other, to show similarities and differences. Making references to details earlier in the same poem, to show how the poem develops, is also an aspect of cross-referencing.

Assessment Objective (v) reads: 'understand and evaluate how writers use linguistic, structural and presentational devices to achieve their effects, and comment on ways language varies and changes'. 'Linguistic devices' refers to the uses of language particularly associated with poetry, explored in Unit 4. 'Structural and presentational devices', in terms of poetry, means the ways the words are set out on the page, the arrangement of words, lines and stanzas, the use of breaks within lines, and the use of punctuation, or the lack of it. Differences in style and tone are what is meant by 'ways language varies and changes'.

Analysing poems

We will now look in detail at two poems from the AQA anthology. We will then go on to discuss how to write examination answers on them.

The first poem was written by the Nigerian poet and novelist Chinua Achebe. He was born in 1930 and lived through a brutal civil war in his country in the 1960s. He now lives in the USA.

VULTURES

In the greyness
and drizzle of one despondent
dawn unstirred by harbingers
of sunbreak a vulture
5 perching high on broken
bone of a dead tree
nestled close to his
mate his smooth
bashed-in head, a pebble
10 on a stem rooted in
a dump of gross
feathers, inclined affectionately
to hers. Yesterday they picked
the eyes of a swollen
15 corpse in a water-logged
trench and ate the
things in its bowel. Full
gorged they chose their roost
keeping the hollowed remnant
20 in easy range of cold
telescopic eyes ...
　　Strange
indeed how love in other
ways so particular
25 will pick a corner
in that charnel-house
tidy it and coil up there, perhaps

even fall asleep – her face
turned to the wall!
30 ... Thus the Commandant at Belsen
Camp going home for
the day with fumes of
human roast clinging
rebelliously to his hairy
35 nostrils will stop
at the wayside sweet-shop
and pick up a chocolate
for his tender offspring
waiting at home for Daddy's
40 return...
　　Praise bounteous
providence if you will
that grants even an ogre
a tiny glow-worm
45 tenderness encapsulated
in icy caverns of a cruel
heart or else despair
for in the very germ
of that kindred love is
50 lodged the perpetuity
of evil.

Chinua Achebe

Discussion questions

The poem can be divided into four sections, indicated by three dots followed by an indented line.

Section 1 (lines 1–21)

➔ What is being described in this section?

➔ What time of day is it in the opening four lines? What is the atmosphere of these lines? How is it created by language and imagery?

Lines 4–13 describe what the male vulture is doing.

➔ What impression is given of his appearance? How is language and imagery used to create this impression?

➔ What change in language do you notice when his actions are described?

Lines 13–21 describe what the vultures did 'yesterday'.

➔ What did they do?

➔ Which part of this description did you find most revolting?

➔ How does the placing of the words add to the grotesque atmosphere of this section?

Section 2 (lines 22–29)

➔ What is this section about?

➔ The first line consists of a single word. What is the effect of this?

➔ 'Love' is personified here. What is 'love' described as doing?

➔ What is the significance of the words after the dash in the last two lines of the section?

Section 3 (lines 30–40)

➔ This section begins '... Thus'. Why?

➔ In line 30 the time, place and focus of the poem changes. What is happening in this section?

➔ How has the poet made the Camp Commandant seem revolting by his use of language and imagery?

➔ How does the language change in line 35?

➔ What connections can you make between the description of the vultures in the first part of the poem and the description of the Camp Commandant in this part?

Section 4 (lines 41–51)

➜   The message of the poem is brought out in this final section. What are the two ways of viewing the glimpses of humanity described earlier in the poem?

➜   Is the ending optimistic or pessimistic?

➜   What is the effect of the images and figures of sound in this section?

General

➜   What do you notice about the punctuation of the poem?

➜   Several descriptive phrases are separated over two lines, like 'smooth/bashed-in head', 'swollen/corpse', 'hairy/nostrils' and 'cruel/heart'. What do you think is the reason for this?

➜   Why do you think the poem is called 'Vultures'?

The second poem was written by Grace Nichols. She was born in Guyana in 1950, and worked as a journalist in the Caribbean until 1977, when she settled in Britain.

ISLAND MAN

(for a Caribbean island man in London who still wakes up to the sound of the sea)

Morning
and island man wakes up
to the sound of blue surf
in his head
5   the steady breaking and wombing

wild seabirds
and fishermen pushing out to sea
the sun surfacing defiantly
from the east
10 of his small emerald island
he always comes back   groggily groggily

Comes back to sands
of a grey metallic soar
                        to surge of wheels

15 to dull North Circular roar

muffling muffling
his crumpled pillow waves
island man heaves himself

Another London day

Grace Nichols

This poem can be divided into two main parts, or six stanzas of different lengths. We will discuss it in stanzas.

Stanza 1 (lines 1–5)
→ The first line is a single word. Why do you think it is separated off like this?
→ The island man is hearing the sounds of the sea in his dreams. How is the sound and movement of the sea created by the use of language and the rhythm of the words?
→ In the word 'wombing' the poet creates a verb from a noun. What feeling does this invented word create?

Stanza 2 (lines 6–11)
→ What impression of the island is created in this stanza? How does the poet use language to create this impression?
→ Why do you think there is a big gap before 'groggily groggily' in line 11?
→ What is happening to the island man at the end of the stanza?

Stanza 3 (lines 12–15)
→ Line 12 carries on the statement begun in line 11. Why is the statement spread over two stanzas?
→ In lines 12–14 words about the island and London are mixed up. Which ones and why?
→ How do the words used to describe London differ from the words used to describe the island?
→ Why do you think the word 'Comes' is capitalised when it is repeated?
→ What is the point of the placing of 'to surge of wheels'?
→ Both repetition and rhyme are used in this stanza. What is the effect of this?

→ If the whole statement beginning in line 11 had been set out in prose, it would read like this: 'He always comes back, groggily, groggily, comes back to sands of a grey metallic soar, to surge of wheels, to dull North Circular roar'. Is this significantly different from setting it out in verse form as Grace Nichols does? If so, in what way?

Stanza 4 (lines 16–18)
→ What is happening in this stanza?
→ Why is 'muffling' repeated?

Stanza 5 (line 19)
→ Why is this line placed on its own?
→ What is the effect of starting it with a capital letter?

Writing about poetry from different cultures and traditions

In each AQA specification you will be asked to write about two poems, as already explained. You will be expected to compare the poems in some way. In AQA B and B (Mature) the poems chosen for you to write about will have some features in common. For AQA A, since you are required to choose one of the poems to write about, you will have to make sure you select a poem that has some relevance to the question.

You can be certain that the question will require comparisons between poems in terms of their subject matter and the ways they are written. If you are taking the AQA A examination it would be a good idea to work out in advance a list of pairs of poems that have features in common.

Comparing poems

Comparing two poems involves analysing a range of similarities and differences between them. There are two ways of doing this:

→ writing about each poem separately
→ writing about the poems together.

If you choose the former approach, you will have to refer back to aspects of the first poem you wrote about when you are writing about the second, pointing out how it is similar or different.

If you choose the latter, you will move from one feature to another, showing how it is treated in both poems.

Before beginning your answer you should write a plan, summarising the topics you are going to deal with in each paragraph.

Once you have decided on your essay structure it would be a good idea to pick out quotations from the poems on which to base your answer. Your discussion of the poems must proceed by making reference to the detail of each. This can also be done in two ways:

➡ explaining ideas in the poems in your own words
➡ quoting directly from the poems.

Sometimes you may combine the two, explaining a section of the poem in your own words, and fitting a brief quotation into the explanation. Here is an example:

The Camp Commandant from Belsen goes home to his family and stops to buy some chocolate for his 'tender offspring'.

The way you set out quotations on the page depends on their length. If the quote is short, it is best to simply fit it into the statement you are making, as illustrated above, rather than separating it off on to a new line. If a short quotation runs over two lines in the poem, you need to show the line division with a forward slash, like this: **they 'ate the/things in its bowel'.**

If you are using a longer quotation, it is better to set it as it appears in the poem, starting on a new line. Here is an example:

After describing how the male vulture's head 'inclined affectionately/to hers', Achebe goes on to describe the couple's grotesque and revolting activities the day before:
> **'. . . Yesterday they picked**
> **the eyes of a swollen**
> **corpse in a water-logged**
> **trench'.**

The way you structure your answer should follow standard essay structure, whether or not you are specifically asked to write an essay. This involves writing an introduction, a series of main paragraphs and a conclusion.

Here is a specimen question:

➡ Write a comparison between 'Vultures' and 'Island Man' that includes a discussion of:
  – the presentation of people and their lives
  – the language and structure of the poems.

Here is a possible paragraph plan for an answer to this question:

Intro: people and theme in each poem
Para. 2:   use of nature to reflect on people's lives
Para. 3:   messages about people in poems
Para. 4:   contrasts in language
Para. 5:   contrasts in structure
Conc.:   purpose dictates forms and style

The introduction should relate both poems to the question, whether or not you are going to discuss the poems separately.

Here is a sample introduction to this question.

Both 'Vultures' and 'Island Man' describe people and their lives. The use of these people in the poems, however, is very different. Chinua Achebe in 'Vultures' compares the Commandant at a concentration camp in World War II with vultures, to deliver a message about the nature of evil. Grace Nichols' poem 'Island Man' describes a Caribbean islander living in London waking up to reality. She is also making a point, but a much less grim one, about dreaming of your roots when you are far away from them.

A substantial part of the main body of your answer must be taken up with anlaysing the language and structure of the poems.

Here is an example of how the second part of the specimen question, dealing with 'contrasts in language', could be answered:

In the first half of 'Island Man', the visions of his island in the man's mind are captured vividly by Nichols' use of language. The sibilants in the phrase 'the sound of the blue surf' capture the sound 'in his head' for us. The sun is personified in the line 'the sun surfacing defiantly', capturing a sense of its fierceness. In the third stanza, a mixture of types of language is used, creating an impression of the man being half-aware of the harsh sound of the London traffic as he dreams of the breaking waves, in phrases like 'sands/of a grey metallic soar'. The harsh sounds eventually take over in the 'dull North Circular roar'. There is also a mixture of harsh and soft language in 'Vultures'. The description of the Camp Commandant with:

> '... fumes of
> human roast clinging
> Rebelliously to his hairy
> nostrils',

creates a grotesque impression, with the obscene metaphor of 'human roast', representing the incinerated victims of the concentration camp, and the harsh-sounding, ghastly personification of 'clinging/rebelliously'. This is followed by the description of him picking up chocolate on the way home for his 'tender offspring'. Here the language is in total contrast with what has come before, creating an almost idyllic impression.

Notice that the discussion of the quoted phrases includes technical terms: sibilants, personification, metaphor. You should try, if possible, to identify such figures of speech and sound. A word of warning here, though! You should never just 'spot' such devices, without going on to explain the effects produced by them. Any use of language is worth mentioning, even single words, as long as you can comment on the effects of the language.

Examination practice

You might now try to write a full answer to this question, using the paragraph plan suggested, or a plan or your own.

EXAMINER'S TIPS

Before beginning to write your poetry answer, it's best to make some brief notes on possible quotations you might use, ideas you might include and possible links between the poems you could make. You should spend approximately the same time on each poem you are writing about and should always include some brief quotations from or references to the poem. Remember, examiners don't want to read large chunks of copied extracts from the poem. They are also always looking to see whether you have made some cross-references both between and within your chosen poems.

APPENDIX

The following is a list of features of the book that crop up in various units, rather than just in the unit which is dedicated to them.

Coursework suggestions

Speaking and Listening:
- group: pages 1–8, 11–15, 45–51, 52–57, 212
- individual: pages 15, 76
- drama focused: pages 112, 121–122, 151

Writing:
- to explore, imagine, entertain: pages 16, 76, 91–92
- to inform, explain, describe: pages 16, 51, 57, 192, 201
- to analyse, review, comment: pages 166–167, 185

Examination practice

Writing to argue, persuade, advise: pages 51, 57, 212, 215
Writing to analyse, review, comment: page 218
Writing to inform, explain, describe: pages 192, 200
Reading: Media: pages 162–167, 181, 184–185

Syntax, punctuation and spelling

Syntax: explanation: pages 23–27, 86–88
exercises: pages 27, 77, 152, 186
Punctuation: rules: pages 16–18, 42–44, 58–60, 93–94
exercises: pages 117, 151, 186
Spelling: rules: pages 122–3, 134, 167, 202, 219
exercises: pages 9–10, 27–28, 228

Literary, linguistic and rhetorical devices

Literary devices: explanation: pages 29–37
exercises: pages 37–41
Rhetorical devices: pages 175–176, 213

Genres of writing

Essay writing: pages 204–212
Magazine article writing: pages 192–196
Letter writing: pages 215–218
Speech writing: pages 213–215